Vice Squad

ROBERT H. WILLIAMS

THOMAS Y. CROWELL COMPANY

New York   Established 1834

Acknowledgment is made to Alfred A. Knopf, Inc., for permission to quote from The French Quarter: An Informal History of the New Orleans Underworld, by Herbert Asbury, copyright 1936.

Designed by Abigail Moseley

Manufactured in the United States of America

ISBN 0-690-86010-2

1 2 3 4 5 6 7 8 9 10

Library of Congress Cataloging in Publication Data

Williams, Robert Hunter, 1933-
    Vice squad.
    1. Police corruption—United States. I. Title.
HV8138.W62   364.1'3   72-7583
ISBN 0-690-86010-2

INTRODUCTION

This book, by design, execution and general appearance, is about police corruption in America; and that statement, the first in the book, is only partly true. Instead, what emerges is a story—or several stories—about policemen functioning in a corrupt America.

It had originally been my intention to examine the phenomenon of police as criminals or grafters by going into finite cases from recent history in certain cities where police corruption had become a public issue in the past—where a beginning, a middle and an end could be presented and the proper inferences drawn. This idea, carefully planned by myself and my editors, began going down the drain as the past, in many cities, began to meld with the present. In Seattle, for instance, I knew that a deputy police chief had gone to prison for perjury in connection with a bribery investigation in 1970, and that his federal conviction had shaken up the department. What I did not know was that a reform district attorney there would bull through and get fifty-four indictments during the spring and summer of 1971—well after the supposedly "finite" Seattle story had ended.

In New Orleans, I dipped safely back to the early 1950s to show the well-documented systematic corruption of a police department, and to show, in passing, how a simple bit of graft can lead to the take-over of an entire area by the forces of organized crime. As I was putting the finishing touches on that 1953–54 situation, the United States Department of Justice surprised me and everybody else in late 1971, by indicting the New Orleans district attorney and the head of the New Orleans vice squad for the very things about which I had been writing—and there went that bit of finity.

I had planned to do New York City in terms of Harry Gross, the gambler who rocked the department a generation earlier; but then along came Frank Serpico and Waverly Logan and the Knapp Commission, and again I was propelled into 1972 before I had quite finished with the tied-up-with-a-ribbon story that had gone before.

Louisville and Philadelphia both broke, essentially, after I had done my research; but both are included, even though an end is not in sight in either city. I never even got started in Detroit, where late in December, 1972, the Detroit *Free Press* reported that a special police squad, after months of investigation, had made a dawn "raid" on a precinct station, and seized heroin and other drugs and evidence implicating about twenty-five Detroit cops in drug trafficking. And Miami, or rather Dade County, Florida, may never be clean enough to get a totally historical view of the corruption that has gone on there since Carl Fisher pumped Miami Beach up from the mangrove swamp it once was, better than a half century ago.

The only city truly represented as a closed case in this book is Utica: the one city that lived up to my original expectations and did not surprise me by breaking out anew even as I did my research.

I would like to make a disclaimer at this point: This book is by no means intended to be a definitive history of police corruption in America. It is very likely that no such history will ever be possible, given the secrecy of police departments everywhere and the reluctance of community leaders to attempt to relate, one to another, what appear to be isolated incidents involving policemen and vice figures. I have relied largely on interviews, personal observation and newspaper libraries, drawing heavily from government affidavits and testimony taken in open court;

historians who attempt to go deeper will face the challenges of dockets, law reviews and indices, jurisdictional crossovers and lost records. This book may give one of those historians a starting point, at least.

For assistance in gathering material for *Vice Squad* I am indebted to Bruce Carrick, who first saw the value of the material; Cynthia Vartan, the editor who helped pull it all together; Harold Foner, Waverly Logan and the late Horace Lord; Lieutenant Frank Alioto, Deputy Inspector Hugo Masini and First Deputy Commissioner William Smith of the New York Police Department; the editors of the *Miami Herald;* Hank Messick; Chief George Tielsch and Captain Richard Schoener of the Seattle Police Department; Louis R. Guzzo, managing editor of the *Seattle Post-Intelligencer*; Will Jarrett of the *Philadelphia Inquirer*; Leighton McLaughlin and Ralph Otwell of the *Chicago Sun-Times*; Virgil Peterson and Aaron Kohn, who know more about crime and politics than is humanly bearable; John Quinn, Richard B. Tuttle, Mason Taylor, Gilbert P. Smith, Neal A. Bintz, John Daugherty and Bill Lohman, all of Gannett Newspapers; Elwood M. Wardlow of the *Buffalo Evening News*; Charles Stewart of the *Metro-East Journal*; Miami Beach Police Chief Rocky Pomerance; King County, Washington, Prosecuting Attorney Christopher T. Bayley; Clarence Jones of WHAS-TV, Louisville; Congressman Claude Pepper and his staff; William Claiborne of the *Washington Post*; and a raft of others without whom this book could not have been produced, including the Washington, D.C., police inspector who tipped me off when the New York City cops were trying—unsuccessfully—to get my personnel records from the *Washington Post*.

CONTENTS

1

The Valley
and the Dolls

One of my earliest recollections is of being handed three or four nickels by my mother at Johnny Perkins' Playdium, where she went each week to bowl in the Alcoa League, so that I could put them into the slot machines which guarded the long entrance hall like so many policemen. I remember slipping the nickel into the slot (the Playdium also had dime and quarter machines, and, at that time, one monster that accepted half-dollars) and hopefully waiting for two cherries and a whatever to roll up—meaning that I would get three (or was it five?) nickels in the cast aluminum tray (even the slot machine manufacturers were customers of the company that employed my mother and made it possible for me to invest three nickels in their machines)—but most often watching a plum, a lemon and a cherry, or another unrewarding combination of fruit salad, come up.

This was in East St. Louis, Illinois, one of the toughest towns in American through the mid-1950s (and still the toughest in terms of a black man getting a decent-paying job, in an area victimized by industrial antirevolution), where if you lived to be twenty-one you were considered by your peers to have enjoyed a rich, full and happy life.

I did not know, as a child, that the slot machines were illegal, or that they were owned by the southern branch of the Al Capone syndicate in Chicago, or that the East St. Louis police were being paid not to interfere with their operation; I knew only that they were there, and that by slipping a nickel into one of them and pulling down on the handle, I had the chance of joining the ranks of those who had—what was the jackpot in those days?—maybe $18 in their jeans. My mother, wise woman, never let me have more than four nickels to hand over to the syndicate, which was run then by a man named Frank (Buster) Wortman, a vicious, mean killer who controlled everything illegal in East St. Louis and her sister city across the Mississippi—St. Louis, Missouri—and whose shirttail relative, a near-midget in both physical composition and mentality, terrorized the city; and whose henchmen pumped bullets into syndicate soldiers as well as honest law-enforcement officers (the few that were around in those days); and who, incidentally, was a hero to every schoolboy who ever hoped to do more with his life than grease cars or go to Brown's Business College. In junior high school one fellow student even started collecting money to charter a bus so that a few of us might make a pilgrimage to the grave of Scarface Al.

The mob ran East St. Louis. Nobody who was ever stationed at Scott Air Force Base (in the old days called Scott Field, a training base for, among others, Chinese nationals who were expected to fly for us against the Japanese) or at Jefferson Barracks, a noted drying-out spot for army colonels, ever recalls his tour of duty without mentioning East St. Louis and (a) the wild good time he had there, or (b) the screwing he got at the hands of either a prostitute, a pimp, a saloonkeeper, a B-girl, a taxicab driver, a card dealer, a cop, or all of them simultaneously. Most often it was (b).

The city was run by a tightly knit little "coalition" government, neither Republican nor Democrat, and it was run to suit the mores of the citizenry, which, although a little bit more honest about things, were truly the microcosm of the national moral scene. In East St. Louis, money would buy anything—literally anything. If you were tall enough to see over the bar, and you had a dollar clutched in your hand, you could buy a drink of anything in the house. If you had three dollars and were old enough to get a hard-on, you could walk through the Valley and get one or another prostitute to take you on—like on a Saturday night one hot summer when the stars were still big and the river full and barely polluted, with the black whores standing just inside the screen doors of the dreadful shanties, the deplorable shanties down there below Third Street (they didn't number the streets below Third, it was simply "the Valley"), their white bras and panties gleaming in the reflection of auto headlights like disembodied Freudian dreams, and old Peet Marie holding you in her fat black arms and telling you to hurry on and get it up because Mr. S. had said the place had to be quiet by midnight; and you would hear Frankie Laine singing "That Lucky Old Sun" on the jukebox (which was also owned by the syndicate, even then, when it still cost only a nickel to play), and then, walking outside into the street—which the pimps had spent all day Saturday digging up so that the nighttime traffic had to move very, very slowly to avoid busting a spring—you would find your buddy's brother, a sergeant on the vice squad, telling you to get your ass out of there and by God he better not catch you there again, and then you saw him take the three bucks you'd paid to Peet Marie out of her hand and warn her not to go fucking around with white kids anymore.

There wasn't anything you couldn't get. The old Club Parlay, a cinder-block building on the outskirts—really in St. Clair County, not the city—where we all hung out, was a hotbed of booze and dope, and I would come home glassy-eyed from beer and maybe a twelve-hour poker game (at stakes varying from a quarter to pot limit), and my mother would inspect the insides of my arms for "tracks," just to make sure I wasn't popping worse stuff than what would eventually kill my old man, who worked nights on the Southern Railroad and spent his days gambling, whoring and drinking. Nobody over nineteen ever showed up at Club Parlay, to my knowledge, except a thirty-year-old named Randy, whom we used to beat up and rob occasionally, just to stay in practice. When the sheriff would change (St. Clair County in Illinois is like many other counties in the state—you don't succeed yourself, so the sheriff and the county treasurer would take turns in the two jobs, today's treasurer being tomorrow's sheriff) it didn't really matter, because the payoffs to the department continued. At Club Parlay we even had an honorary chair at the poker table with the sheriff's name spelled out in brass-headed upholstery tacks, in case he staged a raid and needed someplace to sit while we were being terrorized and the proprietor was trying to raise enough money to square the deal. (The sheriff was furious when he saw the chair one afternoon on a casual, nonofficial visit.)

The Valley, below downtown, had not always been black—before World War II it had been the home of dozens of white prostitutes, some of whom were handled by a relative of mine who was also a gambler— and it is not even black anymore, the entire area having been scalped away by "urban renewal" and a new bridge and interstate highway—the latter of which also ruined Collinsville Road (old Route 40), once a par- adise of brothels, hot-sheet motels (some of which are still operating, or at least were in the summer of 1971) and gambling casinos.

The mob influence in East St. Louis was no joke; it was real. Wort- man operated his pinball, jukebox and handbook empire from a spot called the Paddock, at Fifth Street and St. Louis Avenue—a steak house where Mr. and Mrs. Average Citizen could go for a fine meal, if the temper of the mob that evening was to present a fine meal, or for a horri- fying experience, if one of the members of the Wortman gang decided to take offense to the necktie the poor dude was sporting. The cops never entered the building, except for a free drink or to pick up an envelope.

Throughout this period the vices prevailed. Hard-core crime—mur- der, burglary, robbery—was not common except when it concerned members of the Wortman mob. Gambling, prostitution, liquor violations were rampant. A reporter for what was then the *East St. Louis Journal* is reported to have had an eye put out by mobsters who resented his appearing in federal court to take notes during the Kefauver hearings. He was beaten severely fifteen years later because he dared to report on a dice game which had been in existence in Brooklyn, Illinois, a grimy suburb of East St. Louis down by the National Stock Yards, since the end of World War II (as a young man, I rolled dice in this game, which featured a taut rubber band in the middle of the table, across which the dice had to hop or it was no throw, and I won, but I also watched a sucker in the hot spot be told that he had thrown craps when, in fact, the stickman had whisked the cubes up so fast that nobody in Christ's world could see what was on them). Bar dice were ubiquitous, as were punch cards, and "smoke shops" abounded, those little rooms where you could buy cigars and go through a back door and find a card room six times as big as the smoke shop and where a hundred times the money changed hands.

All this, of course, was regulated and controlled by the police department, through its vice cops, or plainclothesmen. The department was organized along classic lines, and a beat cop never had the authority to arrest anyone he found breaking one of the victimless crime laws. If he saw a card game in operation, or heard a loudspeaker blaring the results of the fourth race at Santa Anita, or if he saw a hooker take a John into the Broadview Hotel, he was expected to notify the vice cops, who, supposedly, had files on such things and would take what is referred to in police department vernacular as "appropriate action." What appropriate action means, of course, is to warn the offender not to be so goddam blatant after this, and to cut the beat man in on a little of the ice, just to keep his esprit de corps alive and functioning.

In later years my awareness of my old home town grew. As a newspaper reporter on the *Journal*, I would sit in Keiflein's Tavern across the street until three or four o'clock in the morning (closing time was 1 A.M., but now Teddy is closing around eleven because the downtown streets are so unsafe), having played rum, a game played at anywhere from a penny to a dollar a point, at the Century Smoke Shop next door (owned and operated by the father of one of the editors at the *Journal*); and then would go off in a converted City Lines bus, owned by the city engineer, to play cards the rest of the night while parked on the levee. Alternately, we would adjourn to Millie's, an after-hours brothel-turned-saloon out on Route 50, where, around 5 A.M., we would be joined by vice cops just getting off a harrowing tour of duty. They would sit in on the card game, play the jukebox or hustle one of the two or three hookers who would have landed at Millie's because there was no place else to go, and who would wind up balling the cops for free because they said so. And then there was Helen's, a bar on Fifth Street, around the corner from the newspaper, a saloon that doubled as a rest stop for diseased or pregnant prostitutes who traveled in the syndicate brothel circuit. They worked as barmaids at Helen's, or else kept out of sight and did nothing, and on Christmas Eve of 1958 it was a warm scene when the girls joined the few of us who were out that evening and then in turn were joined by the vice cops, who had come in to pick up their Christmas presents and stayed long enough to admire the little Christmas tree the girls had decorated and to sing a couple of choruses of "Silent Night."

That was an election year, too, and on election day we had sent a reporter around to see if there was any clandestine drinking going on in the saloons, which were supposed to be closed as long as the polls were open, and in the first one whose alley door he tried he found the sheriff of St. Clair County and a couple of deputies, waiting for the unofficial returns to be phoned in from City Hall, half a block away. The reporter,

Curt Matthews, then a cub and now a distinguished journalist for the *St. Louis Post-Dispatch*, wrote his story, and the next day got an irate call from the sheriff, who said he didn't mind having been caught drinking illegally, but did Matthews *have* to report that the drink was crème de menthe? It had almost ruined him around the county courthouse.

The following spring the state police called the city desk and said they were going to knock over a gambling casino just outside the city limits, in the sheriff's jurisdiction (the sheriff at that time was operating with essentially a one-man vice squad, a man responsible for overseeing the control of everything illegal in the county). I never found out why they did it, unless it was to embarrass the sheriff politically, although they could have found a way to try to do that ten times a day and it still wouldn't have made any difference at the polls because the machine coalition could deliver 70 percent of the vote in any precinct for or against any man or proposition that ever got on the ballot. It is more likely that the men running the high-rolling crap game in the little house in the woods did not try to find *somebody to pay* before they opened up. When I walked in the cops were counting the confiscated money and the gamblers were on their way to a justice of the peace; and there was a huge pot of fresh chicken and dumplings (they were the flat, Belgian dumplings) on the stove in the kitchen; and somebody had finally called the sheriff's chief investigator to inform him of the raid. I asked the state cops which one had called the newspaper, and was told, "Shit, boy, nobody called your newspaper, you got that?" and so I said what the hell, and the sheriff's man rather glumly said what the hell, and we sat down and had a bowl of dumplings, rather than see them go to waste.

I never really knew until I left there that all cops didn't get paid off by gangsters and ordinary businessmen, or even that they weren't *supposed* to. The community of East St. Louis and its suburbs, really all of St. Clair County, was really more of a fascist city-state than a democracy, and in that respect perhaps could be looked upon as a bare-bones microcosm of the entire United States of the first half of the twentieth century: All the meanness, brutality, petty ambitions, selfishness, greed and hypocrisy just hung out there, naked and frank, and I mean in *every* aspect of life and living, not just in the area of police corruption, which was taken for granted. So you would find one of the big, old industrial complexes (there are precious few of them there, now), the Monsanto Chemical Company, making no bones about incorporating the village of Monsanto, whose corporate limits *just* took in the plant, plus acreage for expansion, plus a little cluster of pink-and-white ticky-tack, to keep from ever having to have its property-tax rate set by an assessor from, say, East St. Louis. The mayor, also a clerk of Monsanto, was allowed, with the village board members, also Monsanto employees, to decide whether the police car should have automatic or manual transmission and where the new clock on the village hall would be located. It was an area where great companies—Alcoa had a marvelous factory there—found tax havens in other communities where thus-freed capital could be invested in newer, more modern, more fully automated operations. Alcoa found its friends in Arkansas, and moved out lock, stock and barrel, leaving a thousand, two thousand more souls out of work and getting the community at large, through the newspapers, to believe, *really believe*, that it was the labor unions who made it too tough for the companies to stay. It was an area where if you wanted to run for office you walked in and talked to Dan McGlynn, or met him while you were rolling "horses" at the cigar stand just across the street from City Hall; and it was an area whose idea of a liberal was somebody who thought niggers were all right as long as they stayed in their place and didn't bother anybody. The city then was 60 percent black, and today it is closer to 80 percent, and when my mother visited me in Miami in 1965 she seemed upset because we let the blacks there drive buses and everything.

It was a town in which, until it began to die of starvation, *everything* went, and did even in 1960, when *Look* magazine picked it, incredibly, as an All-American City, and I'll be goddamned if, looking back, that isn't precisely what it was.

You see, it was *exactly* what the body politic wanted it to be. The railroads and the factories wanted protection and profit, and they got it. The blacks wanted gambling and after-hours activity, and they got it. The Catholics wanted bingo and a later closing hour for saloons, and they got it. The night-club-lounge-roadhouse-motel-hotel-convention people wanted prostitution and gambling, and they got it. The downtown merchants wanted gambling to be illegal, and they got it. The whites wanted segregation, and they got it (this is considered a Northern town, and the first black face in what was then the city's white high school showed up in the 1950 yearbook—and there was one, not two or three). The blacks wanted integration, and they got the whole bloody pie—the whites simply moved out and left the blacks with a municipality that was paying city employees in anticipation warrants.

All of these freewheeling, laissez-faire activities were more or less regulated by the police department, which, in terms of a fascist city-state, was just one hell of a good police department; and I thought this even as I left for good, again, as I say, not knowing what a cop was supposed to be like, although maybe, all things considered, the East St. Louis cops were just like all the rest of them. They were tall and tough and smart, and quite able to take care of the city. The crime rate, as I recall, was not extraordinarily high, and the kinds of crimes a community finds most repugnant—arson, burglary, robbery, murder, rape—were solved quickly and convictions secured easily; and everybody knew about the basement of the police station and the rubber-hose artist who obtained confessions there, but everybody also knew that the cops wouldn't be beating around on anybody who didn't deserve it. The only time serious crimes weren't solved was when they involved syndicate or mob-related figures, and I think that is the basic premise of this book: If a man is paying the cops to protect one aspect of his operations, say his handbook, the coverage is automatically extended to other areas of endeavor. You have to hand it to the downstate Illinois mob of the midcentury—they seldom let violence spill over into the legitimate community.

The heart of the police department, regarding the regulation of illegal, immoral and popular activities, then, as now, in most American cities, is the vice squad—the men who, by the demands of their calling, have to know who is operating what, and where, how long he or she has been doing it there and where he or she did it before, newcomers to the area, how much business is being done, who the customers are and whether there is a danger that immoral activities will spill over and affront a community that prides itself on its white churches, its clean streets, its 6 percent passbook savings accounts and the loudness of the roar at the Lion's Club luncheon. Because the vice cops know all this, they are in the unique position of being able to control all of the victimless illegal activity in a community, and, as you know, the power to control has its corollary: the power to tax. And the power to tax, as any prostitute, gambler, dope pusher or student of government will tell you, has its own corollary: the power to destroy.

N o American city is less corrupt than East St. Louis, Illinois, and there is growing suspicion among the aware that American society as a whole—all of its institutions—is hideously and hopelessly corrupt, with indications that the corruption has not been what the Smithsonian Institution likes to call a "short-lived phenomenon," adopted temporarily by the America of the 1970s, thus becoming a societal freak; but rather that the corruption has been absorbed into the genes and chromosomes, producing a mutant society whose children, if anything, will be even more courrpt in finer, more subtle ways. I am speaking now about the corruption of the democratic process by Mayor Richard Daley of Chicago; the corruption of the political process when such close-to-the-earth, solid American types as dairy farmers bribe the government in Washington to increase the milk support price; or when a giant corporation offers to underwrite the costs of the Republican National Convention in return for a favorable ruling from the Department of Justice in an antitrust case; the corruption of the judicial process when men such as Clement Haynesworth and G. Harrold Carswell are nominated to the Supreme Court; the corruption of basic decency by banks, grocery stores, newspapers, broadcasters, the chamber of commerce, civil servants, politicians, lawyers, accountants, farmers, labor leaders, construction companies, railroads, shippers and the people who serve you dirty, tasteless food and don't put ashtrays on the counter because they want you to choke it down and get the hell out and make room for the next unfortunate sonofabitch, who is scared, like you, because he has heard that there may be corruption on the police force.

They're all we have, you see, between us and chaos: the police. Naked. A man points a gun at you and demands your money, and there is a chance another man, a cop, will point a gun at the man and say, "Oh no you don't," and if it weren't for that, well, the guy behind the counter wouldn't bother serving you any food at all, he'd just take your money and kick your ass out into the street. We arm a man and put him into the street to protect our property and our lives, as an alternative to walking around armed ourselves. It is possible, even now, to protect ourselves now and again from corporate corruption, through the intervention of honest men; but against the random street hoodlum or organized-crime figure we are helpless. It is a tribute to some moral restraint surviving in twentieth-century America that General Motors *only* relentlessly investigated Ralph Nader; had he taken on a mob-controlled corporation he surely would have been eliminated. So when our basic institutions become corrupt, we tend to feel that we have recourse, somewhere, or at least that we won't be killed, although this, too, may be a transitional phase, if one recalls the basic institutions run amok in Nazi Germany. But when we discover that the men we have set out on the streets to protect us on an *individual* basis are corrupt, the men at the very first level of personal safety and well-being, we view it with a visceral reaction, like the feeling you get watching a parade, only inside out.

During 1971 police corruption to one degree or another was found in twenty-three American cities. You can be sure that it is suspected, probably with cause, in another twenty-three, and that it is not suspected, although it probably exists, in God knows how many other cities.

Some generalizations need to be made:

1. Investigation and the existence of police corruption recurs in the same cities over the years. Some cities, on the other hand, have never experienced the phenomenon. The former seems to be particuularly true in large metropolitan areas, such as Cook County, Illinois, Dade County, Florida, and King County, Washington, where the major city (Chicago, Miami, Seattle) is only one of up to a hundred municipalities in the county, and where, because of this, police jurisdiction is fragmented. In King County there is not even a countywide communications network among the different police agencies. So it is that Cicero in Cook County became the headquarters and refuge of the Capone syndicate, while nearby Oak Park remained virtually off limits for gangsters and their activiites; that the sheriff's department ran roughshod over the unincorporated areas of Dade County, while the city of Miami Beach—not a Protestant's idea of good clean family fun under any circumstances—remained relatively clean. Cicero today, I am told by Virgil W. Peterson, retired managing director of the Chicago Crime Commission, is about as ugly as it was in the days of Rocco Fischetti, although not nearly so wide open. "There develops in a city with a long history of corruption a philosophy that permeates the force," Peterson told me, adding that he believed the Chicago Police Department proper had cleaned itself up considerably since 1947 and particularly since the police scandals of the early 1960s.

Just *why* some cities seem to be corruption-free seems to be a mystery, but I think it is safe to assume that the honesty of a police department is directly related to the degree to which the police chief is allowed to function within his own boundaries of professionalism, regardless of the political motives and ambitions of the mayor or aldermen. For instance, the Democratic machine in Chicago decades ago made a satanic covenant with the police department, a deal that included laissez-faire for the captains in return for patronage and "favors" for the ward heelers and precinct leaders. The Los Angeles Police Department, on the other hand, seems to have held out for professionalism above all other considerations, and it is possible that Mayor Sam Yorty, who surely must do *something* right, has seen that an honest police department is far more valuable to a political machine than a dishonest one, even if there is danger, from week to week, of a machine pet being taken off to prison.

2. The exposure of corruption, and even corruption itself, tends to reproduce on a cyclic basis—and the cycle seems to base itself, not so oddly, on the human generation, somewhere between fifteen and twenty years. Many times an investigation of a police department will be touched off by a serious crime, believed to have been committed by the police, with their knowledge, or simply in a vacuum of law enforcement created by a lack of police concentration on the *important* areas of crime. An aroused public—or at least an aroused local government— aided by the local newspaper (most of whose reporters will have long ago known most of the intimate details of the corruption at hand), will schedule public hearings, enjoy a parade of witnesses including cops, madams, prostitutes, bookies and, possibly, narcotics dealers. Out of this will come reassignments within the police department, demotions, suspensions and transfers, perhaps an indictment or two, if victims can be found, rarely a conviction and, inevitably, the "tossing in of papers" of up to a dozen high-ranking officers, who will be allowed to retire instead of being fired, since they've got their twenty years in anyway. For the next year to five years, depending on the public's memory or its proclivity for vice, the department will be fairly clean. Orders will be issued from the new chief (the old one will have resigned or retired with a lovely, glowing letter of tribute from the mayor), who, over the protests of the International Association of Chiefs of Police, usually will be the former second or third in command, rather than a new man from outside, the way the IACP would have it, to rigidly enforce the laws concerning bribery of public officials, gambling, prostitution, closing hours. So during this period the motorist who, in keeping with custom, offers a ten-dollar bill attached to his driver's license to an arresting motorcycle cop, will find himself in the lockup charged with attempted bribery. A local Friday-night poker group, which has been meeting for years over a candy store, will find the door broken down by a dozen raiding vice cops; and a poor hustler who made the mistake of wearing too-tight hot pants and boots downtown will get thirty to ninety days and a $500 fine.

For the next ten years, several things may happen: The community, bored and without anything to do, will reinstate its old card rooms, its brothels, its after-hours joints, and they will do it whether or not the police know about it—no business ever stayed open without customers, and if a bookmaker exists a year it is because somebody is patronizing him. At the same time, the men who were only patrolmen and sergeants during the last investigation will have moved up to lieutenancies, and the old lieutenants have become captains and inspectors, and all of them have carried with them to their new jobs the knowledge and memory of how the old men used to do it (and occasionally they get a postcard from one of the old captains in Miami Beach, or St. Thomas, or Acapulco), and the techniques of collecting and distributing graft can now be polished, refined and utilized for the final three to five years of the cycle until it is time for the next exposé and the beginning of a new cycle.

3. Almost all police corruption has its roots in the area of victimless crime, defined by the National Council on Crime and Delinquency as "crime based on moral codes in which there is no victim apart from the person who committed it." In this category fall the vices: liquor, prostitution, gambling and narcotics, plus the fifth emergent vice, pornography. The traditional dabbling with laws attempting to prohibit or control the vices unquestionably has ruined more lives and caused more misery to the public than the open practice of the vices could possibly have done. For openers, remember that it was Prohibition that led to the sophisticated organization of criminals in the 1920s and the ultimate rise of organized crime in America in the 1960s, even while the per-capita consumption of liquor in the United States was not reduced by the Volstead Act by so much as an ounce. Now, the churches and the civic leaders and the district attorneys and the cops will tell you that there are no victimless crimes. At the tail end of the Knapp Commission hearings in New York in 1971, the police department released a study of Manhattan prostitutes showing that 40 percent of the hustlers arrested over a three-month period had been previously arrested in connection with other crimes, including murder and burglary, and the study was released with a "so there" attitude for the benefit of those who would like to see the police department disband its "pussy posse," the cops' own name for the vice officers who have a "quota" of one, two or three hookers to arrest a night.

The danger of such a study lies in the compiler. A district attorney and a police chief, by the very nature of their calling, want *more* laws, not fewer, and you might ask the police why, if a prostitute has been arrested for murder, she is out on the street hustling and not in prison, if the charge, in the first place, was legitimate, which you may have reason to question.

Attitudes may be changing, rapidly, on gambling. The legalization of some form of gambling is under consideration or a fact in almost every state, in the form of lotteries, off-track betting and bingo. Early in 1971, New York State Senate Majority Leader Earl W. Brydges of Niagara Falls (itself a Mafia favorite), a long-time foe of legalized gambling, said he would introduce a bill that would result in legalized casino gambling in the state by 1973. His reasoning, he said, was that since the state had gone so far—lottery, pari-mutuel betting, bingo and off-track—it might as well go all the way.

In February, 1971, former United States Supreme Court Justice Tom Clark, speaking to an audience at the University of Florida, urged that all laws prohibiting drunkenness and prostitution should be repealed, and that the nation should stop trying to prosecute what he called "personal crimes." The former justice, who served on the high court from 1949 to 1967, said, "I would be willing to try permitting these actions between consenting adults. I know it's revolutionary—but we have failed."

Along thsese same lines, Justice Clark's son, Ramsey Clark, a former United States Attorney General, wrote in his 1970 book, *Crime in America*:

> Society has thoughtlessly dumped the enforcement of unenforceable laws on police with tragic consequences. Legislatures blandly pass and retain such laws, knowing they are honored most in the breach. Our hypocrisy in refusing to face the truth catches police in the middle. The alcoholic, the bookie, the whore, the homosexual, the unmarried pregnant teenager and the addict fear—and come to hate—the police. Society sends the police against them to do what cannot be done by force. Under many conditions people will drink prohibited alcoholic beverages, gamble, seek illicit sexual relations, incur unwanted pregnancies, take dangerous drugs and borrow money badly needed at any rate of interest. History shows that these practices will not be stopped by mere force.

You will notice that narcotics is lumped in with these so-called victimless crimes, and quite easily could be if the narcotics crisis is seen from a historical point of view and it is recognized that the "crisis" has been created out of a multiplicity of harsh laws, old wives' tales, horror stories and plain lies. The fact of the matter is that in Great Britain, where junkies are treated as sick people and given enough drugs to satisfy their habit until a turnaround can be made in the life-style that produced the habit in the first place, crime in the streets, from desperate addicts trying to raise enough for a fix at exorbitantly inflated street prices, comes nowhere near the rate of such crimes in even the smallest, cleanest American city. (It should be noted that toward the end of 1971, when New York City's Knapp Commission was finishing up its look at the interrelationship between the police and narcotics dealers, the heat went on, with the net result of driving the street price of heroin up by 20 percent or more, making the day's "nut" that much harder to raise by an addict with only a borrowed pistol but a fixed number of dry cleaners and drugstores to tap.)

Before the twentieth century narcotics were not considered a problem at all, except as a curious phenomenon somehow related to myth, magic and man's soul. Etiologists are almost certain that parts of the *Odyssey*, for instance, reflect drug experiences of the Homeric age, particularly the segment on the lotus eaters. Western Hemisphere aborigines had introduced hallucinogens into their religious rituals centuries before such magic mushrooms were to make the "dangerous drug" list of the various United States. By the 1970s, the real furor over drugs had passed in America, leaving only a hopeless snarl of legislation, statutes, ordinances and attitudes relating to what was never true about narcotics, and in this way the antinarcotics scramble resembles the Red scares of the 1930s and 1950s. J. Edgar Hoover was still ferreting out Communists long after the American public had realized that there was never any real internal danger from the Red Peril, much in the same way policemen are busting addicts and pushers alike, with one important difference. Police became aware that narcotics were much less dangerous than had been believed much earlier than did the general public, so that while America, in the late 1960s and early 1970s, still carried images of the Robert Mitchums and Gene Krupas being hauled off to jail for smoking marijuana, thereby falling into lifelong (it was believed) disgrace, the cops *knew* that the college kids and the faculty and the law students and the intellectual trend-setters throughout the nation were routinely turning on, and that the best deal of all was for the policeman's friends, who could come over to his house on Saturday night and fire up unlimited quantities of Acapulco Gold confiscated perhaps that very day from a downtown user or seller.

The Advertising Council, on one of those puerile television commercials that urge Americans to prevent forest fires, get a pap test, volunteer to work with deaf children and stamp out drunken driving, presents a household scene where a mother, father and daughter are waiting to begin dinner while their fifteen-year-old son is upstairs feverishly giving himself a late-afternoon fix, and as the son hurries down the stairs the announcer asks, "Why should a junkie's parents be the last to know?" when really, if they were the *first* to know, what could they do about it, other than see Household Finance about a loan to support his habit? Certainly they are not going to have him arrested, nor will they send him to the federal hospital at Lexington, Kentucky, one of the abysmal failures of the Great Dope Scare of the mid-twentieth century; and they are certainly not going to find the kid *something better to do* than pop heroin in a society where the President of the United States has his own private bowling alley, a grown man can spend as much as ten hours on a single Sunday watching football on television, where a women's leisure time is *ideally* spent reading aloud to hospital patients, preferably white.

Oh, the cops know. And society is catching up, a little. In June, 1970, the Washington, D.C., City Council voted 5 to 2 to relax narcotics laws in that city—one, incidentally, plagued almost beyond belief by street crime directly related to the high cost of narcotics—making "use" or "being under the influence of" marijuana a misdemeanor with a maximum $300 fine or ten days in jail or both, a statute which would have superseded the existing, tougher ordinance simply outlawing possession, conviction for which carried a $1,000 fine and/or a year in prison. The ordinance was vetoed in July, 1970, by Deputy Mayor Graham W. Watt, a white man, while Mayor Walter Washington, a black man with the knowledge that narcotics-related crimes have as victims mainly the residents and shopkeepers in the ghetto area, was out of town.

That same month, on July 15, 1970, the U.S. Court of Appeals in Washington said, in sending a dope case back to district court for resentencing, that an addict's possession of narcotics intended solely for his own use should not make him subject to criminal penalties. In remanding the case, involving a Washington man then serving a ten-year term for possessing thirteen heroin capsules, the court relied on a 1962 United States Supreme Court decision overturning a California law which made narcotics addiction itself a criminal offense. There is no way of telling, however, how the Supreme Court as constituted in 1972, after four Nixon appointees were aboard, might have ruled—or might in the future rule—in such a case.

The fifth vice, pornography, has become its own cause célèbre, and the cops know all about that, too, except for the most part it is too new, too unorganized and in too much of a legal mishmash for anybody to graft any significant amounts of money from it. The limbo in which the Supreme Court has kept the issue of obscenity has helped keep the cops out of it—as soon as a dirty bookstore opens up in a community, for instance, a handful of Concerned Citizens will attempt to outlaw it, only to be reversed, finally, by a higher court, leaving the cops, in the interim, baffled. If some way could be found to ban, once and for all, books and movies showing naked girls or sexual acts, implied or specific, the cops would have an easy time of it, because they could be assured that the sale of such materials was in fact illegal, so that anybody wishing to buy or sell (or, ideally, possess) such material could be regularly hit by department extortionists. Such direct, total prohibition might also interest the leaders of organized crime in going into the area of production and distribution of pornography, for this is native stomping ground for those men.

In fact, Gail Sheehy, writing in the November 20, 1972, issue of *New York* magazine, said that in New York "today, police estimate three of New York's five major crime families are responsible for 90 percent of the pornography in the metropolitan area: the three family heads are Carmine Tramunti, Samuel (Sam the Plumber) De Cavalcante, and Joseph Colombo."

It is not clear which direction we will be taking in pornography. On October 20, 1970, the United States Circuit Court of Appeals in New York, in the first decision of its kind, ruled that the law may not restrict the mailing of pornographic material between consenting adults for their personal use, although it was emphasized that the ruling did not authorize such exchanges between adults for commercial purposes or between juveniles under any circumstances.

The other point of view was taken just four days later, by President Nixon, who totally rejected the recommendations of the National Commission on Obscenity, which had been created by Congress in 1967 and which had just recommended the repeal of *all* laws regulating the distribution and possession of explicit sexual material.

In commenting on the report, the President said, "So long as I am in the White House, there will be no relaxation of the national effort to control and eliminate smut from our national life."

In one of those tape-recorded interviews in the April, 1972, issue of *Playboy*, actor-director Jack Nicholson was asked why *Drive, He Said*, a movie Nicholson had directed, was originally rated X by the Motion Picture Association of America.

Because [Nicholson replied] it had frontal nudity and it had someone who was fucking have an orgasm. The orgasm is audible, not visible. The person says, "I'm coming." I'm convinced the rating system is 100 percent corrupt. The censors say they're protecting the family unit in America when, in fact, the reality of the censorship is if you suck a tit, you're an X, but if you cut it off with a sword you're a GP.

Whatever you are, you're an American. A little sampler of modern Americana:

■ On December 17, 1969, Criminal District Court Judge Edward Haggerty, the judge who made national headlines as the presiding judge at the conspiracy trial of Clay Shaw in New Orleans, was arrested at a motel stag party and charged with conspiracy to commit obscenity, soliciting for prostitution and resisting arrest. The vice squad alerted the news media, and the TV audience was able to get a look at his honor struggling with the arresting officers. He was acquitted in a nonjury trial, but in November, 1970, was removed from the bench by a 6-to-1 vote of the Louisiana Supreme Court for heavy drinking, gambling and consorting with underworld figures.

■ In February, 1971, 500 persons were taken into custody in San Antonio, Texas, when the vice squad cops raided a gambling and stag party at the San Antonio Homebuilders' Association headquarters. The raid netted civic leaders, including two bank presidents, a steel company president, lawyers, doctors, city officials and the president of an auto agency dealership, and God knows who were among the hundred or so who fled through the back door and out the restroom window. The party had been sponsored by the Cosmopolitan Club, a spokesman for which said the crap games and nude girls on stage were only to raise money for an unidentified charity. Everybody was hauled in and questioned and then released without being charged or their names being released to the press, except the dancers were booked for nude dancing. Meanwhile, police spokesmen predicted that heads would roll among the vice squad leaders because of the raid.

■ In March, 1971, twelve of the twenty-six men on the police force of the city of Falls Church, Virginia, a dollar's throw from the shadow of the White House, were placed on probation for having attended one or more showings of a dirty movie in the print shop in the Falls Church City Hall basement. One of the cops, a lieutenant with twenty years' service on the force, was demoted to private, and all got an "official reprimand" and the loss of ten days' annual leave. The guy who supplied the film to the cops, the owner of a massage parlor in Falls Church, was charged with "offering an obscene film for rent" to the police, a crime that carries a maximum penalty of $1,000 in fines and a year in prison. The screenings had been going on for a number of months, according to City Manager Harry E. Wells. The massage parlor owner—whose business was about to be outlawed by a new ordinance that would forbid massages for a fee by members of the opposite sex— said he never rented or offered films to nobody, but had loaned the movies to the police at their request.

■ In April, 1971, Sergeant John Latin, Jr., a twelve-year veteran of the Washington, D.C., police force, was found guilty by a departmental trial board, fined $900 and stripped of his rank for soliciting a police-woman who was posing as a prostitute to try to entrap suburbanites who might be tempted to come onto the District's Fourteenth Street "strip" in search of a good time and who might, it is feared in police circles, be mugged instead. (I had meant to put part of this paragraph in italics, but as you can see it is difficult to find out which part is the most absurd.)

■ In October, 1971, twenty-one Washington, D.C., policemen including two senior officers, were officially reprimanded for failing to stop several crap games at a businessmen's dinner in June. The dinner, sponsored by the Progress Club, was held in the Regency Ballroom of the Shoreham Hotel, and the cops were there to make sure nobody was robbed. I was sitting a few months later with the owner of a downtown saloon, who happened to be a member of the Progress Club, and he was indignant over the episode. He hollered that the club—all the members of which are businessmen and civic leaders—paid their $500 annual dues simply for the privilege of having someplace to go to gamble, and what-inthehell did the cops mean interfering, because it was just good clean fun, and anyway, the profits all went to charity?

There are four principal forms of police criminality, all, in a way, interrelated.

The first, of course, is outright felonious action on the part of police officers either individually or in concert, usually limited to burglary and robbery, as in the case of some members of the police departments of Buffalo, Denver, Chicago, New York and other cities in the 1960s. In this category also has to be included assault on a citizen, a felony perpetrated by police throughout their history and which has only recently been rec-ognized as something they are not supposed to do. Dr. Albert J. Reiss, Jr., professor of sociology at Yale University, in a 1971 study of three cities, *Our Criminal Police,* found that policemen—under observation by the people who were collecting data for the study—committed criminal violations at the rate of one in five officers in two of the cities, and one in three in the third, and that while misdemeanors far outnumbered felonies, one in ten officers committed a felony—most commonly assault—in the presence of an observer.

Such criminality on the part of sworn officers, while repugnant to society, is not the most dangerous, in the long run, to society. The first form—burglary and robbery—can really be categorized as "freak" corruption, an abnormality of the crime statistics wherein a minute percentage of those committing major crimes against property happen also to be policemen. Vengeance is swift and sure, in most instances, because while police, on the whole, will ignore the grafter in their midst, they are likely to move firmly against the out-and-out thief. (Authorities agree, however, that heinous crimes committed by policemen occur most often in departments where a climate of corruption has existed through the years, where a man might be lulled into thinking that the violation of one law, felony or otherwise, is no more serious than the violation of another, which he sees every day with the blessing and protection of the police.)

The criminal-assault problem stems partly from the public's increasing awareness of its right not to be manhandled when suspected of having committed a crime, and partly from the "them-against-us" attitude which has come to be a part of the psychological makeup of police departments everywhere. In his book, *Violence and the Police* (MIT Press, 1970), William A. Westley writes:

> This is the feeling of the police when they complain so bitterly about the unfair publicity that the city newspaper gives them. It is encompassed in the words of an officer, who said, "You have two strikes against you as soon as you put on the uniform." Almost in spite of themselves, the policemen come to protect the actions of their comrades and to see little in them that is bad. Almost any beating becomes just; even graft becomes permissible. The policeman is thus permitted to breach the law, for to apprehend him would only do the apprehender harm. The prejudice and the stereotype bind the police together and give them a common front against the community.

Public outrage over police brutality has gone a long way toward curing this type of criminality, and one of the principal catalysts for reform was the 1968 Democratic National Convention, during which, for perhaps the first time in American history, it wasn't "just" blacks, Indians, poor people or labor agitators who were being caved in by nightsticks, but the children of the upper middle class, who showed you their bloody heads right there on network television. The Chicago Police Department has reformed itself incredibly along these lines since that summer, and new "attitudes" toward the public are being instilled in departments coast to coast, largely at the police academy level, but sometimes, as in New York City, via the Civilian Complaint Review Board, a device policemen loathe but with which they've had to deal. The Washington, D.C., police force, while far from being free of graft and corruption, has shown itself as one of the cleanest in the nation in terms of criminal assault, handling wave after wave of antiwar demonstrators in 1970 and 1971 with a minimum of busted heads.

The second type of police corruption is practically universal, and it is serious only, I think, insofar as it gives us an insight into the national tendency toward dishonesty. But the bribery of traffic cops is not a crime, ordinarily, that leads to systematic corruption of an entire police force. Where it occurs, it most generally is on a one-to-one basis, the cop and the motorist, and there in the night, in the garish glare of the flashing red light, two souls are searched, one to see if it has the guts to offer a ten-dollar bill to the stern-faced man outside the window, the other to see if it has the guts to take it. In normal times the offer is either accepted or rejected, no hard feelings. (A sports editor I once knew in Long Island carried a pocketful of racetrack passes and tickets to Mets games, and once got out of a speeding ticket with the *promise* of passes for a big Rangers game. The cop showed up at the newspaper office the next day to collect.) In abnormal times, when the heat is on because of an investigation into charges of police corruption, the motorist is apt to find himself charged with attempted bribery, but he must assess the mood of the day himself, before making the offer.

While traffic bribes do little to help corrupt a department (and there is little organized crime can do to turn a buck from a fixed traffic ticket), traffic tickets themselves can do much to corrupt a community or its administration, man being so wise in the ways of self-help. Everybody knows about the speed traps in North Florida and Georgia, where kangaroo court fines go a long way to keep the property taxes down. Fewer know about the city of Waukegan, Illinois, in Lake County (the county north of Cook County, into which the gambler-gangsters fled in the late 1940s when Chicago started to clean itself up), where the mayor, Robert Sabonjian, once said that unwed mothers ought to be locked up, and in an address to the North Shore Illinois Police Association in 1969, said of demonstrators, "There's a lot of talk about understanding these people. Understand, hell. Kick the hell out of them and they won't come back tomorrow." He told them to shoot when the rocks fly, and he received a standing ovation, except that the following year his own cops turned on him, when sixty of them called in sick with the "blue flu" over wage negotiations.

In the ensuing struggle over how much Waukegan cops were going to earn (the top base pay for a patrolman then was $9,400 a year), nine suspended, high-ranking police officials sat around a tape recorder with Art Patacque of the *Chicago Sun-Times* and turned over 1,500 traffic tickets issued since 1963 that had been ordered "voided," some allegedly by the mayor, others by judges, aldermen and the state's attorney's office. One of the officers talking was Lieutenant Charles M. Fletcher, a fifteen-year veteran of the force and, in 1970, chief of the traffic bureau, who said that nobody had talked earlier because of fear of reprisals, but that of an estimated 14,000 tickets written a year, 4,000, or 29 percent, were fixed by politicians. The Waukegan Police Department had 78 men plus the chief, Fletcher pointed out, while Kenosha, Wisconsin, a community similar in size, had 138 men and, in 1969, wrote only 1,700 tickets. It was maintained that the large-scale ticket-writing was done at the direction of City Hall, not to produce revenue for the city, the way they do it in Georgia, but to produce political clout for the administration (the mayor was then on his fourth consecutive term)—the politicians figured, probably correctly, that every ticket fixed was a vote in November.

The third type of police corruption is internal, within the department, and this again, I think, derives from the defensive mechanisms built into police departments everywhere. While internal affairs divisions —if there is such a formal unit within a police department, or an inspectional function if there is not—are primarily set up to police the police, their ultimate function is to maintain the department's status quo, not reform it, reorganize it, change it in any way or destroy it. The men who direct internal affairs squads, and the men of the squads themselves, are all members of the same police department, trained under the same leaders who head the patrol and detective divisions, and report to the same commissioner or chief as do those whom they are investigating. If humanly possible, every attempt will be made to keep infractions of police general orders or of the law within the structure of the department, so that solutions can be found by administrative action—that is, transfer, demotion, reprimand—or departmental trial, where the judge is a deputy police commissioner, the prosecutor a police sergeant and the stenographer on the payroll of the police department. The New York City Police Department has an official who does nothing but hear and rule on such cases; at least one prosecutor who does nothing else; and a full-time team of investigators who do nothing but try to eliminate gross police malfeasance in as unobtrusive a manner as possible. Therefore, while the needs of the *department* may be met, the needs of the *public* are not necessarily fulfilled, particularly as was the case in New Orleans two decades ago, when the good of the department demanded that the public have no idea of what was going on within it.

Yale's Dr. Reiss, citing a New York City Rand Institute stduy in 1971, said:

Granted difficulties in bringing criminal charges against police officers to the point of criminal prosecution and trial (a matter that most police chiefs even refuse to regard seriously, even arguing that the police subculture just doesn't permit it), the departmental trial procedures left almost everything to be desired. Of the two hundred four criminal allegations of criminal misbehavior against the members of the cohort [the sample studied by Rand], only 15 per cent led to a department trial. Of these but six, or 3 per cent of the original allegations (20 per cent of those brought to trial), led to so severe a punishment as dismissal or suspension. Dismissals of complaints, reprimands, probation, and minor fines were common ways of disposing of serious charges against New York's finest. The picture one gets is that the system of police justice is a mild version of the system of criminal justice generally except that unlike common criminals, the officer is left with his job and much of his status.

Later in his report, Dr. Reiss said:

Perhaps the greatest failure in police departments is the failure of internal intelligence units or of any unit that would police the police. Police administrators might well ponder the fact that a small number of observers from outside their police department can gather evidence of police misconduct far in excess of that produced by their own intelligence units in a comparable period of time, as was the case in our police observation studies. Here in New York, investigators for the Knapp Commission apparently discovered by accident police in the act of theft. If outsiders can turn up evidence on criminal violations by the police, why can't units specialized in detection and investigation of them do so?

The fourth, and most important area, over the long view, of police corruption is in the area of vice. And, as I have said, while it is *always* the community and its political power structure that corrupts, the police department is *invariably* the corrupted. And, almost without exception, the vehicle for such corruption is the vice squad, although you will see it in this book disguised as other units under other names, sometimes nonexistent in terms of the formal police flow chart, but always there, plainclothes detectives in New York City, or the chief of detectives office in Dade County, Florida. It is always a unit which is either specifically charged with the responsibilty of controlling and regulating (or, on paper, "stamping out") the practice of the vices in a community, or has taken for itself that responsibility, and, using internal power, has excluded other law-enforcement agents from becoming involved.

Chicago's Virgil Peterson told me this:

When I first came here in 1942 there was a gambling squad, I think it was the Vice Squad, and that was what made it possible for organized crime to take over. For the mob to control gambling. Other officers were supposed to keep their hands off gambling and that sort of thing ... as long as the gambling people were adhering to the rules. Yes. That's the focal point of controlling gambling. I don't mean controlling it from the public's standpoint, I mean, if you have control of or an in with the so-called Vice Squad or the gambling squad, then you can control the whole damned business.

Peterson's concern with the vice squad as a gambling squad has its roots in historical reality. It was gambling, after Prohibition, that served to swell the coffers of the Capone syndicate and make it rich enough to buy aldermen and other politicians who, in turn, would see to the well-being of the mob. And the police in Chicago have *always* been victims, not always involuntary and certainly never innocently, of the kind of City Hall politics played even today by Boss Richard J. Daley, where ward politicians have an inordinate say about the transfer, promotion and reward or punishment of individual cops.

In a report called *Crime and Politics in Chicago*, published by the Independent Voters of Illinois in 1953, based on an investigation conducted by Aaron Kohn (now managing director of the Crime Commission of Greater New Orleans), a policeman is quoted:

Bribery [in 1952] is the order of the day in our police department. Gifts, both money and merchandise, at Christmas time are a "clean" form of bribery. In past years I have seen my district commander receive many baskets and packages at the station during Christmas week. Some gamblers, and even reputable business firms, have lists of their selected police, whether they be in districts, detective, or traffic bureaus. Only last Christmas I was given a three-pound package of bacon by a fellow officer that did not want it. The package bore his typewritten name and was delivered by a Brinks Express truck; one package for each man at his station. I was informed all traffic men received a similar package. Trucking firms also make cash gifts to many members of Traffic Branch at Christmas time. Uniformed policemen walk into gambling establishments once yearly for the same reason and usually are "checked off" by their star number.

In my district, I knew the location of every handbook but I also know better than to molest them (the rooms are now closed and there is only sneak betting). Taverns operate after hours and others open before noon on Sundays but they, too, are not to be disturbed by a patrolman. On rare occasions a complaint from the Commissioner's Office is read at roll call and the lieutenant will sternly state action is to be taken—but then smugly adds "the dicks will handle it." The inference is obvious.

The inference is obvious if you know the structure of the old Chicago Police Department, not that much different from today's. Each police district was commanded by a captain, who was virtually autonomous in his district, and under his command were a uniformed bureau and a detective bureau; the latter (which operated in civilian clothes) was solely responsible for the enforcement of *all* the vice laws, including gambling. The detectives were nominally headed by a lieutenant or higher, perhaps an acting captain, but were in fact run by a "bull dick," a sergeant, or even a patrolman, who answered only to the captain and without whose permission no one—uniformed or plainclothes—including his superior, the lieutenant, could make an arrest of any vice figure or establishment.

Rounding out the triumvirate at the top of each district was the "captain's man," known in New York as the "bagman," usually a patrolman or sergeant in rank, whose sole duty was to negotiate with illegal enterprises and collect money from them on a regular basis. The captain's man was so indispensable to the captain and the bull dick that when the captain would be transferred to a new district, the captain's man would be transferred right along with him. (It should be noted that, unlike in New Orleans during the 1940s and 1950s, and in New York and Seattle during the 1960s, the "bag" was not split with subordinates in Chicago. Because of this, individual patrolmen and other detectives "rooted" for money where they could find it, making private deals with gamblers and madams and bar owners; and everybody knew their leverage was minimal, their worst threat being to make an anonymous telephone call "downtown" to report that a serious crime had been committed in one of the illegal establishments, possibly bringing a headquarters detective squad to the scene. And also, a bookie could never be sure when the cop on the beat might become a captain himself, or a bull dick.)

At this time, in 1952, two years had passed since the late Senator Estes Kefauver had brought his Senate subcommittee to Chicago to listen to testimony on organized crime, and to decide that gambling was the principal source of revenue for the syndicates. The Chicago Police Department, from headquarters, was running a gambling squad consisting of *four* plainclothes policemen, headed by a patrolman (included among the four) named Timothy Allman, who in turn was solely responsible to Captain William Balswick and Commissioner Timothy O'Conner. The squad, according to Allman's testimony before the Emergency Crime Committee hearing of June 4, 1952, operated primarily on complaints "that come to the Commissioner's office which are turned over to me for investigation—and also I get them personally from the people who read the newspapers." Many of the complaints, instead of being referred to the squad, were referred to the district captains, who of course took whatever action they—or their bull dicks—thought best.

The fact that the gambling squad of 1952 was making raids at all —although even then only on those complaints which filtered down to them from the commissioner's office—was a far cry from the morals division of ten years earlier, then headed by Captain Martin McCormick.

A grand-jury investigation in Cook County in 1941 had uncovered "shocking conditions" and concluded that Chicago and Cook County protected syndicated gambling, which was operating "openly and flagrantly" without police interference, and what the grand jury meant was that the downtown horserooms were jammed with as many as five hundred customers at post time, and that you could hear the loudspeakers a block away. The jury specifically blamed the morals division (read vice squad), recommended that it be abolished (it was, temporarily), and charged McCormick and three members of the morals division with neglect of duty and filing false reports; and hearings were scheduled before the Chicago Civil Service Commission, which found, on July 3,

1942, that the charges against the men were unfounded, because, after all, McCormick had given the addresses of suspected gambling houses to his men, his men had visited those places, had found nothing there, had so reported, and therefore could not be guilty of neglect of duty.

The Civil Service Chairman who presided over most of the hearings [Virgil Peterson told me thirty years later] was later promoted to a judgeship. In the course of the hearings we had heard that McCormick had said if he was a victim he'd blow the whistle on everybody. And it was—it was part of the Kelly [Mayor Edward J. Kelly] Machine. They got all kinds of money from the gambling syndicate and that sort of thing. And that is the very base, the essence of organized crime. The mob makes contributions to political campaigns with the understanding they're going to get to put people in law enforcement spots, they're going to have a say in the policies and that sort of thing. It's much easier to control if you've got a Vice Squad [with] exclusive jurisdiction that covers it, but it isn't always just the Vice Squad. You can get rid of the Vice Squad, not have a Vice Squad as such, but still have a bad situation. But it makes for easier control. Now the theory behind the Vice Squad is that you have a certain specialized group specializing in this sort of crime, know all the ins and outs of this particular thing, but the way it was used and has been used in many places it is a very easy way to control the whole situation, makes the control that much easier for the mob, if they're wrong. And of course you've always had terrific problems of corruption in your morals or Vice Squad.

In the McCormick case, the state's attorney's office used, as precedent, the case of Andrew M. Fosse, a six-year veteran of the force, who had been fired for neglect of duty.

Fosse, on November 28, 1941, according to his own previous testimony, had been assigned to

> stop all gambling in two places: 166 West Washington Street and 33 North La Salle Street, [and it was charged that he] failed to stop it at 166 West Washington Street, this evidenced by the fact that other policemen of the department did arrest three persons engaged in receiving bets upon horse racing results, in the said 166 West Washington Street during the time it was Fosse's duty to suppress gambling therein.

As a matter of fact, what Fosse *meant* was that he had been specifically assigned to *Room* 1018 at 33 North La Salle Street and to *Room* *200* at 166 West Washington Street by his boss, Captain Thomas J. Duffy, and by God he had sat in one or another of those two rooms all day on November 28, leaving one only to go to the other, and vice versa, and at the end of the day he filled out a report correctly certifying that there was no gambling in either room.

Another example—one of hundreds brought up in the McCormick case—involved a well-known (in 1940) handbook at 228 South Wells Street, which was visited three times that year by an investigator from the state's attorney's office. The first time he counted 6 employees and 55 customers. The second time he reported 9 employees and 120 customers. And on his last visit there were 10 employees and 100 patrons, a fairly good-sized operation by any standards, even those of prewar Chicago.

A patrolman, Fred Trauth, one of McCormick's gambling squad men, had been assigned, in writing, to make sure that there was no gambling at 226 South Wells Street or 230 South Wells Street—with no mention of 228 South Wells Street—on several days, including at least one of the three days the man from the state's attorney's office had paid his own visits. The situation was described like this for the Civil Service Commission:

> The gambling place at 228 South Wells is on the first floor, and the entrance to 228 South Wells is about ten feet from the entrance to 230 South Wells, and 228 South Wells is approximately seven feet from 226 South Wells. Furthermore, 228 and 230 South Wells are located in the same building and there is a door leading from the lobby of 230 South Wells into 228 South Wells. It is impossible to go from 226 to 230 without going by 228. 228 South Wells is a well known gambling place. During 1940 arrests were made at 228 by Officer Lynch of the Morals Division on March 28, and by Officer Corcoran of the Morals Division on August 26. During 1940 Officer Trauth made innumerable visits to 226 and 230, on every occasion reporting that no gambling was in progress. . . . Only on one occasion, July 8, did Trauth visit 228 South Wells, on which occasion he reported no gambling there. This, however, is significant, in that it definitely reflects knowledge on the part of Trauth that 228 South Wells was allegedly a gambling place, and he also would have known by virtue of arrests made there by other officers of the Morals Division, of which he was a member.

At the same time the vice squad guys were turning in phony reports for the record, it developed that they were turning in longhand reports to Captain McCormick concerning the *real* activities of the spots they were visiting. One of them, dated June 12, 1940, from Patrolmen Trauth and Corcoran, read, in part:

> Subject: Places visited on the Commissioner's list.
> 27 South Wabash 4th floor going 1:30 p.m.
> 19 W. Lake St. cigar store going over counter 2 p.m.
> 114 N. Dearborn St., basement front door padlocked, entrance gained through 108 N. Dearborn going in regular room 2:30 p.m.
> 359 W. Madison St. front door padlocked entrance gained through rear door, going in regular room 3 p.m.
> 145 S. Wells St., front door padlocked entrance, gained through side door, going in regular room 3:15 p.m.

The strong implication here is that the gambling squad was being used as a surveillance team for the benefit of the captain's man so that he would know who was running and who was not running and, therefore, who owed the unofficial license money.

After a long hassle—the Crime Commission put a lot of heat on Mayor Kelly—McCormick was dismissed, only to be reinstated by a one-vote majority decision of the Illinois Supreme Court, and he later became chief of the Cook County Police Criminal Division.

In the McCormick case, one loose string seems to be the intervention of the state's attorney office in downtown gambling. Why? Generally speaking, in larger cities, police officers are especially detailed to the district attorney's special squad (in Illinois, the state's attorney is the district attorney), which gives the district attorney the enforcement powers to go along with his judicial mandate to eliminate crime, but it is sometimes true that a district attorney takes money from the same men who have corrupted members of the police department, or at least that his special squad of police officers have set up their own bag, so that for complete coverage, as they say in the insurance business, gamblers have to pay not only the vice squad but the D.A.'s squad.

In 1940, the chief investigator for Cook County State's Attorney Thomas J. Courtney was Daniel A. Gilbert, who had been a cop since April, 1917, and who had been Courtney's man since November, 1932. Gilbert early on had a reputation as a tough cop, and for one brief period, three months in 1935, he left Courtney's office to become chief of the uniformed force of the entire city, which made him second in command to Police Commissioner James P. Allman in charge of Chicago's 6,000 policemen.

In a yellowing clipping dated April 6, 1935, in the morgue of the *Chicago Sun-Times*, it is recorded that "among Captain Gilbert's first official acts was a conference with Captain Martin Mullen, head of the morals and gambling squad. While Gilbert denied that he plans any new drive on gambling establishments, he admitted that the order to 'clamp down' on gambling had gone out several days before." Now, it was reported, Mullen and Chief of Detectives John L. Sullivan would report to both Gilbert and to Commissioner Allman, whereas previously they had reported only to Allman. This little reorganizing move accomplished, Gilbert, in July, 1935, gave up his new job and returned to Courtney's office as chief investigator, and the newspapers reported that under his interregnum the gambling squad had been abolished and "the lid was clamped on the handbooks." What had happened, it is believed, in retrospect, is that the bag had simply been rerouted. In that same year, the Illinois legislature had passed a bill to license handbook gambling, a bill vetoed by the governor, and when asked by a reporter if Gilbert's double transfer had anything to do with either the bill or the veto, Courtney said, "Nothing at all. I was against that bill. The responsibility for gambling now lies in the police department. We will see that the law is enforced as to gambling. I was never in favor of the handbook bill. I think that the licensing of gambling is not a good thing. I was not strongly impressed with arguments for the bill. There will be no compromising with gambling. I am against licensing vice in any form."

The gamblers couldn't have agreed with him more, since licensing implies taxation, possibly an audit. By 1938 there were 15,000 persons employed in Chicago's bookmaking industry, and an estimated 500 handbooks were operating in the county; Gilbert was spending his time cracking down on labor organizers and loan sharks, and had got involved, with the Teamsters Union, in an attempt to take over the scavenger waste pickup business in the city. In 1940, a candidate trying to root Courtney out of office charged that Gilbert had been seen in the same hotel in Hot Springs as Frank (The Enforcer) Nitti, at the same time a massive manhunt was being organized to track down the Capone figure. (Gilbert's link with gangsters was omnipresent throughout his career—he was early linked with Albert (Jake) Lingle, a shadowy *Chicago Tribune* reporter who reportedly had an interest in the *Chicago Turf Bulletin and Sports Record* and who was murdered in 1930; and Gilbert was given "credit" for "solving" the kidnap case in 1933 of John (Jake the Barber) Factor,

for which Roger (The Terrible) Tuohy got ninety-nine years in States-
ville, and later Touhy was to claim—successfully—that the kidnap was a
hoax perpetrated so that Factor would not be deported to England,
where he was wanted in connection with a $7-million swindle case, and
that Tuohy had been framed by, among others, Dan Gilbert; and in
August, 1954, after twenty-one years in prison, he was ordered freed, as
the victim, in the words of the judge, of "perjured testimony." He was
released in November, 1959, and walked the streets for less than a
month before he was murdered. Jake the Barber continued, through the
years, to appear on the lists of campaign contributors to Democratic candidates, and in the 1972 presidential contest gave substantial amounts to
both Edmund S. Muskie and Hubert H. Humphrey. Factor, of course,
has never been deported.)

Gilbert took a leave of absence to run for sheriff in 1950, having
won the Democratic nomination from a machine politician named
Richard J. Daley, then county clerk, who turned around and supported
Gilbert in the general election, saying, "We have never been lacking the
courage to stand behind any candidate in an emergency," a tenet by
which Daley lived until 1972, when, by now head of the machine and
mayor as well, he dumped his own protégé, incumbent State's Attorney
Edward V. Hanrahan, after Hanrahan was indicted for conspiring to
obstruct justice in the investigation of the killing of two Black Panthers.

Gilbert lost heavily, and at least part of the votes against him had
to be attributed to the fact that Gilbert had been called to appear before
the Kefauver Committee that summer, and even though the Committee
had suppressed his testimony, the *Sun-Times* acquired parts of it, and
reported that the investigator had reported income of $45,000 in 1949,
although his income from the state had amounted to around $15,000.
The rest was from gambling, his main bookie being John M. McDonald,
who ran the La Salle Cigar Store at 215 North La Salle, and who had
been described by the Chicago Crime Commission as "king of the layoff
bookies." (A layoff bookie is one who is heavily enough bankrolled so
that he can accept part of bets made by other bookies who find themselves financially overextended.)

In Gilbert's testimony, he said he didn't think it was illegal to bet on
an election (he said he had won $10,000, at least, in the Roosevelt-Lan-
don contest in 1936) or a football game, but admitted that his men—
now totaling more than fifty—hadn't chopped up a handbook since 1939.
He said there were no gambling operations in 1950 in the city of Chicago.

In a thirty-five-page report released in March, 1951, well after the November election and a few months after Gilbert extended his leave of absence into full retirement, the Kefauver Committee described two major crime syndicates in America, one in New York and the other in Chicago, both of which answered directly to Charles (Lucky) Luciano. The committee put the figure of illegal gambling done through the two syndicates at $20 billion a year, and accused the syndicate of paying millions of dollars a year to law-enforcement officers at all levels. The report tied Gilbert in with Tony Accardo, the Fischetti brothers and Jake (Greasy Thumb) Guzik, the heirs to the Capone empire, and called Gilbert "the richest police officer in the world." When he died on August 1, 1970, his estate was expected to probate out to more than $1 million.

It is a full generation now since the Kefauver Committee went to work in Chicago, with the result of astounding America about the extent of organized crime, and a federal strike force has been operating in Cook County for a year. Early in 1972, a special federal grand jury had its sights set on more than sixty policemen from the city of Chicago, up to the rank of district commander. Thirty of them were turned up when the FBI raided a South Side liquor store, alleged to be the front for a network of syndicate bookmakers, and found one of those famous "little black books" with the names of police officers alleged to be accepting payoffs for protection; and the other thirty are being examined under provisions of the Hobbs Act, one of the tools federal law-enforcement officials use when there is no specific violation to be charged. The premise is that a licensed saloon deals with liquor and cigarettes—both products which are shipped in interstate commerce, and therefore subject to federal scrutiny. What happened is that FBI agents were given statements by tavern owners about police payoffs, and as 1972 grew older, eight of the cops—all vice squad-related and one a lieutenant specifically in charge of an undercover unit assigned to ferret out gambling—had been indicted.

The new exposures are shaking up Chicago, which still has a flourishing syndicate, and which has had two unsettling experiences in the last decade, both of which mortified City Hall and led to complete police department reorganizations—neither of which answered to the problem of the corrupt policeman and his link to wider, more sinister evils of society. The first was in 1960, when five policemen went to prison for engaging in a burglary ring, which stunned the city and led to a new police commissioner, Orlando W. Wilson, the author of the classic *Police*

Administration (McGraw-Hill, 1963), and reorganization along the lines of his book; and the other was in 1968, when America watched the televised "police riot" at the Democratic National Convention, which led directly to the establishment of a new set of courses at the Chicago Police Academy to deal with the problems of hippies and minority groups.

A reporter for the *Sun-Times*, William Braden, spent six months studying the Chicago Police Department in 1970, and produced a series of interpretive articles which the newspaper, pleased with itself, reprinted the following year. The series, "Toward a New Police Image," reported on the difficulties of being a cop in troubled times, what the department is doing to get itself pulled together, the functions of the internal affairs division (so new in Chicago that it was only formed after the 1960 burglary-ring case) and the police academy, and the fact that a first-grade Chicago policeman gets $12,120 a year, the highest police salary in the nation. The community—and its newspapers—seemed to be so concerned with the brutality issue that the idea of graft was set aside, only to be resurrected by the federal strike force, which seemed to know that $12,000 a year is chickenfeed compared with the money being banked by dishonest cops simply for letting a genial man in a cigar store accept a few bets over the counter.

Morals laws [wrote the late Orlando W. Wilson in *Police Administration*] constitute a particularly difficult problem for the police because of the frequent resistance of the public and sometimes of officials to their enforcement. Although violations of the laws regulating or prohibiting prostitution, gambling, and the sale, possession or use of narcotics and liquor are referred to collectively as vices, the public often prefers to think that motivation or environment alter the seriousness of the offense; e.g., gambling for charity is fashionable, drinking to excess is excusable when it involves no injury to another persons, and prostitution may be forgiven when it is limited to one person, the prostitute then becoming a mistress. Vice offenses are characterized by the absence of direct harm to anyone except the willing participants, although in some cases the family and associates are indirectly injured. Many citizens and some public officials believe, therefore, that even though a participant is a weakling who cannot control his appetite, he should be free to indulge in his vices in spite of injury to his health, the dissipation of his property, or the destruction of his own life, so that the strong may taste enjoyments that do them no apparent harm.

Modern society, however, has developed the philosophy that the strong must help the weak by protecting them from their own folly. This is public policy, and without regard to whether its practice strengthens or weakens the human race, morals laws have been enacted to shield the weak from their own lack of good judgment.

Wilson waxed somewhat more eloquent on the need for the public to be informed about how organized crime feeds on the vices, ignoring, of course, the idea that if the vices were not illegal organized crime would have nothing on which to nourish itself; but then, he was a cop, and a cop needs as many laws as possible in order to keep his force building and growing. (There are an estimated 1,100,000 laws on the books today in the United States, with the state legislatures creating new ones every day.)

Wilson goes on to recommend that police departments treat vice like any other offense and simply do their best to eliminate it, and the organization he recommends to accomplish this end is the classic, semi-autonomous vice squad, separated from detective bureaus whose job it is to investigate other crimes, with use of a full range of undercover operatives and informants, and the denial of authority to a beat patrolman to make a raid on a vice den without first checking with his superiors to find out if perhaps the vice squad isn't planning something even bigger for next year—or maybe the year after. Along with this tired old structure of the vice squad is Wilson's ideal staffing of the squad—with men assigned on a permanent basis, men who really enjoy that kind of work. It is likely that not one vice squad constituted in this "ideal" manner has ever done more than further entrench the vice operators and corrode the morale and effectiveness of the police department at large.

2

Miami and Her Sisters in Sin

In December, 1970, on the Monday after Christmas, Mayor Frank
Burke of Louisville, Kentucky, without consulting his police chief, C. J.
Hyde, called a news conference and announced that he, the mayor, was
abolishing the police department's vice squad.

At the conference the mayor explained his reasons:

> Our emphasis is upon the involvement of the police officer in the
> neighborhood and the community where he works. Therefore, and
> consistent with those principles, an objective evaluation leads us to
> the conclusion that a Vice Squad, as such, is not the answer to effec-
> tive enforcement of laws against bootlegging, gambling, prostitution
> and similar type offenses. Hence today, effective today, the Vice
> Squad in the Louisville Division of Police is discontinued.

On that day there were no fewer than 200, by local police estimate, walk-in handbook operations in and around Louisville, the kind they used to have in Chicago, with each race being called by an announcer over a loudspeaker, although federal law-enforcement officials put the number of such operations at closer to 350—and estimated that the total handle for illegal gamblers was running at about $30 million annually. And by gambling in Louisville, the horse racing capital of the world, you are talking about handbook gambling, because, even in the ghetto, there is no numbers racket, only bookies, who take bets as small as 50 cents and pay track odds (unlike some cities, where track odds are paid with a maximum limit of 20 to 1, or, in hard times, 10 to 1).

The morning after the mayor's announcement the books opened, for about two hours, and then closed for the rest of the week. The following week they opened on Monday, and operated on a shaky basis all week, with heavy lookouts and several real raids, and on Friday they closed again, and to this time they have not reopened, although some of them had been open continuously at the same location for *more than a generation.*

It was widely suspected around Louisville that the mayor got rid of the vice squad because he had heard that the squad was central to the process of collecting money from the gamblers, and Clarence Jones and James Walker, special investigative reporters for **WHAS-TV** in Louisville, who had started the whole thing, asked Chief Hyde if he had heard that kind of talk about the vice squad.

"Well, of course, this is a rumor that you always have," Chief Hyde told the television audience on February 9, 1971, in the second of a two-part documentary produced by Jones and Walker entitled *Louisville— Open City.* "And I've observed that it is usually the people who are the most active in enforcement of what people term as unpopular laws, uh, that they are, but when confronted with the proof of it . . . I, ah, I have yet to see anyone prove it, or attempt to prove it in this town, during my tenure of office."

The chief admitted that in the nearly thirty years he had been with the department he had known only one person to go to jail for as much as six months on gambling charges, although he got a bit on the defensive, and, like police chiefs everywhere, started quoting statistics: "Your gambling arrests have continuously gone up in the last three years. Arrests is one thing they do know about or they wouldn't have been making arrests in the last, since the 28th, and this is the 19th—say twenty to twenty-two days, they've averaged quite a number of arrests each day now."

"The real question becomes 'why bother?'" commented reporter Jones on February 8.

Police officials in other cities often defend their failure to enforce vice laws by saying that their men must devote their time to more serious crimes. That is not the case in Louisville. Before it was disbanded in late December, the Vice Squad each year made arrests at one hundred to one hundred fifty handbooks and logged between two thousand and three thousand arrests in connection with prostitution activity [the American Social Hygiene Association in 1969 ranked the city among the top five in the nation in terms of prostitution-related problems]. Even though nothing happened to those arrested, this took a great deal of police time.

The police were very active in Louisville, yes.

The two reporters were turned loose early in 1970. Walker was already on the staff, and Jones, who had worked for the Knight newspaper chain for a number of years, was brought in, given a cover name and identity and a little rented office downtown, and told to expose the relationship between gambling, police corruption and the possible intrusion of organized crime. By the time the first two programs were aired in February, 1971, the two men had worked for eight months, shooting clandestine movies from the hip with a small camera inside horse rooms, following bookies in their daily routes as they picked up and delivered scratch sheets and, it was charged, money to the police, and staked out, among other areas, the intersection of Floyd and Market streets, a block away from the Farmer's Market and the center of the city's flourishing prostitution industry. (At this intersection Jones and Walker reported casual greetings between prostitutes and passing cops, who seemed to pay no attention to the women as they grabbed prospective customers by the arm and propositioned them in broad daylight.)

What they found, in the long run, was that Louisville is either twenty years behind or twenty years ahead of the rest of the nation in one respect: The money paid to cops, judges and political parties over the years has bought the local gamblers protection not only from arrest but from invasion by the "outside" elements of organized crime—if a Cosa Nostra type tried to move in, he would not be able to operate for fifteen minutes before being run out of town by the police. Of course, it must be remembered that all Kentucky gamblers have close ties with men like Gil (The Brain) Beckley, another so-called king of the layoff bookies, who got their start in the casino of Newport, Kentucky, just across the border from Cincinnati, and who were inextricably tied in with the men who today furnish sports results and handicap information to gamblers throughout America. One simply cannot be a professional gambler for any length of time, no matter the local situation, without doing business with the syndicates. (Beckley, incidentally, vanished in 1970, after becoming the target of a federal investigation.)

It is largely thought in Louisville that the mayor's abolition of the vice squad was a direct reaction to the rumors that had come his way about "a man named Jones" who was in town to expose the corrupt conditions in the city (security on the Jones affair wasn't as tight as you might imagine: I knew about it almost as soon as he was hired, and I hadn't seen him in years), and that the mayor wanted to "do something" to divert a little of the heat that was bound to come his way. The vice squad was a good target, because it was used in the classic sense of the vice squad, and, besides there was already enough on them to warrant at least reassignment.

In November, 1970, Commissioner Shirley Palmer-Ball, of the State Alcoholic Beverage Commission, went before a grand jury to testify that in a twin set of raids spearheaded by the ABC that June on licensed beverage establishments suspected of allowing prostitution and gambling on the premises, most of the operators, even with a heavy veil of secrecy over the state-run raids, expected the raiders and were ready for them, and Palmer-Ball announced publicly that he felt that corrupt officers had tipped the joints off.

In the February 9, 1971, telecast, reporter Jones said:

What happened inside the jury room is secret. In the jury's report there was no mention of the document, or any investigation concerning it. Palmer-Ball also carried into the grand jury room an anonymous letter. The letter was signed, "A Policeman."

[The camera now swings to Palmer-Ball.] In this letter he [the policeman] stated that there were over one hundred twenty-nine handbooks operating in the city, and then, ah, went down the line through each district and the vice squad setting out the amounts of money that are paid off to the various, ah, people in the districts and in the vice squad, ah, each month. I felt that with the knowledge of what took place with the June raids in Louisville, the fact that there was a tipoff, ah, very apparent, and, ah, with other bits and pieces of information, ah, that, ah, were available, and, ah, that we discussed to some extent there before the grand jury that day, that a letter of this type, whether it is anonymous or not, ah, should be looked into.

JONES: To your knowledge did they do this? Has there been any effort to ...

PALMER-BALL: No, they gave the letter back to me. They didn't even keep it.

Jones managed to get a gambler and after-hours joint operator to appear on television. He was Cleve White, owner of the Key Club at 1015 West Market Street, and his session with Jones went like this:

JONES: Can you run a place in Louisville without protection money?

WHITE: I don't see how.

JONES: Why?

WHITE: You've just got to have money if you violate the law, if you violate the law, then you've got to pay.

JONES: Are the police that sharp? Can they find you as soon as you start violating the law?

WHITE: Yeah, yeah, they can find you.

JONES: How long would it take if you set up a new place, with gambling and bootlegging ...

WHITE: For them to find you?

JONES: For them to find you.

WHITE: The first night.

JONES: And then what would happen?

WHITE: They'd just come by and make like a complaint, come around, look around, see what you doing, you know ...

JONES: Would they arrest you the first night?

WHITE: No, no, no, they not going to arrest you the first night. They gonna make, you, they want you to talk to them, come in.

JONES: Come in to the station?

WHITE: No, come in to them, and then if you don't come in then they'll arrest you and raid you.

JONES: You mean by comin' in ...

WHITE: Money ...

JONES: Come across ...

WHITE: Yeah, come across with some dough.

JONES: And is there any set rate for this? Do you pay a certain rate for bootlegging, a certain rate for prostitution?

WHITE: Yeah, it's according to what you're doin', you know, if you're not doing nothing but just bootlegging, it's not going to hurt you too much. They'll take bootlegging money, but if you go in bootlegging, gambling, prostitution, everything, then you got to come in good.

· JONES: And what is coming in good?

WHITE: Ah, around a hundred dollars a month for each one of them.

JONES: For each policeman?

WHITE: Well, not no sergeant and beat police, you know. A sergeant usually get twenty-five dollars, maybe fifty.

JONES: Is that a month, now?

WHITE: Yeah, a month, and the, ah, beat police usually gets five dollars, ten dollars apiece, a car.

JONES: Now the beat police, that's the patrolmen?

White said yes, the patrolmen, plus the sergeants, and the lieutenants and all the way up to a colonel—and up to as high as $100 a week, and that the money bought you protection from day-to-day hassle plus advance warning of raids.

JONES: When you buy protection does part of the price include the service to be tipped off?

WHITE: Oh yeah, oh yeah.

JONES: When you pay protection, you expect to be tipped?

WHITE: Yeah, you expect to be tipped and everything. And well they will tip you to protect their interest, you see. Yeah, see, they got an interest in the joint.

JONES: The interest is just the monthly ...

WHITE: Monthly payment. See, they're your partners.

Louisville never really seemed to mind the bookie joints and the whores, and several of the city fathers had gone on record as saying that if you're going to attract conventions to a city, you had to have something for them to do except sit in a hotel room and watch old movies on television. And even after WHAS began its series trying to show the dangers of corrupting your police department the way Louisville was corrupting hers, not a great deal happened, except that the walk-in handbooks shut down (and the telephone books started up, greatly intensified). The feds sent in a strike force, which was still functioning in late 1972; and a federal grand jury had been sitting since April, 1971; and a police court judge, who for many years threw out all gambling charges or allowed pleas of guilty to lesser charges is doing his time for income-tax evasion (and will be eligible, under Kentucky law, to return to the bench when he is released); and not too long after the mayor disbanded the vice squad he removed C. J. Hyde as chief of police for general incompetence, nothing serious, replacing him with a thirty-year veteran of the same, tired police force. Immediately, Chief Hyde announced his candidacy for mayor in the 1973 city election, and it was reported that he had an odds-on chance of winning, since he is a hot man on the civic-club luncheon circuit, and particularly if the federal grand jury fails to return any indictments—something it has had trouble doing, partly because everything shut down so tightly after the television exposé.

The newspapers in Louisville, early in 1972, were just starting to become interested in their city's problems of morality (they had treated the early WHAS-TV documentaries as television fare, and handled the stories as reviews), and only then got around to hiring investigative reporters of their own, the *Courier-Journal* being steeped in the tradition of the Columbia Graduate School of Journalism, which seems to hold that if the gangsters have taken over a community it is by God up to them to call a press conference to announce it if they want it covered. On February 12, 1971, three days after the second telecast, the *Courier-Journal* editorialized:

> Because of the televised documentary, one supposes, we'll now have another of those periodic and temporary crackdowns that always are forced on officialdom when somebody pries up one of these rocks and points at the sin beneath. And we may not even have that for very long, since Mayor Burke has turned the matter over to his Citizens Advisory Committee, a fine group of civic-minded people who will be fatally handicapped in investigating crime by their lack of subpoena power and the right to grant witnesses immunity.
>
> But wasn't it a helluva town for conventions?

There is a touchy feeling in Washington, D.C., because the metropolitan police department has been praised to high heaven for its work in crowd and riot control (although in times of stress, the army always has a few battalions of paratroopers ready to drop in, and the tanks are always just outside the Beltway, ready to clank in and settle things); and any hint of wrongdoing by police officers seems to be taken as a personal slur against the black mayor, Walter Washington, or against the white police chief, Jerry Wilson (who had been mentioned as one of two or three possible permanent successors to the late J. Edgar Hoover and his interim successor, L. Patrick Gray), or against Capitol Hill, whose House and Senate District committees rule the District of Columbia with an iron hand, or against the White House itself, which hates to think of anything evil occurring in the shadow of the executive mansion, even though several people were murdered or raped in executive office buildings during a short period of time in 1971. I am even reluctant to mention the uniformed sergeant who comes into the saloon where I regularly eat supper, who parks his cruiser out front and who sits at the bar and enjoys his free coffee or whatever, and who sometimes just stands by the dumbwaiter leading to the kitchen, forcing everybody in the place to wonder what it is he is waiting for and why he is not out supervising whoever it is he is supposed to supervise; and it is with some reluctance that I tell you about a woman I know who for years has run a house-cut, all-night poker game in a low-rise apartment building within walking distance (or running distance, at night, in a city with so many junkies-cum-muggers chasing you around) of a police station, because, while I am certain this woman is not paying off the cops, they know that she is in business, and figure what the hell. On a warm summer night, with the window open, I have heard cops holler a greeting to this woman from the street, even though she does not answer. The same woman plays the numbers, at the rate of one dollar a day, on the same number every day (I believe it is 2-1-5, the number she believes, rightly or wrongly, to be the first slip drawn from the first social security pool, when she was a young woman back in the 1930s), and in order to get the same number every day she must pay by the month, in advance, which she does with a check.

In the Washington ghetto alone, which roughly comprises everything east of Rock Creek Park (most of the city's politicians, white federal workers, social elite and communications employees, the last of which comprise 22,000 including journalists, live in the Maryland or Virginia suburbs or in the narrow strip that starts in Georgetown and ends in Chevy Chase—it is one of the rare Northern cities with true, solid, well-defined segregation), it has been estimated that there are from 2,-500 to 3,000 employees working full time in illegal occupations. According to Paul Valentine, writing in the *Washington Post* on March 5, 1972, these employees meet schedules, attain new skills, compete with each other, seek promotions and work, through a hierarchy, toward positions of power and authority. There are 3,000 full- and part-time prostitutes, forty well-known pimps, utilizing a network of rented rooms and hotels (and greatly utilized by the State Department and the various embassies, particularly those representing nations of the Middle East, whose diplomats reportedly can barely keep their hands off the stewardesses on the way over), churning about $12 million a year. The numbers racket turns over anywhere from $150 million to $300 million a year, according to who is doing the estimating, working through fifty top writers hiring hundreds of runners six days a week. There are an estimated 15,000 narcotics addicts with an average daily habit of $25, which puts that total turnover at more than $136 million a year. Several hundred full- or part-time bootleggers and after-hours joints are in business, many of the sort where you buy a pint of whiskey at a dollar markup over the retail price, but many of whom net up to $35,000 a year.

How much of this is related to the larger evil of organized crime is not as much a matter of conjecture as it seems, either. In February, 1972, Daniel Packtor, an official with the District Office of Criminal Plans and Analysis, prepared a report on organized crime which was presented with an application for a grant of $1.8 million to the Justice Department's Federal Law Enforcement Assistance Administration. The four-volume report indicated that organized crime in Washington is increasing rapidly, with narcotics, gambling and loan-sharking more and more being controlled by the New York syndicate (referred to in the report as the Cosa Nostra). Further, the swing toward organized crime has accelerated since 1969, before which, it was noted, most heroin in the city came from Baltimore, but after that time began moving to Washington directly from New York City. In February, 1971, an $18-million-a-year gambling operation in the District was directly linked to a New York syndicate.

> There is an increasing amount of evidence that the rackets extant in the District are interdependent. They are not independent narcotics groups or numbers groups—they know each other—and there are cases here where there is financial interdependence [the report's author, Packtor, was quoted as saying by Lance Gay, a reporter for the *Washington Star*]. While this is standard La Cosa Nostra practice, there is no indication that an LCN family is based in the district. But while the underworld is not staffed by LCN soldiers [in Washington], the question is whether they are being controlled by La Cosa Nostra.

Former Supreme Court Chief Justice Earl Warren was quoted by *Parade* magazine in December, 1970, as having said, concerning the narcotics traffic and its effect on the American way of life, "It is my firm belief that organized crime can never exist to any marked degree in any large community unless one or more of the law enforcement agencies have been corrupted. This is a harsh statement, but I know that close scrutiny of conditions wherever such crime exists will show that it is protected."

On September 18, 1970, a squad of Washington police, armed with sledgehammers, broke into four homes and arrested a half dozen people charged with everything from possession of lottery slips and maintaining a gambling premise to destroying evidence and possession of unregistered weapons. In a fifth raid that day, the police knocked at the door of Roger W. (Whitetop) Simkins, then seventy-one, who had headed the city's list of known gamblers for more than a generation, and who the police suspected of directing the operations of the other joints the other teams were busily busting up. While Whitetop drank a glass of orange juice for his diabetes and took a pill for his heart condition, police searched the old man's house, for which he had paid $50,000 fifteen years earlier, and came up with eight pistols, four shotguns and two rifles. He was charged with possession of weapons after having been convicted of a felony, maintaining a gambling premises, setting up a gambling table and possession of horse bets, and then driven to police headquarters, where, four hours later, he was released in $3,000 bail. On October 6, D.C. General Sessions Court Judge Charles Halleck found that there was no probable cause to hold Whitetop, and returned the bail money to the old man, even as another General Sessions judge, Harold H. Greene, held two of the people from the other raids—alleged to have been Simkins' accomplices—for grand jury action.

Whitetop next popped up in the news when FBI agents arrested his son, Roger William Simkins, Jr.—his first gambling arrest—in a sweeping series of raids that bagged fifty-six people, including nineteen in the Washington area besides Whitetop Junior. United States Attorney Thomas A. Flanner said the raids were part of a major crackdown against organized interstate gambling activities and that the operation that included Whitetop's son was doing $18 million a year in the District of Columbia alone and $700 million nationally. Arrests were made in Washington, Maryland, Virginia, New Jersey, New York, Oregon, Florida and Pennsylvania, and Flanner said there was a large layoff action between the Washington bookies and two New York men believed to be tied in with the Genovese family.

(The Department of Justice always likes to go into some detail about its mass coordinated raids, but in 1971 became unusually open about such operations, partly because it had been decided in Room 5114 of the big gray building, the room where the public relations people sit, that the newly flexible use of wiretaps could be sold to the public if it could be shown that they were really a useful tool in combatting organized crime, not just a harassing mechanism for peacemongers and homosexuals and hippies. In all sincerity, the local cops might plead that they, too, might have pulled off such a coup if they'd been allowed to wiretap, but who would need a wiretap to catch the son of a seventy-one-year-old whose first arrest was in 1948?)

I bring all this up because it has been suspected, and announced publicly, that there is more to the Washington Police Department than meets the eye. On January 12, 1972, Representative Claude Pepper said staff members of his House Select Committee on Crime had uncovered what he called "concrete evidence of police corruption" in Washington during a three-month investigation, and nobody knew exactly why he chose Washington as a place to investigate except possibly that he is a Democrat and President Nixon is a Republican and 1972 was an election year. The chief counsel for the committee, Joseph A. Phillips, said that the staff had no idea how extensive the corruption had gone in the 5,000-man department, but that there was "substantial evidence." That day and the next the Washington newspapers reported that they'd found out that besides Pepper's staff, a grand jury, the United States Attorney's office, the police department's own internal affairs division and, possibly, the FBI were investigating the possibility of graft in the department. Hinted at by the Pepper people were shakedowns of businesses along Fourteenth Street, the heart of the city's prostitution and nightclub center, and payoffs involving narcotics and gambling. Pepper's men said that he would request from his full committee independent financing for a commission much like the Knapp Commission in New York to hear his allegations and others, and was greeted by a statement from Mayor Washington that the police department was the best in the country and that it had its own internal division to take care of things like that; but the latter statement may not have been as true as he thought it was, considering subsequent developments. (In 1970, the internal affairs division had conducted investigations of 122 cases of alleged corruption, resulting in 5 arrests of policemen, 136 trial board charges and 33 "separations" of policemen from the force. In 1971, the IAD carried out 96 investigations, as a result of which 3 policemen and 4 civilian employees were arrested, and there were 59 separations—plus fines or temporary suspensions for 70 policemen from a newly formed police disciplinary review board.)

The day after Pepper's announcement, Chief Wilson reached into his desk drawer and pulled out a report on his own investigations, and announced that he was suspending six members of the vice squad of the Third Police District, which encompasses a ghetto area of about 100,000 persons, and that two other members of the squad had already resigned since the beginning of the investigation in June, seven months before the Pepper announcement.

One of the vice squad cops suspended was the lieutenant in charge of the detail. On January 21, a federal grand jury indicted all eight of the men—including the two who had resigned—on charges that they had conspired, over a six-month period, to make false arrests on morals charges. Specifically, the indictments mentioned eight false arrests, all occurring in the wee hours on the streets of the inner city, known to be areas of vice and prostitution, where most of the residents are black and poor (with a few white enclaves), but where most of the prostitution clients are white suburban residents or white businessmen in town for conventions (including more police chiefs than you would imagine). The vice cops (only two of the eight are black), the indictment said, would hang around the area in plainclothes and wait for a proposition, and if they got one they would make an arrest, and this way bagged two men, who were charged with soliciting for lewd and immoral purposes, and six women, charged by them with soliciting for prostitution. (Early in November, 1972, D.C. Superior Court Judge Charles W. Halleck in another case ruled as unconstitutional the soliciting law, calling it an invasion of privacy, a First Amendment violation and, as enforced, discriminatory against women. Halleck pointed out, in a sixty-page ruling that is being appealed, that prostitution per se is not illegal in the District, even though the act involves fornication, sodomy or adultery, all of which are against the law. Judge Halleck said they shouldn't be illegal, either.) The indictment said the cops reported falsely each time that they were approached by the people they later were to arrest, and that the policemen later filled out false prosecution reports for the police department, lied to prosecutors assigned to the case and gave perjured testimony in court. Six of those charges were dismissed, and two of the eight were convicted, and guess who were the two convicted: the women or the guys?

On the face of it, it looks like just another ghetto hassle. But the reward came, according to the indictment, when the vice cops would apply for overtime for the court work when they would show up to testify against their suspects—overtime that amounted to thousands of dollars a year.

The trial for the eight vice cops (including an extra indictment for Lieutenant Harold F. Crook, the squad commander, charging him with perjury) was scheduled for June 12, 1972 (although legal maneuvering continued into the late summer and a trial was ordered to begin November 1, 1972, by United States District Court Judge Gerhard A. Gesell), and it is not likely that the case was exactly what Congressman Pepper had in mind, although the chief gave him the best thing he had going at the time. (On February 15, 1972, Inspector Shirley F. O'Neil, the commander of the third district, announced that he was either abolishing his vice squad or abolishing his detective squads, whichever way you take his merging the twenty-five men of the first with the fifteen detectives of the second, and said that the reorganization would give the new vice squad commander, Lieutenant Robert T. Keahon, forty investigators and five sergeants. "We have found that when we get rid of vice, we get rid of crime," O'Neil was quoted as saying. One unique facet of the move was that the head of the former detective squad—in Washington they handle burglary, larceny, robbery and sex offenses—would perform all the old functions but would report to the vice squad commander.)

In the meantime, a big political fight was going on over the Pepper allegations, with the mayor and the head of the city council, both virtually powerless, considering that the city is run by Congress, anyway, calling it a "witch-hunt," and the District's nonvoting delegate to Congress, something less than powerless, if possible, seeing it as a good thing; and the White House was mum—until January 17, five days after Pepper's announcement, when a deputy assistant to President Nixon let it be known that Mr. Nixon believed the police department should be allowed to handle the matter itself, in its own way, which is right in line with the administration's thinking on state control of pollution, Detroit control of auto safety and local control of school busing and integration. The following day Congressman Pepper caved in and said he was confident that the police department could do the job, and so he turned over his evidence to Chief Wilson and let it go at that.

What finally developed was that Pepper's men had uncovered a really hot, but isolated, situation that shook up high echelons of the department because it involved the second in command of the internal affairs division.

It turned out that Captain John E. Drass, the number-two man in the IAD, had borrowed $2,000 from Ernest E. Byrd, the owner of several topless bars in Washington, who at the time, in 1971, was under indictment and charged with assault with intent to kill in connection with the shooting of two men: his own attorney and the president of the Restaurant Beverage Association. During the time of the loan, Byrd was acting as a police informant, and it was Byrd who had made allegations of all sorts of public corruption to the Pepper investigators. The upshot was that Drass was transferred out of the IAD and found guilty by a police trial board of taking the loan, and fined $1,500. Lieutenant Hamilton W. Shoop, Drass's partner on the IAD, was transferred and filed his retirement papers; and the head of the unit, Inspector Thomas F. Wert, was sent to the division that dispenses belt buckle polish. And that is as far as the investigation had progressed by the end of March, 1972.

In the meantime, however, the Third District's vice squad commander, Lieutenant Crook, decided to "cooperate" with police department investigators, allowed himself to be wired for sound and then went around visiting old acquaintances, chatting about their former and present activities, and these chats led, in January, 1973, to the suspension of another twelve policemen, including an inspector, two lieutenants, six sergeants and three plainclothesmen, most of them involved in vice and morals control. As Chief Wilson was preparing departmental charges against the dozen, a federal grand jury was getting ready to indict at least some of them, and it seemed to be a race over which jurisdiction—the department or the courts—would handle the matter.

None of the foregoing should be taken as an implication that there is widespread, organized corruption in the Washington Police Department. It is intended to show that all of the *groundwork* for such corruption has been laid, and the *climate* in which such corruption can flourish was, in 1972, at optimum conditions. (As previously noted, it is illegal to make a bet of any sort in Washington or its Virginia and Maryland suburbs, except at a race track. Yet the Washington newspapers continue to publish, on a daily basis, race entries and results from other cities, on the off chance, you might be expected to believe, that a reader might want to leave his breakfast table and head up to Aqueduct or Saratoga on a given day. And the *Washington Post*, one of the great all-time breast beaters on the subject of journalistic integrity and morality, in September, 1971, proudly announced that "Jimmie (The Greek) Snyder, billed as the 'King of the Oddsmakers,' will size up National Football League games twice a week in *The Washington Post*. His line and comments will appear each Wednesday. On Sunday, the odds of the games will be brought up to the minute, due to injuries and personnel changes."

Surely in one of those Wednesday editions through the football season, on another page, we might find a report of the police department knocking over a bookie joint using the same "line" on Sunday's games as provided in the *Post.*)

And it should be noted that even as hanky-panky rumors and reports abounded in the nation's capital, the crime rate throughout 1971 and early 1972 was dropping at an amazing rate, particularly crimes of violence; and if that is what a police department is *really* for, then Washington's is doing a good job, even considering the wasted man- and woman-hours corralling hustlers along Fourteenth Street.

T hroughout the nation, the story is similar, although in many areas petty graft by cops is taken quite for granted. In Buffalo, a major stronghold of organized crime (so much so that the city, in 1966 and 1967, was the target of the first coordinated federal effort to combat organized crime—the strike force), the police department has been allowed to police itself ever since a state crime commission, making its final report in 1961 after three years of study and hearings, recommended a shakeup and reorganization in the department, particularly in the vice and gambling squads. Many of the commission's recommendations were implemented in 1963, under a new police commissioner (appointed when political control of the city shifted at election time), who, among other things, abolished the vice squad; but he was to last only three years, moving on to a better job, and when the old regime returned to power things returned pretty much to the conditions they were in at the time of the commission report. An insight into Buffalo comes in testimony at a 1961 hearing of the United States Senate Subcommittee on Investigations, which listened to three members of the State Commission of Investigations, who told of one Buffalo bookie who had operated in one location for many years and who, because of citizen complaints to the police and their subsequent harassment of him, went to the police captain in charge of another part of the city and asked for permission to set up there. A report on that hearing, as carried in the *Buffalo Evening News* on August 22, 1961, says, in part:

> Commissioner Myles J. Lane told the committee that at the Buffalo hearing they had heard testimony about a police lieutenant who had been making book in a station house. Mr. Lane said the commission subpoenaed the lieutenant, but he resigned from the force the day he was to appear and invoked the Fifth Amendment when he testified. Senator McClellan said the hearings are being conducted to find out if changes are needed in federal laws to curb gambling— which he termed "organized crime's most profitable source of money."
>
> The New York commissioners said federal laws were needed to deal with the interstate activities of the professional gamblers. In an exchange with Senator [Henry M.] Jackson, Mr. [Goodman] Sarachan said there are certain elements in professional gambling "we can't touch because they are out of the state."
>
> Senator Jackson said he realized this, but he thought the nub of the problem was in local law enforcement. "Let's not kid ourselves," the Seattle senator said. "You know the problem as well as I

do. They buy off the judges. They buy off the sheriff and they buy off the police officers."

The commissioners agreed with Senator Jackson's analysis, and Mr. Sarachan pointed out that when the commission made its simultaneous statewide raids on October 23, 1959, not a single district attorney or local police chief was notified because commission members knew that if there was a single leak, the whole operation would be endangered.

All of this just rolls off Buffalo's back. After that story, the police commissioner, Frank N. Felicetta, denied that any police officer operated a handbook in a station house. He said that a desk lieutenant was found to have conducted a betting operation in his own home, but certainly not in the station house.

A few miles east of Buffalo is Rochester, where Frank J. Valenti, reputed boss of gambling and organized crime in that area, lives and enjoys his life without a great deal of hassle from the police department. (Valenti is one of those Cosa Nostra figures who appear occasionally for a standing ovation from the Italian-American Civil Rights League.) Every time Rochester starts to look into the matter of its police department the situation gets bogged down in the Republican-Democratic quagmire, and instead of asking why the Valentis of Rochester are not in prison, City Hall, in that quaint custom that pervades New York State, turns on itself, and, like a wounded wolf, begins gnawing on its own exposed entrails.

As recently as October, 1971, an on-again-off-again vice cop named Lucien DiGiovanni was indicted by a Monroe County grand jury for second-degree grand larceny. The charges stemmed from a gambling raid, led by DiGiovanni, on Joseph Lippa's West Side Laundramat on April 20, 1971. Investigators from the district attorney's office, who got into the matter in a complicated way, found that, after the raid on the laundramat, $28,000 in cash and $17,500 in checks seized that day were turned in to the property clerk at police headquarters. Lippa, however, complained that another $153,000 was still unaccounted for, and the grand jury thinks DiGiovanni knows what happened to it. (A revolver, also seized at the scene, also vanished; photographs taken at the laundramat show a modern handgun, but the one turned in to the property clerk was older, smaller and of a different color, it was charged.) The way the district attorney got into the case was through a check for $200, reportedly given to Lippa, the accused gambler, sometime before the raid in April. It was reported missing after the raid, and in May was deposited in the

bank account of Dee's Auto Sales of Rochester, a used-car agency operated by Sergeant DiGiovanni's brother, Anthony, a city fireman who was
also indicted by the grand jury. The man who had originally written the
check, it seems, was astonished when it came back with the others
accompanying his monthly statement, particularly when he saw the auto
agency stamp on the back.

DiGiovanni, for some reason, has been around the Rochester Police
Department a long time. He joined the force in 1955, became a detective
in 1959, quickly gaining a reputation for toughness in the areas of vice
and narcotics, and by 1965 he was running the vice squad—which, in
Rochester, had just been established.

At 11 A.M. Sunday, May 23, 1965, an FBI agent happened to be in
Rochester, tailing an associate of Stefano Magaddino, a Mafia figure
from Buffalo, who parked his car on State Street, a short distance away
from Chuck's Cigar Store. Now, Chuck's had been identified by the state
investigation commission as a bookie joint that allegedly made regular
payments to Frank J. Valenti, the Italian businessman, as he prefers to
be called, to continue to operate. As the FBI agent sat there and
watched, he saw Valenti go into the cigar store, and then he saw Lucien
DiGiovanni and another vice cop, John A. LiPari, walk in, and in the
three-week upheaval that followed, DiGiovanni finally said yes, he had
met with Valenti—and this is where the New York State politics syndrome comes in—because he had been asked to conduct a confidential
survey of crime in the Rochester area by Leonard L. Schieffelin, then
Monroe County Democratic chairman. All hell broke loose among the
Republicans, of course, and both LiPari and DiGiovanni resigned from
the force, both claiming that the resignations were forced by Public
Safety Commissioner Harper Sibley, Jr., when the two officers denied,
originally, having met with Valenti. A short time later, in September,
1966, the state investigation commission issued a seventy-two-page
report on its investigation of the meeting (the governor, you will have
guessed, was a Republican), and said it had failed to uncover any reason
for the meeting, but that whatever the reason was, the meeting was not
held "for any lawful and proper police function."

Both men finally were ordered back to duty by Arthur B. Curran,
Jr., then city manager (who ultimately would become a city court
judge), with a one-rank demotion on the condition that they sign a loy-
alty oath that read, in part: "My superiors can be assured that I will
respectfully and with integrity perform any assignments entrusted to me
and I will do my best to bring honor to the public trust given me." LiPari
decided not to take the reduction from grade-B to grade-C detective, and

instead quit and went to work for a tree surgery firm (he was later, in 1966, to return to the force as a patrolman); and DiGiovanni took his reduction to grade-B detective.

DiGiovanni turned up in the news again in September, 1970, when he was indicted by a grand jury which said it was investigating organized crime and police corruption (and which was eventually to charge Italian businessman Frank J. Valenti with contempt for refusing to testify) for conspiracy and soliciting a bribe. DiGiovanni, then forty-six and a sergeant, was accused, with another cop, of putting the arm on a restaurant owner on State Street and trying to get him to provide two free meals a week for the men under them. The restaurant owner taped the alleged meeting with DiGiovanni and the other cop, and part of that tape read:

> Out of the goodness of your heart . . . as a good business practice. It'd just be one or two times a week, Bob. Only the men who work the area regular . . . they wouldn't abuse it . . . just the guys on the 4 to 12 shift . . . anybody else comes in, Bob, you just give 'em a check. What they want is someplace decent to eat. There's just yours, Bob and Ray's and Bolo's in this district, and, oh, once in awhile they go down to get some chicken at Bull's Head. . . . If anything gets out of hand, you call me.

Toward the end of the tape a voice says, "This is no shakedown, Bob . . . we're not offering protection or anything like that."

In November, 1970, the charges were dismissed, after a series of motions presented by the defense attacking the "sufficiency" of the charges—specifically, that no free meals were ever accepted, and that the statute under which the men were charged was "silent" regarding future acceptance of gratuities. On November 6, 1970, both men were returned to duty (they had been suspended since the indictment) and given back pay to September 14.

That same grand jury also took a look at William Hamill, who in February, 1970, had been sworn in as a deputy police commissioner to head the division responsible for intelligence and vice control. Hamill by then had been a policeman for twenty years, and had been a captain since 1963. His brother, John, also had been a police captain, before his retirement, and for several months in 1970 had served as president of APO International, Inc., a travel firm that organized international gambling junkets, and a partner and secretary-treasurer of which was a convicted gambler named Angelo J. (Oskie) DeMarco. John Hamill was quoted as saying that he sold his thirty shares in APO to the other owners on June 10 because the company wasn't making any money. The other owners were Pat DiPolito, vice-president, and Orlando Lompo, second vice-president, both of whom had been linked by police to the 44 Club, which police refer to as a gambling spot.

William Hamill was finally called before the grand jury to explain his own relationship with Oskie DeMarco, if any. It turned out that at 8 P.M. Friday, July 3, 1970, the vice squad, which was Hamill's responsibility, had busted a bookie joint in an apartment over a liquor store on Broad Street. The police said they found bettors' slips and records of dollar amounts running into the thousands, and confiscated them, and they said the bookie operation was a branch of one run at the 44 Club by Oskie DeMarco.

Over the weekend, it was reported, Hamill called one of the arresting officers at his home, and asked for the details of the arrests and the names of the vice squad supervisors who authorized the investigation. On Monday, Hamill ordered the supervisor to his office, and when the detective arrived, DeMarco was with Hamill, and, at that point, Hamill ordered the detective to get the betting records of the bookie operation and make copies of them. The detective complied, mad as hell, no doubt, and gave the copies to Hamill, who in turn gave them to DeMarco, who in turn stuffed them in his pocket and left. (An honest bookie always tries to pay off his bettors if he can recover the notes he made before the raid.)

The grand jury fooled around with this for a while, plus another reported meeting between Hamill and another gambler (the detectives were keeping records on Hamill, it turned out, in their daily activity reports), and did nothing, except to mention in its final report, made public on August 12, 1971, that the Hamill-DeMarco incident "reflects extremely poor judgment and non-criminal misconduct on his [Hamill's] part."

DeMarco, it might be noted, was indicted for possession of betting records—the records given to him by Hamill.

And in the end, Police Commissioner John A. Mastrella suspended Hamill for fifteen days without pay, at the end of which time he was restored to duty as deputy police commissioner, only this time not in charge of intelligence and vice, but central services—handing out handcuff keys.

There are thirty-five top gamblers in the city of Philadelphia, and they hire hundreds of employees and do an annual business estimated at $107 million, and God alone knows how many policemen are on their payroll, although the suspicion is that there are plenty. That is dangerous talk around the City of Brotherly Love, where it took a court injunction in November, 1971, to get the organized wives of policemen to stop picketing the *Philadelphia Inquirer*, where the trouble started on November 16.

It was just another November day in Philadelphia, smoggy and depressing, and the difference was that the *Inquirer* chose that day to break a story on which it had been working for three months. The staff had talked to gamblers, cops and former cops, hookers, the FBI and the Internal Revenue Service, and had put a reporter-photographer team on the street hidden in a panel truck with holes drilled to take pictures through, and what they finally published that day probably came as not much of a surprise to the street people in Philadelphia—many, not just a few, cops were on the take, and were hauling in money in the same, precise, systematic method used in New Orleans a generation earlier.

On the first day of the exposé (there would be more details to come, but the thrust would remain the same—the gamblers and the bar operators were paying off for protection), the newspaper published parts of a seventy-six-page statement given to the office of District Attorney Arlen Specter by a former policeman named Carl V. Johnson, who detailed his own collection of graft and that of others, in the by-now-familiar question-and-answer format used to draw information from those not quite willing to give it. I mention Johnson because, as the initial stages of what was to be a double-barreled investigation came to an end, nine cops had been arrested on corruption-related charges, and one of the nine, as you might suspect, knowing how police departments work, was Johnson, who was bagged in mid-December on charges of illegal use and possession of heroin.

Johnson had given his statement to the district attorney's office because a special grand jury had been sitting for three months trying to sort out the narcotics thing in Philadelphia. After the *Inquirer* broke its stories, Specter announced that the jury would immediately turn its attention to the matter of police corruption, but that didn't get very far because it was speculated by some very sharp legal minds that the law would not allow a grand jury summoned for one purpose to expand its interest at midstream.

What happened, however, is that Governor Milton Shapp, late in November, ordered the Pennsylvania Crime Commission to go to Philadelphia and hold public hearings, a move that drew all sorts of comment from Mayor-elect Frank Rizzo (who had been police commissioner before resigning early in 1971 to run for mayor) and Specter, often mentioned as a possible candidate for governor.

As the *Inquirer* continued feeding what it had learned to the public (and it had good pictures of police cars parked outside gambling locations), and as the crime commission listened to testimony from gamblers and cops, both crooked and honest, the police had become increasingly upset over being tarred in public, and by the end of March, 1972, lawsuits filed by policemen (individually and as class actions) against the *Inquirer* totaled something like $181 million, which made the editors of that newspaper very happy—if a showdown actually came, the paper would have the power of subpoena regarding the private affairs of the cops.

On Saturday, February 6, the crime commission made public its initial report on its findings, and announced it would conduct a "full-scale, in-depth" investigation as a result of the initial probe and report, which named thirty-five major gambling operations which it said had existed in Philadelphia for decades, and that "the commission concludes that patterns of corruption exist within the Philadelphia Police Department," that "these patterns are not random or isolated but systematic and that they exist citywide," and that "these patterns are not restricted to low ranking officers."

"The problems of police corruption," the report said, "cannot be solved by massive transfers of personnel from one district to another," an obvious reference to a kneejerk move by Police Commissioner Joseph O'Neill, who on December 17, 1971, reassigned the commanders of nineteen of the city's twenty-two police districts, an unprecedented shuffle in the city's history described by O'Neill, for public consumption, as "routine."

The crime commission offered up a ten-point list of recommendations for reforming the police force, including the filing of financial statements by all officers from the rank of captain up; "detailed reporting of all contacts, phone or personal, between any police officers and gambling racketeers, narcotics figures, bar owners or operators and prostitutes ...," and the reorganization of narcotics, gambling, vice and organized-crime units into strike forces acting in conjunction with assistant district attorneys, with the emphasis on getting Mister Big rather than the little guys, which is all right. But somebody wants to play those numbers, and if there were ever a clear-cut case for the legalization of numbers it is in Pennsylvania—which, for openers, is bankrupt and could use a share of that $107 million a year, not counting the advantages of having a police department where the men could hold up their heads again.

T he heads were bowed in Seattle, too, starting with the indictment in April, 1970, of an assistant chief of the Seattle Police Department; and before the smoke had cleared, another four dozen men, mostly law-enforcement officers, but—surprisingly, in this day and age—also a former city council president and a former prosecuting attorney, were under indictment on various charges of conspiracy or bribery. If there were ever a case of a police department being raped by the body politic, it is in Seattle.

The trouble actually began in 1909, when the Washington State Criminal Code was adopted, making gambling in all its forms illegal, despite the state's pioneer history and the waterfront atmosphere of its main city, Seattle, where, early in 1971, I walked into a saloon across the street from the King County courthouse and found seven men sitting at the bar, all engaged in a single game of liars' poker—a common but exorbitantly expensive gambling game utilizing the serial numbers on dollar bills (or five-dollar bills, in high-roller games) instead of cards. Liars' poker, too, is illegal in Seattle, and I was assured in an interview with Captain Richard Schoener, then head of the vice squad, that if his men found such a game they would bust it.

Out of the juxtaposition of total illegality of gambling and an almost inbred love of gambling by the citizens emerged a phenomenon in Seattle known as the "tolerance policy," which operated much like the old Storyville prostitution policy of New Orleans, and which had the dual (and dubious) advantage of more or less controlling gambling, while at the same time funneling a bit of the revenue from it into the city treasury. The policy was initiated in 1947 by Mayor William F. Devin, and nobody ever really knew what it was, exactly (at one time in the early 1960s three memos were circulating within the police department saying three different things about the suppression or nonsuppression of gambling operations), except that it was a city ordinance providing for the *licensing* of multiple-coin pinball machines and card rooms and a fee schedule for the licenses, but making no mention at all of whether the activities were or were not legal. For a brief period beginning in January, 1963, Mayor Gordon Clinton partially undid the policy, with a letter to city license-holders saying that the state laws were going to be enforced, and the response from the public was enormous—and adverse. The next mayor, J. D. Braman, lifted the lid again and it remained lifted until 1969, when the tolerance policy was abandoned, a year after the police payoff system was abandoned (or at least temporarily shelved, depending upon who is speaking). The attorneys for the indicted men in Seattle have been trying to present the tolerance policy as a shadowy co-conspirator, or, really, the true villain in the piece, and they are correct, although it does not really matter if it turns out that one or more Seattle police officers did, in fact, take graft from gamblers.

In an affidavit which is a part of a brief filed by the defense in connection with one 1971 indictment (which named nineteen defendants), the attorney for a police captain made an eloquent statement of the tolerance policy.

The affidavit went into detail on the history of the tolerance policy, and spelled out the license fees collected by the city of Seattle over the years. One paragraph showed that in 1968 the Washington State Department of Revenue announced that 3,500 licensed pinball machines in the state had grossed $7.2 million, and that in the same year the proceeds to local government amounted to just over $250,000.

In July, 1969, the city council voted to end the tolerance policy, and at that time there were 51 card rooms with a total of 229 tables (down from 1962, when there were 70 card rooms), and 1,172 multiple-coin pinball machines, which were grossing something like $5 million a year for what were called the "master license holders," the 38 distributors, who paid $500 a year each for their licenses. In 1967, in unincorporated King County, there was only one master license holder, and that was Farwest Novelty Company, operated by a man named Ben Cichy, and it was with Cichy that things really got hot for the cops in Seattle in 1968, when the *Post-Intelligencer*, in its August 21 editions, published a story about a meeting between Charles O. Carroll, who had been the prosecutor of King County for more than twenty years, and Cichy, whose organization had held that county master license since 1942. The newspaper said Cichy was a regular visitor to Carroll's home, showing up once a month at the same time each month, and a picture prominently displayed on page one showed the beginning of the meeting, outside Carroll's home.

Now Cichy (who was to drown a year later) had been living in the grand manner off pinballs for decades. He lived in an attractive home on Lake Washington's Cozy Bay, with a fifty-four-foot, twenty-nine-ton seagoing yacht docked just off his front yard, and, in 1949, Cichy had conceded during his divorce trial that he was making $60,000 a year. His son lived next door to him in an expensive brick home. And at the same time, the King County prosecutor had almost absolute control over criminal prosecutions in the county—there was, at the time, no regularly sitting grand jury, so that the prosecutor either filed or did not file informations with the court; he set the charges in each case; and he also was by law the attorney for county officers. The *Post-Intelligencer*, rightly or wrongly, thought it had something very big in connecting the two men in a series of late-night, almost clandestine meetings.

The story was to be the opening salvo in a full-scale presentation of what the newspaper, in a three-month investigation, had learned about civic corruption, including payoffs to police officers from gambling figures; but three things happened to dull the *Post-Intelligencer's* cutting edge and put the newspaper again in the role of a reporter rather than an investigator—the ownership of the paper, the Hearst chain, smelling court trouble, ordered the newspaper's editors to lay off; a trio of high-ranking police officers, reading between the headlines, sensed a scandal that might result in one of them winding up as chief of police; and the mayor, J. D. Braman, invited the International Association of Chiefs of Police to send a team around to survey the police department.

The IACP report, in part, stated:

A permissive attitude toward certain types of vice, including prostitution and gambling, exists in the community. For instance, the licensing of card rooms by the city for "friendly games among strangers" is nothing more than a license to gamble. This attitude provides the essential environment for the growth of an even more serious social cancer—organized crime. Present police department vice control mechanisms and the number of investigators assigned to gambling enforcement are inadequate. A formal inspection program does not exist. In fairness to the city and the department, however, we must note that steps were taken recently to improve vice enforcement efforts. . . .

From an organizational standpoint, vice investigation in the Seattle Police Department is misplaced. It is in a position where it is hampered in its functions of keeping the chief of police informed of the status of vice operations in the city. At the present time, a lieutenant is in charge of the Vice Investigation Bureau consisting of the vice investigation unit, the intelligence unit, and the narcotics unit. Results of these activities are passed through the chain of command upwards from the lieutenant to the deputy chief in charge of the staff division. This deputy chief then relays the information to the chief or the assistant chief. In our proposed organizational structure the vice control section will report as an integral part of the Inspectional Services Division directly to the chief of police. This positioning of this important function should result in improved overall effectiveness and better communication with the chief.

As a matter of fact, the vice squad at the time was reporting to M.

E. (Buzz) Cook, assistant police chief, and had been reporting to him for a number of years, regardless of where in the department he happened to be transferred; and as Chief Frank C. Ramon set about to initiate the changes recommended in the IACP report, the officers involved in what was to come to be known as the "palace revolt" saw their opportunity, and within a year, moved: On September 24, 1969, the recently reorganized vice squad busted the Lifeline Club, a multifaceted bingo operation which was doing an estimated annual business of $1.5 million. The raid was well coordinated and brought off in top secrecy, with the vice squad commander going so far as to plant false information in his own desk before the raid, hoping to throw other cops off the trail; and the raid was successful—partly because a large percentage of the Seattle police force was distracted by a major disturbance on the University of Washington campus, where black contractors were shutting down construction projects. As this confusion reigned, the new vice squad made its move, and carted away four vanloads of records and documents revealing payoffs to police, campaign contributions to political leaders and loans to public officials.

On the local level, the raid never made much of an impact—some of the people who were in the Lifeline Club chatted with members of the police department—but a strange thing happened: The operator of the Lifeline was indicted by a *federal* grand jury, sitting in Seattle, in January, 1970, a few months after the raid, for transporting gambling devices interstate and using them in violation of state law. The late Richard McBroome, who was an assistant United States attorney in that matter, told me that the owner had paid something like $3,300 a month protection to the cops, and then

> he told the grand jury about the protection, and from talking to people who had worked in the Lifeline Club we gathered information about that, we found out . . . that since the indictment said that money was paid for protection, the inquiry turned to how that protection was provided, and that's why the federal grand jury got into the act at all. And also, there were policemen getting money for not performing their duty as they should have, and there were some other violations that the federal grand jury was looking for, income tax violations, civil rights violations, due process violations and the like.

So they called in Assistant Chief Buzz Cook and asked him under oath what he knew about payoffs for police protection, and he said he didn't know anything; and in August, 1970, Cook was sentenced to three years for perjury in a federal penitentiary after a summer-long trial that saw one cop after another and one bar owner or gambler after another parade to the witness stand in the United States District Court and tell his version of how and why payoffs were or were not made, depending upon the witness. (Cook subsequently appealed his case to the United States Circuit Court of Appeals in San Francisco, largely on technical grounds.)

The *Post-Intelligencer* covered the trial thoroughly, so much so that whatever seemed to be wrong with Seattle's police department troubled the voters enough that in November, 1970, they elected a new reform prosecutor named Christopher Bayley, who immediately set out to put people in prison, if possible. In February, 1971, Bayley asked for $150,-000 and got it from the King County Council to set up a special county grand jury to be presided over by Superior Court Judge Stanley C. Soderland, and on April 3 the jury, consisting of six women and eleven men, began its work (after being selected from a list of thirty-six prospective jurors, who were questioned in open court by Judge Soderland, while Seattle detectives, at least three of them from the intelligence division, sat in the courtroom taking notes).

Before the grand jury finished its work in September, 1971, it had indicted a total of fifty-four persons, mostly police officers and former cops of all ranks, mostly on bribery charges, with the really big indictment, for conspiracy, dropping like a bomb on July 29, 1971 (the date was to become important later). Named in the indictment were former prosecutor Charles O. Carroll; Charles M. Carroll, president of the city council; former police chief Frank Ramon; former King County sheriff Jack Porter; Buzz Cook; William F. Moore, former acting police chief; Charles K. Waitt, manager of the King County business license department; Lee Scott, former superintendent of the King County jail; William J. Walsh, former undersheriff; and a handful of present and former Seattle police officers, including a man who, earlier in 1971, was a captain and serving as head of the department's internal affairs division.

The indictment, whether or not there was a word of truth in it, pretty much spelled out the trouble Seattle had been in for a number of years without knowing it (or did they know it?).

Young Chris Bayley and his assistants, having secured the indictments, began to prepare for what surely would be the lengthiest, most complex trial in the history of Seattle, when they were bashed with a double reverse—on October 21, 1971, Visiting Superior Court Judge W. R. Cole of Kittitas County dismissed all but three of the fifty-four indictments, including the conspiracy charge against the nineteen, on the grounds that a new grand-jury law, which had become effective on May 11, 1971, nullified any action after that date by the grand jury, which had been constituted under the provisions of the grand-jury act superseded by the new one. (The new grand-jury law also made it illegal for an attorney to accompany his client inside the jury room—a point approved by many prosecuting attorneys because so many organized-crime figures have the same lawyers, and hence can consult between appearances—and prohibited a grand jury from issuing a final report on its investigations and deliberations.)

On December 20, 1971, Bayley took his case on appeal to the Supreme Court of Washington, confident of winning. On August 3, 1972, the nine-man court unanimously upheld his position, and on September 1 lawyers for the defendants petitioned the court for a rehearing, which Bayley expected to be denied. Late in September his staff was preparing a bill of particulars to be handed over to the defense, and Bayley anticipated that the trial—surely good for three months at least—would begin around the first of November.

It is interesting to note, however, that Patrolman Ellsworth J. Robinson, indicted earlier in May, 1971, before the cutoff date, on five counts of asking and receiving bribes, the only one of the fifty-four to come to trial by April, 1972, was convicted. In sentencing the former Seattle police officer, the judge, Francis A. Walterskirchen, had something to say for anyone who is apt to view police corruption as just another piece of civic hanky-panky:

> When the King County Judges established a criminal division of this court, one of its principal purposes was to achieve greater uniformity in the sentencing of offenders. Being one of the judges assigned to that division and being very much aware of the desirability of the greater uniformity in sentencing, and since this is the first of the indictments—fifty-four persons being indicted and now being tried—I deemed it important to talk with the other members of the criminal division and see what their views were as to the type of sentence that should be imposed in this case. I submitted to them the pre-sentence reports of both the prosecuting attorney and defense counsel, the note which the jurors had given me in response to the permission to seek clemency for the defendant, and asked them to give me an idea of what their views were as to the sentence to be imposed. All of these judges agree that this case involves more than a mere violation of the criminal statute by the run of mill offender. They agree that this is a case of great public interest because it concerns public officers becoming corrupt in matters of official duty and public trust. They agree that the public has a much greater stake in the outcome of the instant case than it would fol-

lowing any of the average cases. Three of my associates also pointed out that this case is further distinguished from the average case by the fact that the criminal conduct in this case extended over a period of years, not just a few isolated instances as in most criminal cases.

They agree in cases affected with great public interest as is this one, the major concern is not the rehabilitation of the offender, which is of prime concern in most cases in which we sentence today, the major concern is to let the public know that they can have confidence in their public servants because if these public servants become corrupt, they will be punished. The public must know that officers may not become corrupt and expect to be treated like first offenders. They cannot betray their trust and expect to be treated lightly.

This is the view of the majority of the judges in the criminal department. In addition, the officers who have lived up to the trust that has been placed in them have to be vindicated in their choice to live up to their trust and not betray their honor.

Over the years that I have been connected with public service I have met many police officers, many sheriffs, many other law enforcement officers, and I am still convinced that except for a very few, they are all conscientious dedicated men and women of whom the public can be proud.

I think these factors distinguish these cases from an average case of a young fellow who goes astray and there is every reason to believe can be rehabilitated and made a useful member of society. I agree with my brother judges in the criminal department that this is not a proper case for probation or suspension of sentence, deferment of sentence. It is for these reasons that I intend to impose the sentence that I am about to impose.

The sentence was ten years, the maximum allowed under law, and, if there is any deterrent power in harsh sentences at all, it might make a difference in Seattle—unless the gamblers and racketeers can find a way to get themselves some new judges.

What can I tell you about Miami? Again, like Utica, it was one of those cities where I had planned to draw upon a finite, open-and-shut case of police corruption, mostly based on (a) the 1950 Kefauver Committee investigations of the city and the old S&G Syndicate (out of which Lee Hills and his *Miami Herald* won a Pulitzer Prize), and (b) the investigations of the mid-1960s—a generation later—by the *Herald* and a handful of courageous television newsmen, who got not a Pulitzer Prize but a laugh a minute from a community grown cynical and brutal, hotel owners who thought the *Herald* was getting just a little bit uppity in its search for the mandrake root of honest police administration.

At the very heart of the trouble in Dade County has always been the fact that people have always gone there to have fun, and by fun, by and large, they do not mean fighting off jellyfish and sunburn at the water's edge, or seeing a life-sized bas relief replica in wax of "The Last Supper," all of which is legal. What is not legal is fun—you can bet on a horse running anywhere in the United States, you can take a chance on the Cuban or Puerto Rican lottery, via any of a thousand sellers, you can get laid at prices ranging from ten bucks to a hundred and fifty, although if you want to be whipped, photographed, burned with cigarettes, high-heeled or lathered with some sort of Xaviera Hollander confection the price goes up. Dirty books and pictures are available, and the old Havana crowd, now in residence in Miami, keeps that traffic moving.

The official stance in Dade County is that vice—meaning prostitution and gambling—are not needed to make the cities an attractive lure for tourist dollars. Unofficially, vice is very much worthwhile, and that is what has happened to the cops over the years there.

In the mid-1960s things got hot for the Dade County Sheriff's Department—the force that has long handled major felonies and communications and crime-lab work for the smaller police departments of the twenty-seven or so communities that make up Dade County. The sheriff's department—having been run for years by one after another bumbling sheriffs, either elected or appointed, as the mood of the county happened to prevail during a given year—was horribly corrupt, and one of the corrupting influences was Major Manson Hill, a brutal but dapper man with a broad smile and bad teeth given to expensive shoes and luxury cars, and it was widely reported that when Hill ran the divisions concerning themselves with the enforcement-regulation of vice in Dade County nothing was too grim to contemplate.

A man named Hank Messick—author of a half a dozen books on organized crime and whose father had been murdered by the syndicate —came to town and convinced the editors of the *Herald* that he could uncover corruption they wouldn't believe. Before he was finished, cops fled the county and the state like so many cockroaches going down the drainpipe, the man who was sheriff then is now reportedly practicing law in Miami and Manson Hill—who had been chief of detectives—moved to Georgia, where at last reports he had gone into the business of selling pornography in partnership with Red Vaught, formerly the biggest whoremaster in all of South Florida.

(Late in 1972, Clarence Jones, who by that time had left Louisville to clean up itself and had returned to become an investigative reporter for Channel 10 in Miami, told me that Hill had been seen poking around Miami and speculated that the old detective might be trying to get something going for himself there again. Jones said a federal strike force looking at Dade County thought the same way.)

It had been Hill and Vaught who had provided prostitutes for the out-of-town police witnesses who came from as far away as Texas and Arizona to testify in the Candace Mossler 1965 murder trial (she was acquitted of slaying her wealthy husband, Jacques), and the girls were taken home from the orgy at the Biscayne Terrace Hotel in unmarked county cars afterward.

What had happened in Miami essentially is what is ready, at any moment, to happen in Louisville. The old gamblers, running the numbers rackets (called bolita in Florida) were essentially independent of the rest of organized crime, although people like Meyer Lansky and the Falcone brothers maintained homes there. The syndicate, like that in Louisville, was "home grown," and as such fairly well protected by the sheriff's vice squad—under the direction of Manson Hill.

What brought Hank Messick in with such apparently quick results was the fact that there was too much money churning in South Florida for the major New York, Cleveland and Chicago syndicates to keep their hands off. So as the out-of-towners got pushy, some of the local gamblers, the ones who'd been doing business for a generation, got resentful, and some even talked to Messick and told him some of the details of their operation—including who was being paid off in the various police forces. (It should be pointed out that Hank Messick, after consulting with experts in many parts of the country, chose Fort Lauderdale to make his own home, since, to the best of his knowledge, that city had the only totally honest police force south of the frost line.)

Hank made arrangements, through the local syndicate people, to buy a whorehouse and to pay for the attendant police protection; he visited numbers counting houses and bookie joints, and he discerned who the bagmen were for the various operations and the various police jurisdictions, and before it was over Manson Hill was gone, a handful of his top officers were out, in disgrace, the sheriff was in virtual disgrace (although he had been acquitted of perjuring himself before a grand jury); and by the time 1970 rolled around the evils of police corruption in Dade County had virtually been forgotten, except for the after-the-fact warbling of a deputy sheriff named Charles Celona who, for one reason or another, started telling about how the sheriff's department had operated during the years when he was a vice cop, and as late as mid-1971 former deputies were still coming to trial, based on Celona's allegations. He never discussed anybody really big (although he had hinted darkly that his revelations would shake up even high county and state offices), and it seemed, in the bright sunshine, that Celona, for all his apparent sincerity, was about three years too late and $1.98 short.

The kind of corruption practiced by members of the Dade County Sheriff's Department was classic, of course: A stolen bracelet, a one-of-a-kind number made of thirteen gold Mexican pesos, turned up at a race track adorning the wrist of the wife of the chief of detectives, Manson Hill; a gang of torture robbers, apparently acting on information furnished right out of the Public Safety Building, operated along the waterways of Miami Beach with impunity, until Rocky Pomerance's Beach cops put an end to it; Georges LeMay, the first international jewel thief to be caught via Telstar, bought his way out of the Dade County Jail, and Murph (Jack Murphy) the Surf and his crowd of charismatic cutthroats ran rampant with or without the help of the sheriff's department.

All in all, a dozen deputies went to prison; a dozen or more left town, some for Broward County (once upon a time the two sheriff's departments were interchangeable), where the sheriff, John Stack, told me in 1971 that as far as he knew the entire department was "clean." (For a look at how "clean" the Broward County Sheriff's Department has been, read Hank Messick's book *Syndicate in the Sun*.)

Actually, all of South Florida thinks it's pretty clean right now, except for the realists, who are simply reluctant to start investigating again, since the body politic generally gets what it wants—and deserves.

And no matter what you think, the city of Miami Beach, long considered a hotbed of sin, may be the cleanest of the two dozen communities in Dade County.

> The chief is the one political appointee in the department. He is appointed by the mayor of the city and is directly responsible to the mayor and to the Civil Service Commission. The nature of his appointment gives to the chief his basic, though not formal, function in the department. He is expected to function as the departmental public relations man, and to keep the department under control for the political organization to which he is responsible, no matter what their ends. [Underline added.]
>
> —William A. Westley, Violence and the Police

Rocky Pomerance and I sat down for breakfast at the Dupont
Plaza Hotel in Washington, D.C., just before Christmas, 1970. He is the
chief of police of the city of Miami Beach, Florida. We ordered coffee
and let the tape recorder run, and I later transcribed it because at some
point it is valuable to get a kind of free-flow look at a man who is in
charge of carrying out his community's ideas of righteousness. The following are excerpts.

POMERANCE: You know, our community has an unfortunate
heritage, because years back it was a wide open city, had bookmaking establishments, the hotels where the cigar stands sold for forty
thousand dollars, the lease, let's say. You know that the entire community was a part of this web of corruption. The newspapers advertised, over in town [Miami], illegal gambling clubs, euphemistic
phrases suggesting, you know, that that's what it was, has big stars
and suggested that there was other entertainment. The religious
organizations, the synagogues and so forth, accepted huge contributions from the group of people who controlled this syndicate. The
people ran for office based on a so-called liberal policy, which really
meant that corruption was okay, right through the entire spectrum,
the entire power structure was involved. And so they take some
policeman, and he commits a transgression, and everybody's
shocked and they call for his scalp, and so—well, why should we
call for his scalp, what about the scalp of the community? Now
gradually, this changed, I look at it as a sign of maturity, that gradually the community grew up, and realized that this is not an
answer, that if you're a tourist community you need not depend on
illegal activity to get tourists. In fact, I firmly believe that we do
better with—well, the proof of it is that the community has
improved over and over and over again since they stopped that
kind of activity. For one thing, the convention business has
increased tremendously. It's taken up a lot of the slack. For another
thing families like to come to a community where there's not this
kind of vice activity. We recently had a question of a referendum, to
legalize gambling. It was interesting to me that the hotel industry
almost unanimously—I say almost because I would imagine somebody in the hotel industry opposed it, I don't know who it might
have been, though—they supported this kind of legalized gambling.
The mayor violently opposed it. I opposed the legalized gambling. I
opposed it—of course, the illegal gambling has been curbed over the
years I've been there—and I felt that legalizing it [was wrong].
This speaks not just from a Puritan ethic, but from a really deep

feeling that what it will do, what legalized gambling does, although it legalizes people's immorality or vices and so forth, it also brings with it a whole new spectrum of problems attendant to it. Who in the country today knows how to run [legal] gambling? No businessman, very few businessmen. It boils down to bringing in hoodlums, bringing in an element I think ultimately destroys the community. And so I took a position in opposition to it. Which is not easy when the greater part of your community seems to be in favor of it. Surprisingly enough, in a referendum it was defeated. That referendum, by the way, was really a poll, the state still would not have permitted it, but the theory was if they could show the state the city wanted it, the legislature would have possibly passed something. I don't believe they ever would have. I looked over the people who sit on the committees, and they just wouldn't have gone for legalization of gambling. . . . In any event, the greatest majority of people voting against it were the old people, the so-called senior citizens. I don't know, I would assume the mayor, who is highly regarded in that area, was able to reach all these people. The media were all opposed to it except for one newspaper which publishes twice a week, the *Reporter*. They were very much in favor of legalized gambling, and they had some sound reasoning behind them. But for a police chief, we're better off without any form of gambling. But in our community there *is* legalized gambling. Three, four dog tracks, three, four race tracks, two jai alai frontons. I don't think I've ever been at a race track.

· · · · ·

To go back to one of the original premises that if we didn't have vice we wouldn't have corruption. Well, if we didn't have greed we wouldn't have murder and robbery. I don't know if you can legalize it and then say that it will go away. I don't think you can legalize robbery, and then say, now . . .

INTERVIEWER: Well, now, I'm not trying to build a case for legalization of this. But there's a point where a police officer is efficient, and really is getting into good detective work, and there is no way to pay that police officer not to make an arrest in a robbery or a murder, or a kidnapping, or a crime that is repugnant to society. The same officer, it seems, might be prone to accept money not to arrest somebody a judge is doing business with.

POMERANCE: Uh huh, yeah. I'll tell you, I've always felt that the policeman who'll take a five-dollar bill from a hustler, a hooker,

you know, tomorrow may look the other way when a robbery has
been committed, because he'll get a bigger portion of the ...

INTERVIEWER: This is exactly what happened in Dade County.

POMERANCE: That's true, that's right, and you see, you can't
have a little bit of corruption, because it's like being a little bit pregnant. There ain't no such animal. Once the attitude becomes acceptable, to the community, or worse than that, to the policeman, there's
no telling where it could—where it will lead to, and it does lead to
greater and greater involvement, and a general—well, I don't want
to make up all kinds of pretentious-sounding [metaphors], but you
stretch your moral fabric here it's going to pop over there. And
that's exactly what happened in some parts of the country. The
policeman who thought it was no big deal for the corner bookmaker
to operate later could have easily been involved in a burglary raid.
He was now conditioned for it. Really, when these kind of things
come up, that's one of the fears I've got. For a resort community
we're kind of tough on prostitutes and illegal activity. I know
Miami Beach, y'know, you say oh boy, it's a resort community, wow,
people are talking of a community that existed twenty years ago,
not one that exists currently. The median age of our local population, the 1960 census showed it was fifty-nine point two. Nationally,
it was twenty-three. Now, I haven't seen the latest figures, but it's up
around sixty-four, I guess. In the 1970 census. That's the *average
median age*. People like that, they could care less about hustlers and
gambling, it's not a factor in their lives.

· · · · ·

Let me tell you an interesting point. Shortly after I became
chief [in 1963], I determined that this kind of attitude—you could
go to the top hotels and get a hustler—was a bad one for the community. If a prostitute feels she doesn't have to take a chance on
arrest, and she can work with impunity, in a bar, pretty soon that
bar is hers, and when you come in with your wife, or your business
associate, or your sister who's visiting, that lady is the outcast, and
the hustler is the boss. The hustler is, you know, she'll look down on
the lady with you. To reverse this process, we've determined that
we're going to have a very heavy campaign on antiprostitution. Now
you know it's the oldest profession in the world. You're not going to
stop it, but you should make enough arrests so that they don't think
that it's *so* simple, it's *so* wide open that all they have to do is walk
in and tell the bartender, "I'm in business" and then wait. And so
we've met with some of the hotel owners individually and told them

that we've planned a very active campaign and that we wanted to let them know about it first, and secondly we wanted them to alert their help, their bartenders, to the fact that if they participate by either tipping off the hustler or certainly if by sharing in their proceeds, we're going to make arrests of the bartenders. We've done this, by the way. Now you know there are a hundred ways a bartender can tell a prostitute, particularly in a community where after a while he'll know all the police, know who they are by sight. I'll give you an example. I'm the bartender and you're the prostitute, and I look over and see a vice detective or some other, and I just walk over and drop an ice cube into your drink. Natural, perfectly normal, nobody would have noticed anything in a million years, but that hustler knows that as soon as she can gracefully get out of there or stop what she's doing, she's been alerted. So it's just one of hundreds of different ways. So in speaking to . . . one of the hotel owners who is known all over the world, he said, "Rocky, why are you telling me all this?" He said, "Do you think I want hookers at my bar?" So I said, "Well, judging from . . ." [laughter], "you know, it kind of caught me a little off," I said, "Well, I guess I always had the impression that it was good for business," and he said, "Let me teach you something about business." He said, "A hooker is bad for the hotel bar business, and I'll tell you why. I've got conventioneers, there's four or five fellows sitting there drinking, and a hustler comes in and what does she do? The first thing she does is she takes one of those fellows out of there, the others leave, to wherever she's at." He says, "I've now lost an evening's business." He said, "She sets up people for blackmail and extortion." That's a possibility, her pimp—and this part I throw in—she may be on junk, her pimp may be a burglar, in other words, I came to the conclusion that he agreed with us. Since that time we've had a *load* of arrests, a *load* of arrests. . . . Now, at the beginning of our campaign I anticipated a problem with the leading hotels, and there was none. The hotels all agreed: they don't want 'em in there. You know, in our city you can lose your telephone service, your license to operate, your liquor license, the whole. . . .

. . . . .

[Back in the middle of 1963] you had the Life Bar, you had five joints on 23rd Street, on 22nd you had two or three, two at least, there were loads of stripper bars and such . . .

INTERVIEWER: Place Pigalle was one.

POMERANCE: Pigalle was one. Pigalle, by the way, is still run-

ning. It's the *only* one that's still running. And although it's a strip
joint, they now take in tours, like they'll take in the Morton Towers
residents, you know, like all the old people that live there they
come, they see the show. However ...

INTERVIEWER: Do they still run B-girls there?

POMERANCE: No. And 'if they do they're subject to arrest. Well,
we've done that, too. What the bars were, they were just flat-out B-
girl operations, you couldn't even call 'em whorehouses because they
never really came through. They enticed and led on the fellow and
took his money, and, used to be a favorite trick they'd give him a
key and you'd see people waiting at six in the morning on a street
corner looking for an address that didn't exist [laughter]. So, going
back to the very beginning, gradually, very quietly, you know we
didn't go in with axes, I think before the community realized what
had happened they were all closed. The interesting thing is that on
23rd Street not only did all of them close, but one—if you go by
now it's still vacant, just west of Collins on 23rd—was so furious at
this continual heavy enforcement that he not only closed up, but
rather than pay taxes on the shell he knocked the building down
[laughter].

·   ·   ·   ·   ·

I'm not prudish and saying gee, they shouldn't strip, that wasn't
the problem. The stripping wasn't the problem, it was the B-girl
operation. That was the problem. Again, if you look at it from the
community's business viewpoint, ultimately, the community, who
knows what kind of conventions we've lost in that area? Because
the president or the head of some committee went in and got busted
out and couldn't complain; imagine the furious anger that attends
something like this. Man sees a night club, and he's in a strange city,
and he's with a friend, and they'll go in, let's say. Now they didn't go
in for something illegal, it's been advertised in the newspapers, they
didn't go into some back room, and they get busted out by some B-
girl operation. He doesn't want to complain, because back home he
would never go into a strip joint, and he's a leading civic figure or
married, which is more often the case, and the wife tells him what in
hell were you doing there talking to those girls. You know. So he
doesn't complain, didn't complain, but that convention of Pythians
or whatever it was, they would never come back to that community.
And so little by little, as this stopped, now they opened up in other
places, they moved to other areas, one of them is right here in

Washington today, again I don't want to—it's Sam ——, you know him.

INTERVIEWER: There's a lot of funny stuff in Washington today.

POMERANCE: Oh God, is there ever! I was stunned [laughter].

. . . . .

You see, one of the things I did administratively was wherever possible I tried to set up a system of checks and balances. And I don't want to seem simplistic, but ultimately that's the answer. The check and balance, if it's not within a police department, I'm speaking now of the corruption area, if it's not within the police department itself, can be the community's public opinion as evinced by the news media. The checks and balances could be the state's attorney, the grand jury, it could be a higher echelon of enforcement. I was pleased to see something recently that Congress did: they passed, I think it's PL 30, they passed a law, I don't know around the country if public officials are aware of it. And this law basically says if illegal activity is taking place and if the activity is over two thousand dollars a day, and there are over five employees, and it goes beyond participation by the public officials, to the point where if he is—he may not be a participant—but if he's not giving every effort to closing it up, he's subject to a federal court case. Ultimately this is another tool, another weapon to stop corruption.

I served on an organized crime committee for the IACP, and [with] the highest officials of the highest organizations in the country, I was very proud to serve on it, and we came out with a recommendation that's in the proceedings of I guess a year or so ago, condemning corruption of police agencies—we didn't limit it to police, because it's *never* limited to the police. That's the secret here. But of all public officials, courts, prosecutors, political officials. Then I was surprised to find out that it was the first time they had addressed themselves to corruption as a factor in American life.

. . . . .

So when we compare America with Denmark, in pornography, for example, or America with parts of West Germany, with the legalized prostitution and so forth, our lifestyles are so different that it's a comparison between apples and oranges. Now ultimately, as television has a worldwide effect, as communications [get more elaborate], the differences between people all over the world [will change], there won't be the cultures and lifestyles of different countries, it won't be as drastically different, one from the other. We've westernized much of the world today. Unfortunately, we give them the worst, we give them the rock, and we give them the hippie, the drug culture, we give them all the garbage along with it. That's kind of sad. But I guess in return we'll be taking some of their worst. We don't always take the best of other cultures. So in any event, when they say, "Look, in this city in West Germany they have prostitution that's legalized," it's probably great there, I haven't examined it, and I don't know. But I don't know that because it works there it would work in a Midwestern city. You see, I don't know enough about the transplant of that ethic to this country. Now, it might be that in a sophisticated, urban community the attitudes might be so different that maybe they could accept these kinds of concepts.

But let's go back to the web of corruption. The thing that's always distressed me about the prostitute is that—I'm not all shook up that she'll take somebody to bed and get paid for it—the thing that distresses me is that it's illegal, and because it's illegal someplace along the line she's going to run into a policeman or a detective, and she'll bed him down as a favor, and maybe give one a five-dollar bill as a bribe, or, as I said, bed him as a bribe, well, that beginning sets this fellow off and he begins to look to other areas as potential sources of corruption. And that's the danger to me, as I see it, in all these illegal acts. Now whether you say that if you legalize it it won't happen, or if you legalize it he won't be corrupted, I don't think that in contemporary America we're ready yet for that step. I think that ultimately that may come, but I don't think we're ready now.

· · · · ·

Bob, yesterday, the mayor of Hialeah, a couple of days ago, was convicted of taking seventy-five hundred dollars of the City of Hialeah's monies, a complicated case, and the counts of grand larceny involved, although he's seventy-two years old, was convicted. *Gerstein*'s office convicted him. And he could have been sentenced to eleven years, and Judge [Carling] Stedman who was about to retire, in his last act of I don't know what you're going to call it, sentenced [Henry] Milander, and I'm sorry I can't recall if it's three months or three years, but withheld adjudication, and by withholding adjudication, he protected his civil rights, and he's going to run for office. He announced—Milander walked out and said that the judge's decision was right and this is my announcement that I'll run for reelection. Okay, now, you take youngsters today, what the hell are they going to think about our judicial system? It's corrupt and it's this and that—how they going to think otherwise? Something— something's radically wrong with the system.

· · · · ·

You know, let me tell you something. I started on the police force January 1, 1950, and I was a mailman on the Beach just prior to that. And they had a ... that was when the Kefauver investigation was just beginning.

INTERVIEWER: How old were you then?

POMERANCE: Twenty-two. So I'm twenty-two years old, and I'm a beat man at Lincoln and Washington, and I'm subpoenaed along with everyone else about the S&G syndicate. I'd only been working a few months on the department, so I go over to the Federal Post Office Building where they were meeting, and I look in the halls, and I see fellows who over the last few months—and years—before, that I knew well enough, hard, tough, old-time policemen. They were running into the men's room, running, throwing up, running in with diarrhea, sitting there, barely talking to one another, a little nervous laughter, all of this kind of registered with me, I can tell you that. And so that assistant U.S. attorney came out, and he saw me, pink-cheeked, and he said, "Son, come here, what are you doing here?" I was in uniform, by the way. So I said I'd been subpoenaed, and he asked how long I'd been on the force, and I said about three months. So he said, "Well," and we talked for a few minutes and he walked me a little bit away, and he said, "Do you know what's happening?" and I said, "Frankly, I really don't, but I've never seen a group of men so upset," and at this point without ... I said, "My God, will you look at that?" Just about that time one of them got up in the hallway, you know, and ran into the men's room again, and cigarette butts, and I said, "These are pretty tough guys, and I never saw ... I don't know what's happening, but they're not talking to each other, they're snapping at people when they talk to them, I've kind of stayed away from them." So he said, "Son, don't ever forget this. We're conducting an investigation, and it's my belief that these people were involved, they're not the only people involved, but that's all we've got," and, uh, I never forgot it. He didn't have anything to question me about. But when I left there that day, I thought, I don't care what they earned, what they stole, got, were bribed, it couldn't possibly be worth the anguish and torture, because if this was happening here Lord knows what was going on in their own home, at night, when they were trying to sleep. So for me that was a great lesson. I wish I could take every young policeman that comes on the department and show him a movie of this and say, "Listen, this is real, this is it, think about this, if all else fails, if all our encouragement and moral values fail, think of this." It made a helluva impression. And so, in later years, when all that was going in [Dade] County, and I was chief, and there were a lot of people kind of rumbling, you know, gee, look at all the money they're making over there, wow, look what's going on, oh boy, look at that stuff, I always thought back to that thing, forgetting all the professional attitudes and everything else, I thought, well, one of these days they're going to be sitting, waiting [laughter], the voice of doom, you know? And it happened, it happened. I even had some of the old-timers on my department say, "You know, all you have to do is relax a little and look the other way, just a little, and nobody would ever. . . ." [And I said] You know, one of these days, these people going to wind up in jail. But as it turned out they didn't.

INTERVIEWER: They're starting to now, some of them.

POMERANCE: Right. And they had to leave the state. You think about, my Lord, what about your children? What does your youngster think when a thing like this happens?

. . . . .

[Interviewer asks about Charles Celona, the singing deputy.]

POMERANCE: I've wondered too. I don't know enough about it. He's the kind of fellow that sometimes you'll pick up a rock and see something like that scurrying around, those kind of people are despicable to me, even, . . . let's say he got religion. I just have that—maybe you do too—wariness of a guy like this. I don't think he really knows the meaning of truth. I don't doubt that a lot of the people he's turning up were involved, but I always have the feeling with a guy like that if it would help him he'd throw in anybody, you know.

INTERVIEWER: Anybody except somebody who might kill him.

POMERANCE: Well, that's liable to come up. You know, the highway patrol just said they're not going to bodyguard him any more. The sheriff's office has to take it over. It's kind of amusing that the highway patrol assigned more men to bodyguard him than were assigned to Nixon when he came down to Key Biscayne [laughter]. . . . That kind of—they turn up continually—it's like the informant [the] police use, he serves a good purpose, but you can't like him [laughter] and you never really trust him.

INTERVIEWER [on informants]: Is it right not to prosecute him? He did commit a crime. There are laws on the books.

POMERANCE: The government has used this [informers] at every level up to the highest, Congress, federal agents, everybody. It becomes a question of your expertise. What do you trade off to get something more important?

Let me just go back a moment, you talk about the makeup of a vice squad. At the time it was so simple, and you look back on it and you say, gee, why didn't I think of that, years ago they had one man who was responsible for gambling. I don't care who he was, the pressures on him would always, you know, be very harsh, and what I did was make a very simple statement that every man's badge is as good as everybody else's. So that the beat patrolman or the guy in the car, if he's aware of bookmaking activity or if he sees it, makes an arrest. *Makes* the arrest. If he feels he has information and needs skillful assistance, fine, he can go to the vice squad and say look, this, this and this, but he has to be later informed what came of his information, and wherever possible, involve him in the arrest, and so now instead of having one man enforcing the vice laws, you've got a few hundred. And each one has a new sense of dignity, he doesn't say, "Oh oh, I'd better walk away from that, that's gambling," or, "I'd better walk away from that, that's liquor," he can do it, he *can*. So by that simple device, people may by power, fear, money, broads corrupt one man, but they can't do it to two hundred fifty. No system is that big.

. . . . .

[Interviewer asks about organization of vice squad.]

POMERANCE: What I do is, it's vice and criminal intelligence and it's also narcotics, liquor and so forth. The narcotics has become such a specialty that although they're available in vice enforcement, they're really more or less specialists, they're all graduates of the Federal Narcotics School. So I've got a captain in charge of the unit, then a lieutenant who primarily supervises the four fellows in the narcotics unit, and a captain in overall command, supervises another four men in the vice, and something that's been forcing us to give a tremendous amount of our time to, and again, it's a community feeling, is the pornography, the adult book stores, the strip shows, and the movies that got so bad that finally they had a play where there was simulated intercourse on the stage. We've made a lot of arrests in this area, and we've done it with the philosophy that I have, that the policeman is not the censor, a literary censor, an art censor, so what we do is take the evidence, present it to the judge, [and if] the judge says yes, it's indecent, then we'll make the arrest. . . .

. . . . .

If it [pornography] is available to adults, it'll wind up in the hands of the young people. And on the youngster who's not emotionally mature, it could have a deleterious effect. It could tip the kid over one way or the other, his whole attitude towards the opposite sex, or her attitude, becomes warped and changed, and Jesus, we're losing a whole generation just on the drug culture, I'd hate to see us lose more of them on some of this sick stuff, I don't know if you've ever seen this, some of it is, Jesus, bestiality, really bad. . . . I'm convinced too that the present trend will lead to the "Superman" shows of pre-Castro Cuba. I'm not going to testify it is okay or it isn't okay. Right now it isn't, and we're going to enforce it that way.

The following is the complete text of an advertisement that appeared in *The New York Times Magazine* on January 10, 1971.

Why Miami Beach Is Changing:

For decades we've had a great thing going. With sunshine, warm sand and a hundred things to do a day.

But now Miami Beach is changing. For one reason. Because people are changing.

There's a new breed who don't remember Sophie Tucker. Tuned into new sounds, new lifestyles, new clothes, new values.

For them there's the new Miami Beach.

With titanic discotheques to turn on every rock generation from bubblegum to underground. Even one with a plastic mountain to climb. Because the fox trot doesn't let much soul hang out.

With scores of great restaurants and clubs where you'll feel just as comfortable in bells and Blass as the old grey bib and tucker.

There's still a lot of the Miami Beach that always was. For our longtime friends who like it that way.

There's still the excitement of the great horses and greyhounds racing and jai alai and Broadway/South theatre and the big revues.

But this year begins the new Miami Beach. With a lifestyle all its own that's somewhere between New York's campiest First Avenue boite and the great joy of old Havana.

Try on the new Miami Beach. It fits.

3

Dirt Storm in Utica

As I waited for the elevator in the motel I noticed that the emergency key to the sliding door was missing from its box to the left of the button. God knows when it had vanished, or who was responsible for inspecting such things, but in the city of Utica, New York, from past experience, it could be missing until the place burned down without anybody being chastised for it. On the way out I passed the bar room-cum-nightclub, which the evening before had been packed with salesmen and air force noncoms and hookers and amateurs. At this time in history, in April, 1971, the best way to tell the professionals from the amateurs was hot pants: the $20-to-$50-an-hour set had adopted them as soon as they'd been invented, with the vinyl boots and the contrasting pantyhose. In the old days in Utica the whores didn't hang around the saloons. Instead,

Irene Burke and Ma Davis sent out for the lobster and filet mignon dinners and the elegant carafes of wine; and after the good-time, gravy days
were over and the entire vice squad, consisting of two men, had been sent
to the thick, high-walled prison over at Attica, one of the two owners of
the old Imperial Restaurant complained to the editor of the local newspaper that the crackdown had cost him an average of $50 a night, losing
those dinners ordered by Irene, who ran her shop literally within a
stone's throw of City Hall and the police station.

The date was April 8, 1971, as I walked north on Genesee Street
toward my meeting with one of the former bosses of the Democratic
party machine who ran Utica with an iron hand for years and years. Old
snow was piled up on the side streets, barely visible under an accumula-
tion of soot and dirt, and a bitter wind from the north blew more dirt
into my eyes. At Oriskany Plaza the dirt got so bad that it filled the gut-
ters, running from the street to the sidewalk in an unbroken sweep, like a
brown beach, mixed here and there with broken bottles, beer cans and
the other debris that surfaces after one of those gloomy cities along New
York State's Mohawk Frontier ends its annual contention with winter.

He was waiting for me at Marino's.

He was one of those in control of the city when the Laino brothers
ran the town; and when the two Falcones moved in there with the
north-central branch of the Mafia; and when the crap games were big
enough to lead to bodies face down in bodies of water as far away as the
East River, 250 miles to the southeast; and when the whores were big
and blowsy and tightly controlled by the vice squad, under the machine's
orders; and it was all run from right here at Marino's, a squat, gray
wooden cafe with maybe eight booths in the main dining room, and a
couple of private meeting rooms off to the side. It is gone now, fallen
under the urban renewal wrecking ball, but this is where the seat of power
in the city of Utica spent its winters and summers for many years; and it
is in one of the side rooms, it is reported, where oil company executives,
trying to get zoning changes to allow a gas station to open up on one
corner or another, would be told to report, to play cards with a boss, and
to lose $2,400 in cash, no checks accepted.

He sat there with his $50 shoes scraping on Marino's linoleum, or
what was left of it, his jeweled cufflinks shot from the sleeves of what
had to be a $350 suit, and ordered a Western egg sandwich on toast, one
of about three entrées offered in the former capitol of Utica. I mentioned
that I had just walked through a dirt storm.

"Yes," he said. "Goddamn it," adding that in the old days the streets
were cleaned by Easter. "And just look out there now," he said.

The talk just naturally turned to the good old days, the 1940s and 1950s, when, he said, the whorehouses were good and they were clean and good for the city, when the girls all had blood examinations every week, at least, and that Utica needed the houses because some guys just naturally couldn't get girls, being ugly or revolting or such, and with a natural outlet like a brothel look at all the rapes we avoided here in the city of Utica. He said the venereal disease rate was now 3,000 percent higher than it was back then, thanks to all the go-go girls and the call girls, and just look at all the *pornography.*

"Utica then was a fun place to come to, and let's face it, the only reason people enjoy going to New York City is because it swings. Utica has been no fun since the investigation, and it's going to hell, too."

He wrote the investigations of 1954 and 1955 off as Republican attempts to discredit a very hard-working Democratic machine, run along the lines of and with the same precision as the old Tammany Hall, and he is a little bit right about the goals of the investigations.

It was the machine, he said, which got Franklin Roosevelt to put the air force base in at Rome, a few miles away, and that brought 11,000 jobs, and which helped bring Univac in, and that brought another 7,000 jobs, and the way to do that is to have somebody running things who knows how to wheel and deal. On July 20, 1959, a special prosecutor who had been appointed to make things right in the city ruled that five firms must be barred from dealing with the city for the next five years because officers of those firms had refused to sign limited waivers of immunity when they were called to appear before a special grand jury. One of the companies partly belonged to one of the old bosses, and that is one indication of the kind of wheeling and dealing we were talking about.

I posed a logical proposition for my subject, as he dabbed tomato from his lips with a paper napkin:

A. If whorehouses and gambling are against the law and you

B. Use your city police force and vice squad to control and regulate them but continue to let them operate, you are

C. Setting up the cops for charges of corruption and the possibility of corruption.

"Sure," he said. And he added that Vincent Fiore was the best cop on the force, and that the police department had never been the same without him. That is probably true, too.

On May 20, 1958, Captain John P. Ronan of the New York State Police, who had just finished a ten-week survey of the Utica Police Department, reported to Public Service Commissioner Boyd E. Golder:

"All members of the police department took an oath to protect life and property and to enforce all the laws," and that "this primary function has been forgotten by many members of the department. Some of their forgetfulness is due to the lack of being properly supervised by commanding officers." He said that some policemen should be "re-educated" about gambling and prostitution:

> Unfortunately, there are some members of the department who are apparently not qualified for the positions they hold. Some members have an idea, which was instilled in them from the time they first became members, that certain crimes can be overlooked, such as gambling and prostitution. Where this occurs, and if neglect of duty by a member of the department is responsible, departmental discipline should result for those members. . . . This condition [disorderly houses] has been brought about by a lack of proper investigation and enforcement by the department members. There are facts available which prove this. Vice and crime conditions as it relates to gambling and disorderly houses cannot operate without some form of protection or immunity. This protection can be given in many ways. The beat man or patrol car assignment who is fearful of making the "wrong" arrest or is not permitted, as he thinks, to take the necessary action against such violators without fear of some reprisals, is unknowingly giving protection. Any gambling locations or disorderly houses cannot operate for long without protection. Any large-scale operation must certainly depend upon a certain amount of protection in order to continue their operations. Constant vigilance on the part of beat men and patrol car assignments with close supervision by the chief and all command officers can deter and control these operations. When the police department resolves, with the help of all the people [in the unified fight against] vice and crime, it will raise its own general character to a high degree.

Vincent Fiore in April, 1971, was working at the front gate of a Utica factory as a security guard, and there is no question but that when you have Fiore as a security guard you have one of the best, because wasn't he the one selected, back in 1951, to supply police protection for the late Albert Anastasia at the Utica wedding of Anastasia's nephew?

Fiore is a native of Utica, and joined the police force on March 16, 1929. Between then and March 1, 1939, when he was promoted to captain, he earned the title of the "singing policeman" because of his performances in local minstrel shows, and gained some fame as a southpaw pitcher in local semipro baseball games.

In September, 1944, Captain Fiore became the acting deputy chief of police, in charge of the night squad, and he continued to sing "Many Brave Hearts Are Asleep in the Deep" at testimonials, and pitched ball in the Twilight League, and the next year 400 citizens turned out to honor him at his own banquet. His reputation might have been tarnished somewhat in 1949 when a grand jury investigating voting irregularities indicted both Fiore and Lieutenant Martin Koslowski, who had succeeded Fiore as night chief of detectives when Fiore was promoted to deputy chief of police. The grand jury said Fiore, Koslowski and others in the police department acted as protectors of illegal activities and that they "conferred, combined and agreed with other members of the conspiracy as a protector of illegal activities during the night hours in the City of Utica." Fiore then was made head of the detective division from 8 A.M. to 5 P.M., probably because there is just not too much of the kind of activity Fiore was proving to be interested in going on during those hours, and anyway it was a daylight job and you couldn't miss the great, sleazy bulk of Fiore if you wanted to keep an eye on him, in case anybody did.

There were never any convictions from those indictments, because there wasn't enough evidence. And for the next five years everything seemed quiet, with the booming defense industry of the area getting a boost from the Korean War, new families moving in, a hustle and bustle not seen since the first band of Italian immigrants came over from New York City to work on the New York Central and the canals. There were rumors, of course. Some whispers had it that a syndicate had moved in, but nobody knew just what kind of syndicate it was supposed to be, always thinking in terms of Chicago and Al Capone, and the gangsters of the 1930s, who, all in all, were a pretty innocent bunch. Utica—and the rest of the Mohawk-Niagara Frontier—had no idea that the elite of organized crime—some call it the Mafia, others the Cosa Nostra—were moving in at full speed.

There was gambling, there had always been gambling. Pinball machines, slots, card games, and then the high rollers would show up from Buffalo and New York City to meet at Reile's Garage, just a few feet outside the city limits, in Oneida County. There were prostitutes in the houses, but that kept the airmen away from the daughters of those new suburbanites, and it kept the college students from as far away as Syracuse out of more devilishness; but there was nothing bad, like criminals. And there were also rumors that the Democrats had made a deal with the Republicans—you take the county, and I'll take the city, and never the twain shall meet.

By the mid-1950s things were wide open. The Democratic machine got its own man, John T. McKennan, elected mayor in November, 1955, and everything came out in the open. The lobster dinners fairly flew across the street to Irene's whorehouse. The pinballs were in every saloon, the kind where free games mean a payoff from the bartender, where you could put in up to five dollars' worth of nickels on a single game. Bookie joints were operating everywhere. And it was, in the words of a former boss, a fun place to be. He was confident that it would not only be fun, but wholesome, and to keep it that way he kept in very close touch with Vincent Fiore, who saw to it that his men—especially the two-man vice squad—kept everything tidy and under control. Fifteen years later one of the upstate city's former leaders was to tell me that the only reason Fiore and his men went after Lee Clarke and her spinoff, daylight brothel operation was because of the deviates she had coming up there, and the narcotics. They couldn't stand that in Fun City North.

Now, the political implications of the situation in Utica may appear overwhelming, as they always are when a situation sifts down through a few years. The Utica *Observer-Dispatch* and the *Daily Press*, which won a Pulitzer Prize for its work on the civic corruption in 1959, really did a job on the city. But it must be remembered that in the long run those newspapers were really concerned with throwing out the Democrats and getting the Republicans in on a reform ticket, and half the battle in getting anything done was first convincing a Democratic governor to do something, anything, and then later trying to stop a Republican governor from doing *everything*. In its Pulitzer presentation the newspaper included all manner of investigatory material concerning the sale of tires by the Laino boys to the city, nefarious snowplow contracts foisted off by the county Democratic leader, Rufus Elefante, and other schemes not relating to what was really going on in Utica; the city had gotten itself the kind of administration and environment it wanted, and in the kind of fascistic "regulation" and "control" the bosses were talking about the city corrupted the police—the only conceivable arm of the body politic capable, if uncorrupted and uncorruptible, of protecting the city from what it really considered undesirable: murder, rape, kidnap, larceny. The city wanted to wallow in bordellos, the more opulent the better; the city wanted to bet on horses and shoot dice and drink and make all kinds of merry, but they wanted it to be illegal, too, and so they set up Vincent Fiore for a free, chauffeured ride to Attica.

The mid-1950s were very important to Utica and Vincent Fiore.

One extra-warm, late-summer Saturday a dozen high rollers were out at Reile's Garage, 5,000 feet over the city line, and packed around the pool table customarily used for the crap game. There were about ten shooters, plus the banker, a man named Corteze, who five days a week put in his time on the New York Central, and a not-too-bright New York City hoodlum named Frank Caputo. When the game broke up the other shooters headed for the street while Caputo remained behind with the bank man, pulled a gun, and said, "I'm taking the money." The banker thought he was kidding, and had every right to think so, since everybody knew, or at least suspected, that the Mafia (nobody called it the Mafia then, just the mob), the sheriff's department and the city cops were taking a three-way split on the game. But Caputo wasn't kidding, and he left with about $1,800, and when one of the men outside shouted at him to return the money he hollered, "Come and get me."

The next day Caputo took his wife out to the Aurisville Shrine, where he obviously got some but not enough divine guidance, because the following day he gave back about $700 to the banker. In September, 1954, his body was fished out of the East River, down in the Big Apple. A lot of speculation arose about this case, and it heightened when a guy named Happy Longo vanished from the face of the earth. It was reliably rumored that Happy had fingered the game for Caputo and that he is now a permanent part of one of the overpasses of the New York State Thruway, which passes Utica a mile north of downtown and which was under construction at that time.

This is one of the well-documented mob murders. There were more, and in 1958, when the New York Legislative Watchdog Committee was trying to get some answers about what was going on in Utica, they called Police Chief Leo Miller and asked him some questions about Caputo. He said that he knew Caputo had been around in Utica for several years, but he had no further information on the man. The committee had already taken testimony on seven unsolved gangland-style slayings in the Utica area, and they asked Miller about them, too. It went like this:

Q. These seven murders, are they gangland slayings?
A. Yes, from what I have heard.
Q. Does the syndicate organize crime in Utica?
A. I have no knowledge of that.
Q. You have no knowledge of any individual who could be responsible?
A. No.

Q. What have you done in ten years as head of the police to run rackets and racketeers out of Utica?

A. We can't get information on who they are. We have no evidence.

Q. And on prostitution?

A. This is a family business.

Miller, under questioning, said most of the girls were from out of town, and admitted knowing about the operations of Irene Burke, Henry Cittadino, Ma Davis and Lee Clarke, and that he had known about them for a long time.

Q. To your knowledge prostitution has gone on in Utica for twenty-five years. The Cuban lottery and bookmaking and seven to twelve gangland slayings in the last twenty-five years, does that not indicate to you as chief of police of Utica that open racketeering has operated? What have you done?

A. We make investigations on all this, but we don't get anywhere with them.

Now, the watchdog committee was on an obvious crusade to link the Democratic machine with organized crime, and there have been countless books about organized crime, and you can read all about the capos and capo-regimes and the like elsewhere, but it becomes important here because without the police force being initially corrupt and corruptible, by the whores and the gamblers, the syndicate might not have become what it has become in New York State. It is quite possible that it was there all the time, but unnamed and unquantified, anonymous but ubiquitous, the way scientists are beginning to think about cancer.

America really has three major landmarks in its progression of awareness of organized crime. The first was the Saint Valentine's Day massacre, which shocked a good bit of the romance from the happy-go-lucky gangsterism that flourished in Chicago during and after Prohibition. The third was when the late Joe Valachi in 1963 turned songbird and described the actual structure of what he called the Cosa Nostra, naming names and showing America that it was, indeed, infiltrated with hoodlums posing as legitimate citizens. (The fourth and final landmark will come when the *organization* of illegal activities is subordinated to the realization that, just as war is an extension of politics, crime is simply an extension of ordinary business techniques, without obeying the arbitrary rules which, anyway, only serve to make patsies of those who follow them to the letter.)

But the second landmark, and the one that rocked Utica, occurred at dusk on the lovely evening of November 14, 1957, when Sergeant Edgar Croswell of the New York State Police shocked the nation by rounding up a couple dozen of the biggest gangsters in America at a summit conference in a lodge at Apalachin, New York. This was a landmark because it was the first *proof* that organized crime was really organized, although people like Hank Messick and Aaron Kohn and Virgil Peterson had been hollering about it for years. Here it was, out in the open (although to the day he died it was not proof enough for J. Edgar Hoover), and—just imagine—among the conferees at that meeting were three solid citizens of the gloomy but happy little city of Utica.

The three were Joseph Falcone and his brother, Salvatore, and a man named Mancuso, all of whom got their start in the Utica area during Prohibition, when the city was openly wild, and when the Falcones were running a cutting plant to water down the bottled smuggled Canadian whiskey, then shipping it to New York City and Buffalo and points intermediate; and the three ran the local lottery, which at the time was based on the numbers thrown in the Cuban national lottery.

Years later, after Apalachin but before Joe Valachi, when the legislature's watchdog committee was conducting hearings in Albany, Vincent Fiore was subpoenaed to appear before a rival investigatory panel—this one appointed by the Democrats and headed by then acting Investigations Commissioner Arthur L. Reuter in New York City.

Committee Chairman William F. Horan asked Fiore if he had indeed telephoned a gambling house operator, warning him to shut down by 5 P.M. because another deputy chief would be in charge of the night shift, and that protection couldn't be guaranteed. Fiore said he didn't remember making any such call.

Fiore the Foxy also went on to say that he wasn't denying making the call, just that he couldn't *remember* doing it, obviously trying to circumvent a perjury charge, and then the interrogators got around to asking about Utica's mobsters. Under questioning Fiore acknowledged that he had known both Joseph and Salvatore Falcone for more than thirty years, and that he and Joe Falcone had seen each other socially over the years.

Q. How many times did you and your wife entertain Joseph Falcone in your home?

A. Three or four times he came to my house when he delivered stuff, a bottle of wine or a bottle of whiskey ...

Q. Do you mean Joseph Falcone acts as a delivery boy?

A. Not always. He has other deliverers, too.

Later on in this session the talk turned to Albert Anastasia, the New York City mobster who had gotten himself in enough hot water with his companions that he was afraid for his life, properly so. In 1951, Fiore acknowledged, he had furnished police protection for Anastasia when he came to Utica for the wedding of his newphew to Concetta Miletto, the daughter of an old, old friend of the deputy police chief. The bride died six years later, in 1957, and it was rumored that Anastasia was going to be hit when he came to her funeral, so Fiore furnished another police escort and saved the good name of Utica. Anastasia lived on until October 25 of that same year, when he was gunned down in a Manhattan hotel barber shop.

But if Fiore was a friend of the big and the mighty, he was also a friend of the small, the family whorehouse operators. Like Irene Burke, and, for many years, until she began letting perverted stuff go on in her place, Lee Clarke, Miss Burke's sister.

When Utica "cleaned itself up" in 1959, what it did was select a handful of madams and pimps and send them off to jail. In 1956, an investigator for the American Social Hygiene Association visited the city of Utica and found what they called "semi-flagrant" vice and venereal disease conditions. The association, which was headquartered in New York City, was organized in 1914, and had conducted social protection services for the armed services since World War I (and was, incidentally, a member agency of the Greater Utica Fund Campaign). In a secret meeting in January, 1957, the agency reported on its findings to Police Chief Miller, who was then also safety commissioner, to a representative of Mayor McKennan's office, and to the provost marshal of Griffith Air Force Base. (During Fiore's subsequent trial, the judge was to disallow the introduction of the report as evidence on the grounds that it was hearsay.)

The district attorney, an ineffectual bumbler named John Liddy, guided an Oneida County grand jury through an "investigation" of prostitution and gambling in the area, and helped prepare the jury's final report that it "has been unable to find sufficient evidence to prove beyond reasonable doubt any violations of the criminal statutes applicable to the existence of vice and gambling," and urged "a continuous and conscientious surveillance by authorities of vice and gambling conditions in this city." They went on to recommend the creation of a separate and distinct vice squad, to be responsible to the safety commissioner himself, and if that has a familiar ring, so be it.

During this time the two newspapers in town, both owned by the

Gannett chain, were getting ready to win their Pulitzer Prize, although they didn't know it at the time. The newspapers were coming under all sorts of pressure, including, naturally, threats on the lives of the editors and reporters, usually by anonymous telephone callers.

It went further—the Utica Common Council demanded a tax on printing and advertising, and requested that the United States Department of Justice investigate the monopoly of the newspapers. City Hall bought a reporter, one who had been covering that beat, by hiring him for a $10,000-a-year municipal job. The city controller refused to let reporters see city records, and, of course, since the whole thing had started with the people who have the funny, inflective names of southern Italy, the Federation of Italian-American Societies got out a special issue of its newspaper *The Vanguard*, Volume I, Number 4, on October 9, 1959, whose first page consisted of an open letter to Governor Nelson Rockefeller demanding an end to the special investigation, putting the ethnic vote on the line. The back page was an exposé of the newspapers in photographs showing how employees block sidewalks to load newspapers, how circulation men double park and other heinous crimes. Without pressures of this sort the Pulitzer committee probably wouldn't even have noticed Utica, which is sort of poetic (although the year before they had noticed Little Rock).

After the VD-vice report hit, after Apalachin, after the crap game holdup, the Gannett powers in Rochester suspected that maybe their editor in Utica had been a little lax in reporting what had really been going on in the town. They made him Sunday editor, a job that involves a lot of going out to lunch with itinerant comic-strip salesmen, and they reshuffled the top staff so that veteran investigative reporters and editors like Gilbert P. Smith, William J. Woods, William Lohden, Mason Taylor and Jack Germond were running things, and during 1956 and 1957 the newspapers printed something like eighty editorials on lax law enforcement and one or another various conspiracies to defraud the public. Mason Taylor, now executive editor of both newspapers, told me in 1971 that he was still sort of ashamed of the press for letting the city run so wide open for so long, but I don't think it occurred to him that the multiplicity of little laws making one thing after another illegal because it is immoral contributed to the decay of the city's ethical fiber.

Several investigatory bodies zeroed in on Utica. One was the watchdog committee, and, immediately after testifying, Chief Miller resigned. In the meantime, the state cops made a spectacular raid on several gambling establishments in Utica and in Oneida County, knocking over one of the old-line bookie joints in the city, sending an old-timer named Pete

Olivadoti to the county jail for six months, and netting his son, Tony, a six-month suspended sentence. It wasn't much, but it showed that the gambling was there if somebody wanted to prosecute it. And after a series of questions posed by the Reuter Commission in New York City on February 8, 1958, Fiore also resigned.

Chairman Horan, after ascertaining the relationship between Fiore and the Falcones, asked Fiore if he knew of the existence of bordellos in Utica, five of them specifically. Fiore said he knew of them and of the suspicions about them, and that he had aided in investigating them.

He listed a pitifully small number of arrests, and then, in response to a question by Chairman Horan, said that he had never asked for outside assistance in cleaning up the city.

Nobody ever *asked* anybody for help around Utica except for a would-be runaway grand jury being guided by District Attorney Liddy, which on February 17, 1958, asked Governor Averell Harriman to name an extraordinary grand jury and provide it with special legal counsel.

"I feel," Liddy said, "that my staff is adequate to handle whatever might be requested or required in the vice probe, as things now stand." In April, 1958, Liddy finally asked the board of supervisors to provide funds for an investigative staff. The following month the board appropriated an extra $10,000 for his use, but on May 22, 1958, Governor Harriman went ahead and ordered a special prosecutor appointed to investigate crime and vice in Utica. He acted on the recommendation of the state crime commission, whose chairman, Myles J. Lane, said his organization "does not feel that a proper investigation and prosecution of the alleged criminal activities . . . can be made by the present district attorney." The commission said in its report to Harriman that "while no evidence has been disclosed of corruption in the office of John M. Liddy . . . there has been ample evidence presented to the commission which indicates that Mr. Liddy's official conduct has been characterized not only by apathy, but by failure to understand and appreciate some of the most fundamental concepts of the duties and responsibilities of a district attorney."

Irene Burke was born Irene Mae Filitrault in 1906. Her baby sister, Mrs. Lee Orlene Clarke, alias Iva Davis, nee Filitrault, was three years younger, so that when Irene, Lee and a prostitute named Pat were knocked over in a raid at 219 Pearl Street in January, 1950, Lee was a solid forty-one. That is probably the first time she had ever been arrested, and the job was started by a sergeant named Koslosky and a patrolman named Gigliotti, who stopped a local businessman while he was leaving the brothel early on that winter morning. The businessman was aghast, and told the cops—who were obviously not among the enlightened few who knew of the vice squad's policy of benign neglect— that he had paid Irene $15 and that he had known her for thirty years. Koslosky and Gigliotti then went and got a warrant, and knocked on the door, but Irene wouldn't let them come in, and so Koslosky notified the chief, Leo Miller, who sent Detective Captain James Laino (brother of the man who was to go to jail ten years later for cheating the city) and two other detectives, who broke down the door only to find Lee Clarke and Pat in bed, and Irene in a clothes closet in the attic (for all she knew, these were robbers crashing in). All charges stemming from the warrant were later dismissed, and naturally—and Gloria Steinem would have predicted this—no charges were filed against the local business-man-customer.

A year later Fiore himself busted Irene, Lee and a third prostitute named Ann. Fiore said the warrant for Irene's arrest was based on infor-mation provided by a man whose identity they declined to reveal. Irene admitted conducting a disorderly house, and got thirty days in the county jail. Lee Clarke and Ann both pleaded guilty to charges of prosti-tution, Lee getting ten days and Ann getting the hell out of town while her sentencing was deferred.

Apparently that night Fiore and Irene and Lee came to an under-standing of some sort. Neither was arrested again until after Lee started that funny business at 211 Pearl Street.

The final case against the sisters began to be built in the summer of 1957, when the vice squad began to pay attention to the heat being gen-erated by the newspapers. Everything was, supposedly, shut down until the heat was off. That included the big crap game and the brothels, which were ordered to stay closed until told to reopen. The cops put a tap on Lee Clarke's telephone, and made a few recordings over a period of months, apparently just to establish the fact that Lee was up to no good.

In one of the early tapes of this nature, Lee Clarke answered the telephone, and it turned out to be a man named Red, who told Lee that Irene had given him the number. Lee gave Red complete directions on how to get to her place, and told him which bell to ring—there were two.

The next call was from Lee's place and was from a prostitute named Bernadette to a cab driver named Herb, who apparently was running business for Lee's illicit illegitimate house. They discussed the prices a cab driver should charge transient customers, and the kind of heat Fiore was putting on the whorehouses, but agreed the rumor was that everything would be open again by the weekend.

Everybody in town was hearing the rumor, it seemed. A few nights later Lee Clarke answered her telephone, and it was a man who did not identify himself but asked that a prostitute named Beverly (really Bernadette, operating under an assumed name, as most of the girls did— probably her real name wasn't even Bernadette) call him, and this means that Lee knew who the caller was even without hearing his name, the way you know it when your friends call you at home. Beverly/ Bernadette returned the call, exchanging all sorts of hellos and how-are-yous, and then the caller said, "I'll be in action Monday."

"So I heard," Bernadette said.

"Yeah. You don't miss a trick, do you?"

"No. But I heard Saturday."

"Huh?"

"I heard Saturday."

"Well, I was talking to what's-his-name, and he said maybe Saturday, or Monday for sure."

"Um-hum."

"So, automatically, I ain't gonna let you open up on a weekend—so, automatically, it will be Monday."

"Oh, I see," Bernadette said.

"You follow me?"

"Yeah, well, me don't care, because me'll be going home Sunday."

"What's that?"

"I'm going home Sunday."

This was a tough period for everybody in town, when nobody would know when he was going to be open or why he was to be closed, but as opening day neared—that Monday Bernadette was talking about with her mysterious regulator, preparations were made to get open. Bernadette called Buffalo, to talk to a prostitute—a part-timer—named Gerry.

"I might call you Friday or something, because I understand that there might be a change, but you know how that is. You know, it's supposed to be definitely this weekend—and ... so try to have your bonnet ready," she said.

In June, a secretary at the General Electric plant at Schenectady who turned tricks part time as "Marsha" called Lee Clarke. Marsha asked about whether the places were going to open up, and announced that she was getting ready to leave town, having made plans to resign from GE. She and Lee discussed the possibilities of reopening, just in case Marsha wanted to make some traveling money. The reopening, of course, was a matter of speculation, and the two looked for the obvious signals: the re-emergence of other forms of vice.

"And, uh, so I understand that—I guess if it's going—it's—the crap game's open," said Lee.

"Yeah."

"Um-hum."

"I suppose that would start first," Marsha said.

At this time, Coke Stefano was running, Henry's on Main Street was running, Ma Davis on Cooper Street was running, Jerry's on State Street was running, and both Irene Burke and Lee Clarke were closed, and they really didn't know what the trouble was. It was double-barreled trouble, as a matter of fact, and it came with two names: Robert Sacks and Crazy Sally (not her real name).

"Sally" was very popular at Lee's. She was a housewife and a member of the parent-teacher association in another New York town, and when she was in her late twenties she asked her husband to take her over to Utica, to Lee Clarke's operation at 211 Pearl Street, to see what it was like, and when she saw what it was like she wanted to join in the fun. She had never before had any sexual relations for money, and the money didn't mean very much to her. She gave it all to Lee, and the parties got better and better until it got to the point where she would do just about anything and let you take pictures of her doing it if you wanted to.

Crazy Sally took the stand as a prosecution witness at Irene's trial in 1959, and by this time she was thirty-six and was wearing horn-rimmed glasses. Defense Attorney Joseph Panzer of New York City got out of her that she had never been convicted of a crime and that she had never been in a mental institution, that she had been married thirteen years and had three children when she first showed up at 211 Pearl Street.

"You want this court to believe your husband took you to have relations at 211 Pearl Street?" Panzer asked, the way defense attorneys ask questions.

"We wanted to have sex parties," she said. And this was something Vincent Fiore and the city fathers could not stomach. It was, somehow, dirty, and so they shut down the Burke-Clarke operations. Robert Sacks helped. In a telephone call between Sacks and Irene Burke, she told him that "Mosca" (a nickname for a runner for the city machine) was coming to see her.

"And—to cause you trouble?" Sacks asked.

"No. He's coming up here, and he said to me, 'I'll tell you what your trouble is.'"

"Yeah. It's me?" Sacks said.

"Well, I don't know," Irene said.

It was simply that Sacks, like Crazy Sally, irritated the vice cops' sense of propriety. They ran a clean town, and Sacks was into a scene they didn't care for—he was a dope fiend, to use the nomenclature of the day, and he was living at Irene's and Lee's and doing a little pimping on the side.

(Another thing that bugged the vice squad about the ladies' operation, like dope and perverts, was that in 1954, when the Pearl Street whorehouse was idle, Irene rented it out to a man named Harry. Harry, who had told Irene he wanted to set up his mistress in the apartment, actually turned it, briefly, into an abortion mill, and of course that outraged the cops.)

Sacks was eventually indicted for living off the proceeds of a prostitute, but in the meantime, he was convicted in city court on December 6, 1957, of possession of narcotics, fined $500 and given a one-year suspended sentence. His was the sole arrest to come out of the wiretaps, and it is probably time to say a few words about them, and how they came to pass—and what they meant.

Utica Police Captain Robert Bogan, who later was to draw a two-to-four-year sentence for conspiracy with Fiore and the other vice cops, was the one who planted the taps.

Bogan, one of the two members of the vice squad, and Detective Frank Macner, the other, both were assigned to District Attorney Liddy and Police Commissioner Miller, as a formality, and Bogan was the one who went to the New York Telephone Company with a court order to tap the telephone at 211 Pearl Street because of suspected prostitution activities there. It should be noted that Bogan did not attempt to tap the phone at 219, Irene's place next door, although every cop in Utica knew that Irene had been doing more business for many years than her sister. She just didn't run perverts and junkies.

The wiretap was set up in a "nearby office building," Bogan said, when testifying at Irene Burke's 1959 trial, which was held at Rome. The tap was on from June until December, 1957, during which time at least twenty-four tapes containing about one hundred conversations were recorded. At this amazing trial of a couple of old madams Bogan testified that he had "erased" some of the conversations from the original recordings, adding that he had eliminated only "any we felt were not pertinent to the investigation, personal conversations." As a result of listening to the expurgated versions of the tapes, District Attorney Liddy decided to make only the narcotics arrest, despite the fact that most of the voices on the tapes were recognizable, most of them substantiated any suspicions anybody might have had that a brothel was being operated, and one of the names referred to in one of the conversations—"Criggy"—was a nickname for Vincent Fiore. The tapes were admitted to evidence in the trials of Burke, Clarke, Stefano *et al.*, and in February, 1961, when Bogan and Macner were on trial with Fiore the tapes showed up again, being entered as evidence, over defense objections, against the very man who had set them up and subsequently edited them.

You must give Bogan some credit—his name only appeared once on the tapes he had edited. You have to take away some of the credit, though, when you realize that he made the mistake of testifying before a 1958 grand jury, between the time of the wiretaps and the trials, that he had no knowledge of brothels operating in the city—during the exact time when he had bugged one of the Mohawk Frontier's finest whorehouses.

The absurd way Bogan edited the tapes shows up in Irene's trial, when Bogan testified that he and Macner had gone to 211 Pearl Street, Lee's place, in June, 1957, and had been admitted by a girl named Suzanne, took her to the police station (a short stroll), photographed and fingerprinted her and ordered her out of town. A playing of one of the tapes at this time showed that Suzanne was not charged, the obvious implication of this being that Bogan and Macner cared less about apprehending and convicting "criminals" than they did about keeping things the way Fiore and the machine bosses wanted them. And it was in June, 1957, remember, when the heat was on Lee Clarke because of the way she was running her operation. Shortly after the raid, the two sisters talked to each other over the bugged telephone, and it turned out that the two vice cops had come back to the upstairs parlor of Lee Clarke after they'd sent Suzanne on her way.

"So . . . they were all right," Lee said. "They weren't fresh or nasty, you know?"

"Well, of course, I told you I know Macner better than I do Bogan," Irene said.

This involvement of cops and prostitutes isn't unusual, but it was long-standing. In making his opening remarks in the Fiore trial two years later, Prosecutor Robert Fischer said Detective Leonard Custodero saw a lot of Suzanne, and said their relationship was quite close. Both Custodero and Pasquale Fragetta were customers of the various Utica prostitutes, Fischer charged. He was right. His star witness, Irene Burke, testified that both men had been customers at her brothel. Both men were also special vice investigators.

"They were entertained in the rooms by the ladies," she said, going on to describe one visit to 219 Peral Street (her own place, not Lee's) by Bogan and Macner while she was closed during the summer of 1957. They asked her, she said, why she wasn't operating like everybody else, and when she told them she didn't know—at this point she was oblivious to Lee's leather-boot and tea-pad operation next door—they left. A few days later they told her she could open, but that Suzanne and Beverly would have to leave town.

"I said I only have another girl, would you give me a few more days, and they said yes," she said. They explained that someone—referred to as "they"—did not want the two girls in the city. A few days later Macner visited her and apologized, saying "I'm not the boss," and old goodhearted Irene put $50 bill down next to him on the sofa and he picked it up.

Irene told about an earlier visit by Custodero, the vice cop who had been so thick with the Suzanne "they" wanted to see leave town. He had a fingerprint card, he said, and wanted to give it to Suzanne (how's this for a licensing arrangement for an illegal operation?), but she wasn't there, so he left and came back when she was and then the two went into a back room together, but Irene said she really had no knowledge of what they did back there.

She said Custodero had visited her establishment eight or ten times to be "entertained," and that Fragetta had been there four or five times, but that Fragetta had never been to her place without Custodero.

Anyway, when the pimps and madams came to trial in March, 1959, in the Rome courthouse, it was finally as a result of a nine-month investigation by Special Prosecutor Fischer, who had been appointed by Governor Harriman. The corruption in Utica had spanned the administrations of Thomas E. Dewey and Harriman and was to continue well into the first term of Governor Nelson A. Rockefeller, who was elected on November 4, 1958, and assumed office in January, 1959. The embarrassment of the Democratic machine in Utica by a Rockefeller, of course, could not compare with the red face of the Harriman faction.

It took four days to pick a jury for the sisters, Irene and Lee, who were charged with six felony and three misdemeanor counts each. The first prosecution witness was Bernadette, who said she made $400 to $500 a week as a whore at 616 Broadway, Irene's location before moving to Pearl Street. She said she worked during 1956 there and later at Pearl Street, and that she also turned a few tricks for Coke Stefano, and had been taking $10 and up per man in the upstate area since 1942. She said she split 50-50 with Irene, which means that to make $500 a week Bernadette had to turn about a hundred tricks a week. Irene also took five bucks off the top every night for board.

This Bernadette/Beverly, who appeared in court in a neat blue cotton dress, a small blue straw hat, high-heeled sandals and long blue gloves, said she had been convicted only once in those fifteen years, and that was when she was working for Stefano in 1955. She was fined $50 and given a 90-day suspended sentence on the provision that she leave town. Instead, she left Stefano and went to work for Irene.

On May 30, 1959, Irene, then fifty-two, and Lee, fifty, were given three to ten years by a judge on the charge of conspiring with unidentified persons to operate brothels and receive protection from arrest.

On December 5, 1961, Irene Burke was released from Westfield State Farm at Bedford Hills, just seven months after her sister was paroled (both were to be under the supervision of the state parole board until the end of 1969), and only a few months after Irene decided to turn state's evidence against Fiore and his gang of regulators.

If you think she made a deal, you are probably right.

But we have to go back a little bit to pick up the thread of Vincent Fiore, who ran the whole creaky thing.

After the Reuter Commission did its work in February, 1958, Fiore resigned from his job as deputy police chief. He wrote out his resignation on Reuter's stationery, after which Reuter remarked that the resignation "lends substance" to charges that Utica was wide open. A few days later the watchdog committee, which initiated the investigations, asked both Fiore and Chief Miller to submit reports of their finances. They did not, but Fiore denied ever having taken any money for protection while he held down his $5,700-a-year job.

Fiore struggled along during the next few months. He was called as a witness before the special Fischer grand jury in April, 1960; he watched as Miss Burke's whorehouse at 219 Pearl Street was shut down forever and ever, not because of its immorality but because the property was taken over by the city as part of the twenty-two-acre Urban Redevelopment Project Number One and as the sisters were being held in jail as material witnesses in the grand-jury investigation, and it must have been with some relief when, on July 26, 1960, the cat fought its way out of the bag in preparation for what would become the longest trial in Oneida County history.

The grand jury returned indictments against Fiore, former Water Board General Manager Dennis P. O'Dowd, Bogan and Macner of the vice squad and Custodero and Fragetta, the special vice investigators.

The same day, a new safety commissioner, J. Carroll Hamlin, suspended the four policemen.

All of the charges centered around the Burke-Clarke brothels. The sisters had been cooperating with the grand jury since losing their final appeal during the winter. Specifically, O'Dowd and Fiore were charged with giving Miss Burke permission to operate in return for cash payments, supposedly made for political dinner tickets; all six were charged with conspiring to obstruct various investigations of brothel operations, a misdemeanor, and all except O'Dowd were charged with lying to the investigators, a felony. O'Dowd was charged with bribing a witness in a little side deal with Irene Burke. The indictment was twenty-five pages long, and contained a total of thirteen counts.

If there ever was a classical bagman in Utica, it would have to have been Dennis O'Dowd, the water commissioner and a bigwig in Democratic politics there. He seemed to be the arranger, the man to see when something had to be done, and he always seemed to have a pocketful of tickets to one Democratic fund-raising event or another.

During Irene Burke's trial, during the playing of one of those tapes from the summer of 1957, Irene and her sister were chatting.

"I just got a call from Fiore," Irene said. "I've got to go down there. . . . I don't know why he can't come here."

"He wants you down there, I suppose, before he goes home," Lee said.

"Yeah. He goes home at 4:30." (The reason Fiore wanted to see Irene was about the arrest of Suzanne earlier that week.)

Earlier in the same day, Lee had tried to call O'Dowd, who wasn't in, but this was the very first time the man had been linked, publicly, to the brothels, and it got no further at the time, not until Irene turned state's evidence at the group trial of the five cops and O'Dowd.

She testified that she gave O'Dowd a total of $1,000 after getting "permission" to operate the old joint at 616 Broadway, that she gave him $500 for tickets to various party functions and another $500 in cash at "election time" in 1955. Besides this, she said, she had to give the tickets back to O'Dowd, and they must have been kind of dog-eared if he was doing this with every madam in the city.

It was O'Dowd who gave Irene permission to operate the house on Broadway, telling her that she would have to pay the vice squad members $20 a month each and the men in the prowl cars in the area $10 a month each, and that she would have to check with Fiore before she opened.

O'Dowd was also the "fixer," the guy who could get action when nobody else could. Once, in 1954, Irene said she had to call O'Dowd and ask that he fix it that police squad cars park a little closer to her whorehouse, which, you'll remember, was right near the police station. This seemingly odd request had more sanity than you would think, however—Fiore had ordered Irene not to let customers leave when police cars were "in sight," and the prowl cars had been parked "in sight" at the street level but just far enough away so that she couldn't look out the upstairs window and tell when it was all right for the clients to leave. O'Dowd took care of it.

Irene continued to operate at 616 Broadway through 1955. She had to close that location the following year, however, because it was becoming too well known, not only in town but in the county and the state. A grand jury was sitting, and was threatening to "run away" from the control of the district attorney and actually look into vice conditions (such a "runaway" grand jury is rare in New York State); and the state attorney general had written to city officials asking about the situation vis-à-vis vice in Utica (Irene was called into the police station and actually shown the letter). The situation was resolved when Irene asked for and got permission from O'Dowd and Fiore to open up at Pearl Street, a less conspicuous location. She began business there on February 1, 1957.

It was about this time that Irene's mother was subpoenaed by the grand jury, because the old lady had been living at the brothel all these years, sort of a madam emeritus. O'Dowd got Irene a lawyer, whose immediate reaction was to suggest having the old woman committed, but Irene didn't want to do that, so she called Custodero, who went down to Marino's to see one of the machine bosses, and came back with a hand-tailored plan. Custodero said to wait until Sunday, when it was difficult to get a doctor, and then give the old lady "something to excite her," and call the police station and report a heart attack and the lack of an available doctor. Irene did that, and the cops were waiting to send the police doctor over, and when he got there he ordered the old lady hospitalized immediately and, of course, she never was released in time to testify before that grand jury, which was going down the drain anyway through inertia. For this, Irene testified at his trial, she gave Custodero $50, not a bad day's work considering the relatively low cost of living back then.

All six of the men were found guilty in April, 1961, and jailed immediately. The trial had lasted a little longer than two months—jury selection alone took thirteen days—and the jury kept the case fifty-six and a half hours. It took Nelson A. Vale, Jr., of Deansboro, the jury foreman, nearly fifteen minutes to read the verdict, and when Judge John S.

Marsh ordered the defendants jailed, the audience of about fifty persons booed.

After all appeals were exhausted, on January 29, 1963, Fiore went off to Attica, in handcuffs. He was taken at 9 A.M. to do two and a half to five years for perjury, and he was then fifty-six years old. Going up with him were O'Dowd, seventy, to do three and a half to seven for bribery; Bogan, fifty-two, Macner, forty-nine, and Custodero, forty-seven, all sentenced to two to four years for perjury; and Frank N. Laino, forty-nine, who was to do an incidental five to ten years for bribery and grand larceny and three and a half to seven years for fraud in connection with tire sales to the city as a partner in Laino-Fisk Tire Service, one of the two firms that supplied tires to the city for many years.

When the men were sentenced, Judge Marsh had this to say:

> You and your co-defendants are men of experience and maturity who sought and were accorded positions of public trust of your home community. The preservation of the honor and integrity of our American way of life in the community and in the nation requires that those discharging the vital responsibilities of government conform to the highest standards of good citizenship. You have been found guilty by a jury of your fellow citizens of crimes involving a planned and deliberate betrayal of the trust imposed in you as public officers of your city.

Judge Marsh was wrong, of course. Vincent Fiore and his associates had done nothing more than carry out the mandate from the people of the city of Utica. But when the ax fell, they were the ones who had to go to prison, and that, at least, made their peers feel a little more righteous.

4

I'll Take Manhattan-
You Get the Bronx

It would have been well within the original guidelines of this book to have limited the chapter on New York City to the Harry Gross affair of a generation ago—many of the methods used to collect graft were the same then as they are now. I elected to update the New York story, however, to include parts of the Knapp Commission hearings and because what happened in the spring and summer of 1971 affords a rare glimpse into what I have chosen to call the internal corruption of a metropolitan police department, in this instance the case of Waverly Logan, former cop.

The New York City Police Department is probably the most totally corrupt police force in America. Man for man, there is not a single police agency in the country that is as humane and at the same time cruel; as self-confident and at the same time almost violently defensive; as conscientious in the performance of daily duties and at the same time so prone to let those duties slide when faced with the more important task, as in New Orleans of a generation ago, of collecting graft; as cynically corrupt and at the same time almost naïvely honest; as furtively secret and at the same time open and easygoing.

Some New York cops will be going off to serve prison terms this year, largely as a result of newspaper exposés, political maneuverings, including the attempt by Mayor John V. Lindsay to head off criticism of his administration by appointing an investigating committee to look into those newspaper allegations of corruption, and the knee-jerk reaction of the top cops in the city, trying desperately to clean up their own house before the civilians could bring it tumbling about their ears.

Some cops will go to jail. They are the victims of politics. The graft will continue, although it will be as deeply underground as the Spartan warhead they tested at Amchitka, and it will be many years before it is blatant again, but it is the generational thing again, and New York City in another decade or two will have another exposé, another reform commission and another attempt to clean up the cops, but that one won't do any good, either, because the force was born in corruption, for corrupt reasons, and it is congenitally deformed. The best New Yorkers can hope for is that the bagmen and gamblers will leave the fairly honest cops alone long enough for murder and rape to be kept to a minimum, and that the ordinary murder, rape, arson and assault doesn't become, too, a negotiable commodity.

The police department came into existence with the Municipal Police Act of 1844, passed during the middle of those unspeakable days of the mid-nineteenth century when immigrant-packed New York was a tower of Babel already, with few rules, fewer real laws and only a handful of men to enforce them. By 1845 there were 800 men on the force, and while the law had called for uniforms, the men would not wear them, and perhaps this was a portent of the twentieth century, when promotion is out of uniform and into plainclothes (where the real money is). During its first six years of operation, according to Gerald Astor in his book *The New York Cops—An Informal History*, the new department made, in one year, 144,364 arrests, including 13,896 for assault and battery, 20,252 for disorderly conduct, 36,675 for intoxication, 29,190 for intoxication *and* disorderly conduct, 14,454 for picking pockets, 11,347 for vagrancy, 1,484 for insanity, 187 for bastardy, 171 for "constructive larceny," 138 for insulting females in the street, 68 for rape and 64 for murder. By the end of this period the force had grown to 1,000 men, and Astor, in his book, points out the conspicuous absence of any significant figure for arrests for crimes against property. What is also conspicuous is the concentration of police activity in the areas of behavior that constitute social nuisance—vagrancy, drunkenness, disorderly conduct; and even the assault cases (remember that at this time New York had a population of about 400,000, largely concentrated in lower Manhattan, and largely immigrants of all conceivable national origins and languages) had to be mostly those which today would be forgotten after the saloon closed, or else settled in civil court. The police force simply had taken over the function of the old night watch, which was supposed to keep some sort of peace, and the enforcement and regulation of licenses, which of course is a natural breeding ground for corruption.

After the Civil War, during which time the police department grew in domain (the boroughs had been added to police jurisdiction) and authority (they were now inspecting boilers as well as grog shops), the Tweed ring came and went, and the Reverend Charles Parkhurst, head of the Society for the Prevention of Crime, decided to try to clean up the vice traps *and* the police, of course not realizing the cause-and-effect nature of these two entities.

Dr. Parkhurst's investigations led to the first major investigation of New York's Finest in the mid-1890s. A grand jury, sitting as a result of Parkhurst's personal findings, found enough on its own to overthrow the superintendent of police, William Murray, who was succeeded by Inspector Thomas Byrnes, who had been named to head the department's new detective squad in 1882. It was Byrnes who was to represent the department in the 1894 Lexow Committee hearings, which, tiredly, had the same sort of political overtones as the Knapp Commission's 1971 hearings were to have, except that the 1894 investigation came out of Albany, where the Republicans were trying (as they have been generally trying over the years) to wrest control of New York City from the Democrats.

The committee began with a study of election irregularities, since at the time another of the police functions was to oversee and regulate elections(!), but eventually got into the matter of ordinary corruption on the street level. One brothelkeeper testified about the collection method: Two wardmen, both in plainclothes (the department had given up and gone into uniform long before this), served as bagmen for the captains, and would collect $25 a month from every operator in the precinct. As a captain was transferred, the new captain would make an initial raid, to shake up the game a little, and then collect a small "initiation" fee of

$500 to get the charges dropped so that the payoff system could continue as it had in the past—usually with the monthly ante raised. (This basic format remains essentially unchanged to this day.)

The kinds of rackets policemen engaged in were almost wholly concerned with the vices and licensing regulations during this period, according to Astor.

As a result of the Lexow hearings, there was the same sort of pitiful reform you will be seeing as a result of the Knapp Commission investigations—the more obvious crooks left the department, or were transferred to "less sensitive" assignments, and, because of the generational nature of police corruption, many cops retired, some resigned and some shaped up under the new police commissioner, none other than Theodore Roosevelt.

Roosevelt tried reform. He walked the streets at night with trusted police officers, seeking—and finding—evidence of daily police corruption, and he came to grips with the liquor laws, including the Sunday closing laws, which nobody in town wanted enforced except for a handful of the godly, and he insisted that, because it was the law, it would be enforced, and that is all right, except that a reformer can't be everyplace at once, and this sort of an enforcement decree against victimless crimes generally just tends to run the cost of protection higher.

It was probably with a sense of relief when, in 1897, with the Spanish-American War about to provide another sort of excitement, the old elephant hunter quit to become Assistant Secretary of the Navy. His reform, then, came to an end—he had tried to enforce the laws, without looking at the laws themselves; and when he left office the discretionary enforcement prerogatives fell back over the department like a veil.

Back into office came William S. Devery, a Tammany cop, who had been either abroad or ill during the Lexow hearings, and who, after Brooklyn became part of the city through the new charter of 1897, assigned an inspector there to teach the Brooklyn cops the fine art of grafting; and The New York Times, in an exposé, reported that gambling-house operators paid more than $3 million a year to cops; and it wasn't long before one of those inevitable New York State legislative committees got up a hearing before what was called the Mazet Committee to investigate the city's operations in 1899–1900. Testimony showed that Devery was running such a wide-open city (at one point, during a departmental trial, one of the phony ones like the one where they got Waverly Logan in 1971, an officer was charged with firing his pistol recklessly in the street, and Devery fined him thirty days' pay for not hitting anybody) that in 1904 the politicians dumped him.

After Devery, one halfhearted police scandal after another broke, one committee or another was assigned to look into it, one commissioner after another bit the dust during the first two decades of this century. Shortly after the telephone was brought into general use a woman named Mrs. Goode invented the call girl in New York, and by 1913 the police force had grown to 11,000. When the Eighteenth Amendment was ratified on January 16, 1919, the stage was set for a pattern of intricate corruption that continues, with embellishments, today. Before that date, there were 15,000 places to walk in and buy a drink or a bottle; the number grew to 32,000 during Prohibition.

In his book, Gerald Astor remarks, "The cops who worked during ... Prohibition policed New York City into the 1950s and trained the men who now command the department. And on the other side of the street, organized crime secured a large enough bankroll through Prohibition to give it permanent financial power and a working political structure."

The department continued to refine its collection techniques, and to delineate the duties of the vice cops—the plainclothesmen attached to the precincts and divisions to do nothing but investigate, regulate and make arrests in the areas of prostitution, gambling, liquor and narcotics (although today much of the liquor-law enforcement is handled by the State Liquor Authority, and the story of corruption in that little agency is still to be discovered), so that by the time World War II was ready to descend upon us (the war tabled much pending business in many areas, including a reassessment of police departments) the city was ready to look again at its Finest, this time under Governor Franklin D. Roosevelt, a Democrat who was forced to investigate the conditions at Tammany Hall, partly because Fiorello H. LaGuardia, in his losing election campaign against incumbent Jimmy Walker in 1929, had shown just how rotten things were.

Roosevelt appointed Samuel Seabury, a Democratic judge whose honesty was above reproach, to head a commission to look into the dealings of Magistrate Albert Vitale, who, among other things, had been known to borrow $19,600 from gambler Arnold Rothstein, and it was during the Seabury investigations that the first breath of scandal began about the "going price" of a judgeship in New York City (the most recent was in 1971, and watch for more of it), and in the middle of it Judge Joseph F. Crater pulled his famous vanishing act. From judgeships the investigation spread out to include lawyers, bail bondsmen, the courts, the mob and, of course, the cops. The interlocking of all these elements ultimately became so obvious that Mayor Walker was forced by his own machine to resign, clearing the way for LaGuardia's election and subsequent efforts, destined to be unsuccessful, at reform.

After considerable testimony, during much of which women were excluded from the hearing room on Seabury's orders, the commissioner suspended twenty-eight vice cops and set up those famous departmental trials, and then Seabury went on to other matters, including Polly Adler. It is reported that on the day she got her subpoena, a vice cop was in her apartment, and she stalled the process server long enough for the cop to get out the window and down ten floors on the fire escape. Polly didn't talk then, but later wrote, "The police [after the hearings, where she had remained clamlike] were no longer a headache. There was no more kow-towing to double-crossing Vice Squad men, no more hundred-dollar handshakes, no more phoney raids to up the month's quota." For the next three years, she said, she never had to break a lease.

Out of all this investigation and testimony came virtually nothing. Seven vice squad policemen were demoted. Two detectives who attempted to rape a shakedown victim were sent to Sing Sing (and people aren't sent to Sing Sing to do long sentences), and gambling cor-ruption continued unabated.

A 1940 grand jury in Brooklyn got fairly close to the refined nature of the corrupt system in that borough, noting that they had uncovered the sophisticated methods used by detectives to produce *almost* a case when it came time to come to court. That's the way they do it today in the Big Apple.

The men in blue still faced two major scandals: one in the early 1950s (just a generation after the one in the early 1930s), and one in the early 1970s (just a generation after the one in the early 1950s).

The first one involved a man named Harry Gross, and it started, the way so many do, with a newspaper exposé. (Newspaper reporters always know pretty much the extent of police corruption in a city, but they are seldom given the time, money and staff assistance necessary to prove it, and when they are it generally is when the money is virtually falling out of the pockets of the beat cop, his bosses already having amassed small fortunes over the years.) This time it was the old *Brooklyn Eagle*'s Ed Reid, who counted something like 4,000 bookies operating in New York, and found that in the first three quarters of 1949 not a single bookmaker had been sent to jail from Brooklyn—although one man had been arrested fifty times in twelve years.

After a series in the *Eagle* alleging that the cops were grafting to protect the bookies in Brooklyn, the Kings County (Brooklyn) district attorney, Miles McDonald, and an assistant, Julius Helfand, investigated, with the aid of a couple dozen recent graduates of the police academy—

men presumably so new on the force that they hadn't had time to get in on the action. McDonald found evidence that the bookies were indeed paying off the cops, and that all of gambling in Brooklyn was being run by Harry Gross, who reportedly was passing out something like $1 million a year to buy protection for his operations, said to be doing $26 million a year in business. McDonald knocked over the Gross operation, and many indictments and trials ensued—more than a hundred cops were hauled into court, and several committed suicide (one, a detective, jumped out of a window at the courthouse). Others filed for retirement, while an additional 18 were to be brought to trial in September, 1951, with Harry Gross himself scheduled to testify against them. He didn't, partly because his family had been threatened with death if he did, and partly because the cops had gotten together a $75,000 fund to be turned over to Gross in the event he failed to testify. This ploy was successful, and Gross drew 1,800 days and a $15,000 fine for contempt of court for his failure to testify. He later appeared at the departmental trials, which got rid of 74 more cops (bringing the total Gross-related departures to 110, counting those who quit or retired before testifying before the grand jury), including a chief inspector, an assistant chief inspector, three deputy inspectors, four inspectors and three captains.

Gross got twelve years for his bookmaking activities, pulled seven of them and then wound up doing five years to life for manslaughter after a fight with his father-in-law in California, which resulted in the old man's death.

The Gross scandals rocked the department, but nothing really changed inside the big gray building, except that the cops got colder and more distrustful of the public, even more inbred and tightly knit, and today it is almost as easy to get out of the Tombs as it is to get into police headquarters, although part of the sign-in-and-sign-out, visitors'-pass and intrabuilding-escort-service procedures can be attributed to a bomb that went off there a couple of years ago. The men who had trained under the old captains were now taking over the department, under the natural system of promotion from within the ranks, and corruption continued.

Isolated cases plagued the department from the last days of Harry Gross until 1970 and 1971, but they *were* isolated, if for no other reason than that they were not vigorously pursued by the city administration or the police department, and considered as no more than a nagging backache by a population beset by civil disorders, school closings and openings and more closings, subway strikes, overcrowding and muggers in Central Park.

The guy who blew the whistle on police corruption in New York was a plainclothesman named Frank Serpico, who refused to be dishonest. They are making a movie about this thirty-five-year-old misfit, supposedly to star Paul Newman, and it will probably be exciting and dramatic, the way Serpico's eleven years on the police force were until the night of February 3, 1971, when a narcotics dealer shot him in the face and—he still has bullet fragments in his brain—ended his career on the rooftops. Serpico by ancestry should have been a garbage man: Irishmen become cops, Italians join the department of sanitation; but he had always wanted to be a policeman, probably for all the wrong reasons, and so he did, walking a beat in uniform for six years before being sent to plainclothes school, and then taking on all the unpleasant tasks that job offered. He seemed to relish the "pussy posse," and would pose as a foreign businessman (he speaks five languages), going so far as to sew foreign labels in his clothing, spending most of an evening just to nail a single prostitute. The quota then, before the crackdown, was one per night.

Ordinarily affecting long hair, a full beard and an army field jacket and an earring in one ear, Serpico carried a field pack and no fewer than two guns, generally three, sometimes more. His reputation is that he walked the beat those years only hearing rumors of the kind of money the plainclothesmen were making, and that when he became one of them and was handed an envelope containing $300 he just couldn't bear the thought, and tried, without success, to tell about that to his boss and other superiors. Serpico finally went to Bronx District Attorney Burton Roberts and testified before a grand jury against eight fellow officers, all of whom were indicted. At the same time, Serpico's brother, who owned a small grocery store in Brooklyn, was being shaken down by a couple of cops for $2 a week because he remained open on Sunday (another case of offering cops a myriad of regulations to enforce—it is not illegal to be open on Sundays to sell bread and milk, but you cannot sell canned goods or other nonperishables, and if a cop is likely to testify in court that he indeed bought a can of peas in your store on Sunday, you are likely to pay him the two bucks a week to keep him from doing it), and Serpico turned in the two cops, who reportedly told him, "I don't care who you are, your brother will pay just like everybody else, or he'll get a summons every Sunday." They were fired from the force, and that tore it as far as the rest of the department was concerned—they had a ratfink bastard in their midst.

It was Serpico who first took his stories of widespread corruption to *The New York Times*, resulting in the series of articles beginning April

25, 1970, that made John Lindsay set up the Knapp Commission, named for the Wall Street lawyer, Whitman Knapp, who was to head it, before the upstate people could get their hands on the situation—it was only a year later, you'll recall, that he was to become a Democrat, and Governor Nelson Rockefeller remained a staunch Republican—and before the federal strike force could move in and take embarrassing action. (Ultimately in August, 1972, the Knapp Commission asked Rockefeller to appoint a special prosecutor to investigate the city's criminal justice system. Rocky was happy to oblige them.) And it was Serpico who laid out much of the story for guiding Knapp investigators in the search for evidence.

The stakeout where Serpico was shot was made deep in Brooklyn, probably on an informer's tip, and Serpico was accompanied by two other plainclothesmen, who voted that he, Serpico, should be the one to shove his way into the apartment where suspected drug selling was taking place. Serpico got only his hand, holding one of his guns, and his head into the door before he was shot, at the same time plugging the man who shot him (the man, called Mambo, was later shot again, in the belly, by other narcotics men, after leaving a trail of blood through his own apartment and out a rear window as Serpico's partners stood looking dumbly down at his prostrate form).

Well, Frank Serpico recovered partly, although he has said he is resigning from the force, probably taking a disability pension. While he was in the hospital he received a lot of hate mail, probably from cops, because the letters called him such things as "scumbag," a cop's word generally not used outside the department; and shortly after he got out, after eleven years on the force, the new commissioner, Patrick V. Murphy, promoted him to sergeant, a deed former Commissioner Howard Leary had sworn would never come to pass. Serpico was even visited in the hospital by Hizzoner.

A lot of people are still wondering what they promised Mambo for the job, and whether he knew he might get a bullet in the belly.

During 1970 and 1971 the New York cops were under almost continuous pressure from the *Times, New York* magazine and the national news magazines, which did everything but put reporters with push-button counters out to keep track of every whore, bookie and narcotics pusher in the city. The *Times* seemed particularly annoyed by the ladies of the evening, especially those brazen enough to accost men in the streets in the midtown area, where merchants were complaining that honest shoppers were being driven away.

Between the pressures generated by the media and the Knapp Commission, which by now was calling all sorts of embarrassing witnesses, Commissioner Murphy on July 1, 1971, initiated a "crackdown," one of those periodic attempts to satisfy the part of the community outraged by immorality.

There are about 4,000 prostitutes believed to be working in New York City full time, although this estimate could easily triple when you count in the girls who turn an occasional trick to help get up the rent, and most of them are streetwalkers—many in the midtown area, far more on the far West Side, and fewer in the one-and two-bedroom apartments that have become minibrothels without the opulence associated with the bordellos of old.

During the 1971 crackdown, the vice cops were given a quota of two arrests a night instead of one, and since the new emphasis was on "quality" arrests, there were a lot of suspicions of perjury on the part of cops when the cases were called; and at least one case of false arrest of a woman who was not a prostitute was reported to have been made by the pussy posse.

Surprisingly, the number of arrests was down from preceding months for two reasons: The prostitutes began avoiding the high-arrest areas, such as midtown, and the cops actually did seem to aim for "quality" arrests. Before the crackdown only 15 percent of the whores arrested went to jail, but during the first three months of the antivice drive this rate soared to 40 percent. The conviction–jail sentence ratio might be viewed with a degree of skepticism on two counts. In the first place, the Knapp Commission was hard at work out there showing how many cops were on the take, and the prospect of a prostitute or her pimp buying off an arresting officer was dim while that heat was on. In the second place, with the demand for "quality" arrests on the blotter, it meant that the revolving door of the courthouse was temporarily blocked, and that a cop would have to get the conviction even if it meant telling all sorts of lies in court, not a new set of conditions for New York's Finest. Martin Garbus, a New York trial lawyer, in an article for *New York* magazine on December 6, 1971, tackled the problem of police perjury, charging that the district attorney's office is fully aware of the situation and even encourages it in vice cases.

> I stress the behavior of police witnesses on the stand for several reasons [Garbus wrote]. First, because the amount of police perjury that goes on is truly scandalous. Second, it goes on in the presence of the D.A.'s men and is rarely—I mean *rarely*—a matter of primary concern to them. Third, as a consequence of the first two,

police perjury under the very eyes of the D.A.'s office brings the law itself into disrepute. The law becomes, in the eyes of the cops, not something one is sworn to serve, but a plaything, something to be manipulated.

A third possible reason for the rise in jail sentences for prostitutes, one that has little to do with cops per se, is the pressure that was generated on judges during 1971, after public allegations of the "price" of one judge or another by street figures who claimed to have arranged through their lawyers to buy off certain judges. In July, 1971, just after the vice crackdown began, two accused prostitutes were even held without bail, almost unheard of in the field of vice.

The *Times* also had its sensibilities offended by the dirty-book people. As a result, Mayor Lindsay ordered a crackdown on that business on July 7, 1971, and in August, in a well-timed series of raids, Captain Daniel McGowan, of what the police department calls the public morals administrative division, led two sergeants and ten patrolmen to half a dozen storefront porno shops where coin-operated peepshows, giving two minutes of a dirty flick for a quarter, had been doing business. The raids were coordinated with the office of Manhattan D.A. Frank Hogan.

There are 31,000 police officers in the city of New York, and that is about the size of two army divisions. This figures out to about one cop for every 230 citizens, although only about 10 percent of that force is on the street at any given moment because of shift work, paper work and the tiered system of management, which Commissioner Murphy is setting about to change a bit.

These 31,000 cops, operating on foot and in a fleet of 1,800 city-owned marked and unmarked automobiles (and in their own private cars, nonreimbursed), in a typical *week* face 3,000 petit larcenies, 3,500 burglaries, 400 assaults, 300 cases involving dangerous drugs, 1,500 cases of what the New York Penal Code calls "criminal mischief," 1,500 auto thefts and 50 to 60 cases of arson, not to mention the 100 to 150 prostitutes hauled in on poor, tired, aching feet.

While statistics might be staggering, what is more incredible is that any of these cases get solved at all, when one takes into account (a) the time and energy spent by police officers at all levels in plotting, engineering, collecting and distributing payoffs; and (b) the quite natural relationship between those arrested for immorality—whores, pushers, saloonkeepers and gamblers—and those arrested for other, more serious crimes: assault, arson, robbery. In what the police department would like you to believe was a significant study, the department said in October,

1971, that they had been checking into the backgrounds of the 1,302 prostitutes arrested since July 1 and found that about 40 percent of them had been arrested previously for other crimes, including use and/or possession of drugs, burglary, robbery and larceny, and that half of those had a history of violent crime, including homicide.

The report was released by Captain Dan McGowan, the department's "prostitution control director," and between him and *The New York Times* a case was made directly that the "victimless" crime of prostitution is not victimless at all. The *Times's* story on the statistics of October 9, 1971, said, in part:

> This [the report] has led the police to conclude, inferentially at least, that there is a direct connection between the easy atmosphere created by widespread prostitution and the commission of many other crimes. Some of these are committed by prostitutes and pimps and others by persons posing as prostitutes and pimps to lure intended victims. "We can't put them all into the victimless crime category," said . . . McGowan. . . . "What we have to do now is go back over the old homicide cases and find out how many involved prostitution or pretended prostitution."

This report presents an argument against the legalization of *anything*, but its true inferences are far more dramatic than those presented by the police department. For instance, the report refers to the numbers of previous *arrests* on charges of more serious crimes. It would be interesting to see a similar report on the number of *convictions* stemming from those arrests, and, further, an analysis of why there was no conviction in cases where there was none. Why, we might ask the police department, since they are answering questions, does a woman or a man arrested on prostitution charges have an arrest record that includes homicide? Or assault? Or attempted murder? Why are these people walking the streets at all, in any capacity, streetwalker or clerk, if they are guilty of more serious crimes? (In passing, it should be noted that a large part of the American Civil Liberties Union's time and money in 1971 was spent trying to expunge arrest records in cases not leading to conviction, and in fact the ACLU has been more than successful in keeping previous arrests from becoming a part of the record during criminal trials. The subject has gotten so touchy that police departments throughout the nation, including the Federal Bureau of Investigation and the Internal Revenue Service, will not release "rap sheets" to anyone but other police officers, unless, of course, it suits their purposes—the FBI and IRS are particularly good at this—to "leak" an arrest record to enhance the possibility of conviction of someone the arresting agency particularly wants sent away. It is not so odd, considering this, to see the New York City Police Department using the same sort of records to "prove" one thing or another.) It might also be inferred that these people had been paying off the cops to ignore their sexual activities and that the protection money bought them a little extra consideration when it came time to face a judge for busting the head of a john, and that when the bag snapped shut with the advent of the Knapp Commission hearings, the extra protection went out the window with the prime protection—and landed the hooker in jail after all, where she could become a moral statistic.

But to make such an inference depends upon the assumption that things along Broadway are a lot more corrupt than any of us have dared to believe. Just how bad are things in Little Old New York?

We get an inkling from the Knapp Commission, and from the New York State Commission of Investigations, whose hearings preceded the Knapp efforts.

By the most conservative estimate, it has been reported, New York City has 100,000 narcotics addicts, a third of them of school age. In his *New York Times* series, David Burnham reported that bookmakers in 1970 were paying off at rates ranging from $1,200 to $2,400 a month each; numbers operators were paying a total of $7 million to $15 million a year; about 10,000 neighborhood grocery stores were being shaken down (mostly to allow them to stay open on Sundays, not illegal) for more than $6 million a year; building contractors were paying off from $40 to $400 a month for each construction site, and one contractor, who was building a new police department precinct house, was hit for $40 a week from the cops whose building he was putting up. Burnham did a good job in the routine shakedowns, although the precinct house construction job is not so routine and added a bizarre twist, but it is likely that he fell for the oldest bit of nonsense in police department legend: that narcotics graft is dirty graft and therefore untouchable.

As a matter of fact, the extent of police corruption stemming from narcotics soars wildly beyond that of gambling, prostitution and liquor, as discerned by both the state investigating commission and the Knapp people. (More fun is to come, if you take the word of Harold Foner, the Brooklyn lawyer who defends cops in departmental and criminal trials, who says that what the New York police are taking out of the multibil-lion-dollar narcotics traffic "is peanuts compared with what the federal narcotics guys are taking." You hesitate to listen to him say that because dreams of Eliot Ness die hard, but he knows more about dirty cops than any other individual in the city, and you can't discount that.)

The Knapp people, led by chief counsel Michael Armstrong, took testimony and fielded a team of thirty lawyers and investigators for eleven months, stopping work late in 1971.

The key witness at a two-week session of public hearings which began on October 18, 1971, in the auditorium of the Bar Association of New York City on West Forty-fourth Street, was a cop named William R. Phillips, a forty-year-old, fourteen-year veteran of the police department. Phillips was the highlight of the hearings, which Counsel Armstrong said were based on evidence from 271 sworn statements from witnesses and 620 subpoenas. As Phillips, a married man without children, spoke, several police officers, not in uniform, sat in the audience of about 200—otherwise composed essentially of news media representatives and lawyers—scribbling notes in their memo books, having been assigned to "cover" the hearings for their supervisors in one precinct, division or another, and at one point the room was cleared by police because of a telephone call saying that a bomb had been planted in the room.

This was the second day, Tuesday, of the two-week sessions. The first day had been taken up largely with tape recordings gathered by Phillips, who, on Monday, had remained unidentified as one of the voices on the tapes. He was being guarded—and had been for months—by members of the department's anticorruption unit and by United States marshals, because he was naming names. Phillips had not been a voluntary witness to begin with—he had been caught with his hand out and had been forced to work undercover for the Knapp Commission—and he was not granted immunity from prosecution resulting from his testimony. But talk he did.

A handsome white man, the way country singers are handsome, well dressed from his soft orange shirt and gray, pin-striped suit down to his patent-leather loafers, Phillips displayed traces of wry humor as he told his audience that in his fourteen years on the force he had never known a cop assigned to a gambling-enforcement unit for more than two months who did not accept graft, and when he was asked what percentage of the plainclothesmen assigned to enforce gambling laws were "on the pad" he said, "Everyone, to my knowledge." He told of being assigned to the East Sixty-seventh Street station in the 19th Precinct shortly after joining the force on June 24, 1957, and that, despite the fact that it was a "slow" precinct with few chances of making extra money, he was taught almost immediately where to get his meals free, and that he could expect, as a patrolman walking a beat, to get $5 or $10 from every bar on his beat on weekend nights. During the time he was in the 19th, until 1961, the average foot patrolman made around $50 a month and the average policeman in a radio car took in up to $100 a month, he said, adding that there was always the opportunity for a one-time "score," such as the night he arrested a drunk who attacked him and in return was charged with felonious assault. A friend of the drunk later came around and offered Phillips $300 if Phillips would fix it so the man could plead guilty to a lesser charge. The price was right, Phillips said, so he made the deal.

But it wasn't until Phillips was made a detective in 1961 and assigned to an antigambling unit in Harlem that the big money started falling in. During the six months he was there he took about $6,000 from gamblers for protection. He said that in one of his unit's precincts about twenty major gambling spots existed, each of which paid a total of about $3,500 a month to the police.

Most of that day was taken up with identifying Phillips and hearing him tell how he was initiated into the world of the crooked cop. The next day, Michael Armstrong got to the heart of the matter in questioning Phillips. Excerpts from that session (as printed in *The New York Times*), are quite interesting:

"Now," Armstrong asked, "can you explain what a share is at the division level in plainclothes?"

A. Well, the individual who is designated to be the bagman—or the individuals—will pick up all the money at a specific time of the month, and it will be distributed to each member of the plainclothes unit [vice cops] equally. The way it's set up, the boss will get an additional half a share. So, in other words, if the pad will be a thousand per month, the boss would wind up with fifteen hundred dollars.

Q. What was the share at that time up in the Sixth Division?

A. Six to nine hundred and a thousand dollars a month.

Q. Is this, to your knowledge, the way it works throughout the city: a normal plainclothesman gets a share and the bosses above him get a share and a half or more?

Phillips replied that that's the way it had been and still was, to his knowledge. Under further questioning, the officer detailed the size of the "nut" in each of the various divisions throughout the city, including the Third Division, which includes midtown Manhattan, where the average illegal income for each plainclothesman amounted to around $500 a month. The nut rose to about $1,500 per month per man in the Sixth Division, which includes Harlem, according to Phillips' testimony. He also described how a cop gets "on the pad":

Q. When you come into—when an officer comes into a plainclothes division unit, is he put on the pad immediately?

A. No, no one is on the pad immediately.

Q. Would you explain how that works?

A. When you're assigned to a plainclothes division, first of all, as I stated yesterday, you have to be checked out. Someone has got to verify you. You just can't walk into a division and go right on the pad. The person who verifies you is responsible for you. Ordinarily, after you have been verified and checked out, it takes approximately two months before you are put on the pad. After you are transferred out, your termination in plainclothes is ended, you receive two months' additional pad after you're back into a new command.

Q. After you have left the division you are entitled to two months' severance pay, you continue to get your pad for . . .

A. Yes, that's right, for two months.

Q. I'm sorry, go ahead.

A. You have two months' coming when you leave.

At this point Commissioner Joseph Montserrat asked a question of his own: "Is that to tide you over before you get onto the next one?"

A. It gets you back on your feet, yes sir.

Armstrong resumed questioning: "If a gambling case arrives at court, is it too late to do business?"

A. No. It's never too late to do business.

Q. With respect to your specific experience in recent months, you said that you were transferred to First Division plainclothes on August 24.

A. Yes. The police department came up with a pilot program . . .

Q. Pilot program?

A. Yes. It was the first time it was ever done. To transfer men into plainclothes who had between ten and fifteen years of service in the Police Department. [During the summer, Commissioner Murphy had been trying every conceivable sort of reorganizational device, trying to fix his force before the Knapp Commission could destroy it. The plan Phillips is describing here is one of those devices.] The idea being that if these men had this much time on the job, they would be a little more responsible and less likely to get involved in the pad and gambling practices or corrupt measures than they were used to before. I was assigned to the Police Academy with thirty-four other police officers. . . . We arrived at the Police Academy for a one-week indoctrination into gambling, A.B.C. [Alcoholic Beverage Control] violations and the new laws involving prostitution. Some of the police officers involved were drafted into this particular operation, and out of the thirty-four men, there were five or six who wanted no part of plainclothes at all. They wanted to be out.

Q. Why didn't they want any part of plainclothes?

A. Well, they figured they had a large investment in the job, between ten and fifteen years, they know what goes on in plainclothes, and they just wanted out. They wanted no part of it at all.

Q. How would it threaten them to be in plainclothes?

A. Well, they figured that they could be engulfed in the situation or in the system, and if division broke, or something like that, they would wind up in serious trouble, and their lives would be jeopardized, and their pensions would be jeopardized also.

Knapp then asked, "What do you mean, the division broke?"

A. [If] there would be a large scandal somewhere, there's a possibility of them being arrested or indicted or something along that line. There were four or five other individuals who were not completely happy with their transfer, but after a few days, they figure, "Why, I'm here, I'll do the best I can and go along with the system." The rest of the class was absolutely elated about being transferred to plainclothes because of the money involved.

Q. In this class of plainclothesmen, was there anyone there who actively stated he would not take money?

A. To the individuals that I talked to, no.

The questioners were also interested in the "code of ethics" among grafting cops.

Q. In all of this, with respect to the money that is taken, do you personally yourself have any lines that you draw specifically, and if so, why, and that you drew when you were on the job?

A. Well, in the area where money is involved, it's like the indoctrination period in the police department, where you have another officer usually older than you who will give you guidelines to go by to keep yourself from getting into trouble. And the guidelines that were laid down for me when I first came on the job were never to take money in narcotics, prostitution, or involving weapons.

Q. Why not in narcotics?

A. It's the unwritten rule that you don't fool around with anything to do with narcotics.

Q. Is that unwritten rule still adhered to, do you feel, in the department?

A. To my knowledge, it's not adhered to right now.

Q. In other words, it's breaking down?

A. Yes, it's broken down to a large extent.

Q. What is the reason for not taking money in connection with guns, loaded weapons?

A. Well, the unwritten rule there is that a man with a gun is a potential killer, and if you end up dealing with him he could be a potential cop killer besides.

Phillips said you didn't deal with prostitutes because they were unreliable and you couldn't trust them.

On this day of Phillips' testimony, the police department chose to announce that 113 plainclothesmen, about 25 percent of all those on the force, were being transferred back to uniformed duty, and that 154 new plainclothesmen had just finished a five-week course at the police academy and were in the process of being sent out to the divisions. The department said the announcement of the move was "routine," and that the decision for the massive shifts in vice-cop personnel had nothing to do with the Knapp Commission hearings.

Even on October 21, the fourth day after the two-week Knapp hearings began, Murphy, acting the part of the loyal commander, got on the police radio system and, in reference to Phillips' testimony, told his closed-circuit audience:

For the last several days the honor of all of us has been under attack. I want to assure you today that I believe in you, that I have confidence in your basic integrity, and that my pride in your courage is without limit. Only last night two of you again displayed that courage which is so routine to members of the New York City police department in a shootout on Madison Avenue. To me, incidents such as this again prove how much the average police officer wants to do a 100 percent job. There is no reason to be ashamed because one or another traitor to the uniform that you wear so proudly seeks to justify his own dishonesty by pretending that none of you is honest. That is not true. There are bad policemen. I ask you to help me rid this department of them. The dishonest cop is not our brother. Don't be discouraged—24,000 times a day the people of New York City call 911 and demand your help, and they get it. A thousand times each hour you justify their faith in you, and mine.

It is revealing that Murphy referred to how much the "average" cop wants to do his job honestly and fairly. It was Deputy Inspector Hugo J. Masini, aide to First Deputy Commissioner William H. T. Smith, number-two man in the department and an old sidekick of Murphy's from their days in Syracuse, who drew for me a simple, normal, classic bell-shaped curve, which he and other experts considered the optimum obtainable in police honesty—the large swell in the middle takes in all the cops who may or may not know about crooked cops, but who nevertheless ignore them and go about their business; the rapidly diminishing arc on the left takes in the small percentage who are not only untouchable but who will turn in a crooked cop; and the equally rapidly diminishing arc on the right includes the rotten apples. "On this kind of a curve, it takes minimum effort by your IAD to root out corrupt practices," Masini said. But then he drew another curve, this one with the bulge moved far to the right, with a correspondingly marked increase in the "rotten apple" segment of the arc. He pushed his pencil point around in the new, enlarged area. "When it gets to be like this," he said, "the main object becomes to shove it back into the classic bell—but it becomes increasingly difficult, because the internal affairs people have a lot more territory to cover." With the new curve, the "average" line—the one that bisects the bell curve exactly in the middle—moves far to the right, and this is the "average" cop Murphy was addressing that day. It is quite possible that he is right, too, and that these men are waiting for somebody to tell them that it is all right to stop being one of the boys who gets an envelope every month.

Phillips became a Knapp Commission witness the hard way: Early in 1970 he was caught—big. A Knapp investigator, a private eye named Teddy Ratnoff, posed as an agent of Xaviera Hollander, the madam of an opulent, successful, three-bedroom whorehouse on East Fifty-fifth Street, in the fourth division. Ratnoff, for the sake of the investigation, was supposed to be trying to set up a package deal for police protection. He was steered to Phillips, and the two men had several meetings, mostly in P. J. Clarke's, a fashionable East Side noontime watering hole for Beautiful People and politicians, and a final meeting in the offices of a lawyer, Irwin Germaise. During all of the meetings Ratnoff was wired for sound, and excerpts from several of the meetings went like this:

RATNOFF: What are we talking about in figures—approximately?

PHILLIPS: So, if she wants to give like two or three hundred for the division.

RATNOFF: Well, how's it work ... division, borough and precinct?

PHILLIPS: And precinct, yeah.

RATNOFF: Two hundred.

PHILLIPS: That's reasonable. .... Well, the precinct you can probably buy for two.

RATNOFF: Two hundred?

PHILLIPS: I think ... I think ... you could wrap the whole thing up for between eight hundred and a thousand.

RATNOFF: Yeah. Look, you gotta have a little for yourself. We appreciate that.

PHILLIPS: Well, listen, she said I got a hundred dollars a month for myself, right?

RATNOFF: Right.

PHILIPS: The only thing that would happen is the chief, something like that, the P.C.—I can't control that.

RATNOFF: The chief of what?

PHILLIPS: The chief inspector.

RATNOFF: Yeah.

PHILLIPS: And the Police Commissioner—I can't control them.

RATNOFF: Who is it—you mean downtown?

PHILLIPS: Yeah. That's the heavies, that's the heavy. A lot of time they get a communication down there and pass it from the chief inspector to the borough—beautiful. But if they come up themselves, then you're fucked. But you got like a 98 per cent guarantee, no matter how, 98.

RATNOFF: That's $1,100 a month?

PHILLIPS: Right.

In the matter of not being able to control the commissioner's office, Phillips assured Ratnoff that they would work up a code warning. "Like if somebody should call and say, 'This is Mr. White from Chicago'— boom, shut down. That's it." In the course of events, $1,000 of the first month's grease of $1,100 was paid in two $500 installments, and Phillips told Ratnoff why he was so anxious to see that Madam Hollander's operation protected was that if she were shut down "the golden goose is gone. You lose, I lose, we're all out of a lot of fucking business. I don't want to see her go; I hate to see her go." These tapes showed that the money paid did, indeed, start making its way up the line, and at least a part of it reached another plainclothesman assigned to the Fourth Division (Phillips was not then in that division, but had just set up the deal for the division).

There were two other negotiations between Phillips and Ratnoff. The first was an attempt to set it up so that a plainclothesman would change his testimony in a case against Madam Hollander.

The other deal involved a friend of the madam's named Larry, who was accused of having a fraudulent check in his pocket. During the negotiations over this one it was decided to hand over $10,000 to lawyer Germaise in return for a guarantee of Larry's acquittal, and this never got very far because immediately the inference was that the lawyer was going to lay at least part of the money on a judge, whose name was deleted from the Knapp Commission tapes, because, after all, the commission was only interested in *police* corruption.

In the final meeting between Ratnoff, the lawyer and Phillips, it is discovered that Ratnoff is wearing a microphone and transmitter, and he is grilled by the two of them but stalls long enough for other Knapp agents and a cop to enter the room, and the last part of that tape has the lawyer asking, "Who are you, sir?" and Ratnoff responding, "I'm with the Knapp Commission." From that moment on, Phillips was also with the Knapp Commission.

They wired Phillips for sound and sent him out to try to establish the "perfect" crap game, first informing Commissioner Murphy what they were up to. (When Phillips first started testifying later, however, Muphy's first reaction was to suspend him and draw up departmental papers. He later changed his mind and reinstated Phillips—for awhile, until Phillips was charged with the 1968 murder of a pimp and a prostitute. Phillips maintained that he was "framed" by police he'd ratted on, and in August, 1972, his murder trial ended in a hung jury. The prosecution said he would be retried, but such a new trial had not yet begun by mid-November.)

The crap game was to be in an apartment or office in midtown Manhattan, and Phillips set out to find the bagman in the Third and Fourth divisions, which cover that part of town. Phillips testified that it took only a few days before he was introduced to a plainclothesman from the Third Division, who, in a series of meetings in the Three Lions Pub in East Forty-first, asked for a total of $4,000 a month, $2,000 for each division. Before negotiations were complete, however, plainclothesmen from the divisions had jacked up the monthly total to $8,000 to split between the two divisions. Phillips, in one of the tapes from those sessions, expressed concern over the figure, but one of the plainclothesmen replied, "I wouldn't take less than four large. You got to be crazy to take less than that."

The mythical crap game was to be operated by a gambler known as Little Artie, a real figure who is a known gambler in police department files. Phillips said he made a down payment of $450 to the two officers, who by now were helping him in his search for the ideal location, the Knapp Commission didn't have the $8,000 for the first month's ice, and negotiations were finally broken off.

The extent of police graft came out a little more at this point. During one conversation played back to the Knapp listeners, one of the bagmen spoke of the commander of one division (whose name was deleted from the tapes because, unlike other instances, the commission did not have independent corroboration of his involvement) who was getting "an envelope."

"He was getting an envelope for like fifteen [$1,500] a month for the thing and God knows what else he had. . . . And he was there for years, he was entrenched in that fucking place and he'd go out and get sides of beef, get some cases of soda."

Earlier that week, before the commission, Phillips had described his entry into the world of the corrupt cop:

Q. In your class in the Academy how many or what per cent would you say of those men were dedicated and had no idea of becoming involved in any kind of corrupt activity?

A. At that time?

Q. Right.

A. Ninety per cent—85, 90 per cent.

Q. Aside from the officers who participated in the Christmas pad and took free meals, how many of the others, or how many offices accepted the kinds of monies that you've been talking about, from bars and construction, to your knowledge?

A. Everyone but one.

Q. How much money did you make when you were in the sector car?

A. Between seventy-five and a hundred dollars a month.

Q. Where did you make that money?

A. From most of the same places—dance halls, cabarets, and most of it was construction.

(It might be pointed out that the construction industry, that symbol of American progress, becomes a sort of a sixth vice when operating in a city of the size and complexity of New York. The working ground space available, for instance, to erect a thirty- or fifty-story office building is less in many instances than a contractor in a smaller city might have to build a simple row of townhouses. It is impossible, therefore, for a contractor to operate in midtown Manhattan without being in continuous violation of one or of more the city ordinances involving barricades, parking, heavy equipment clearance, protective scaffolding—literally hundreds of laws the adherence to which would mean that the building simply could not go up. Since the building *has* to go up, it means that the laws must be circumvented, and once again it puts the power of discretionary enforcement in the hands of a man—the cop on the beat—who is unqualified to exercise it.)

Q. While you were in the 19th Precinct, was money paid inside the precinct between police officers to get services done?

A. Yes, it was.

Q. Did you pay the clerical man?

A. Not in the 19th Precinct. There was—on these citations that I received [Phillips had been commended several times for outstanding police work], they have to be written up in a special form, and it was customary for the officer who was seeking departmental recognition to pay the clerical man who did the typing five dollars if he typed the thing up. The first one I was involved in, I was told that this is the right thing to do by an oldtimer in the precinct. He said, "Did you take care of the clerical man for the writeup for your recognition?" I said, "Gee, no I didn't." He said, "You should go down and do that."

. . . . .

Q. How much did you pick up around Christmas time?

A. The 19th, I guess about four hundred dollars, plus a lot of whiskey.

Q. And does your reputation follow you as you go through the department? Do you know who the people are who will take money and who won't take money?

A. In this particular department you can make a phone call and find out in five minutes who the individual is, what his hobbies are, what his habits are and whether or not he takes money.

Q. What happened with respect to the police officer who is straight?

A. Well, he's in his own little group. He's not accepted into the group of people who engage in this type of activity, because they

are afraid they can't trust him, to begin with, and they are not going
to tell him what they are doing on the street.

. . . . .

Q. In describing these operations, officer, in your estimation,
were the police officers who served with you in the 19th good police
officers?

A. They were the best cops I've ever seen since I've been on the
job.

Q. What do you mean by that?

A. Arrests, responding to assignments, a spirit of closeness
between one another.

. . . . .

Q. When you say "runners coming in and dropping off work,"
maybe you could explain a little bit what that means?

A. In one specific location that we were assigned to, as a matter
of fact, it was the first day that he had been assigned to the Sixth
Division, my partner and myself got in our private automobile and
we proceeded to a location on 120th Street and 8th Avenue. We
were to suppress a gambling operation there. The individual's name
was Eggy.

Q. Eggy?

A. Eggy. He was a colored man. We pulled our automobile up
at 120th Street and 8th Avenue. And this fellow who was a known
gambler was waiting for us to arrive. He knew that there would be
new men coming up in the area that day. It was on a Monday
morning. He walked over to the car and he says, "Are you the new
. . . men?" Never seen him before, never seen us. He says—we
said, "Yes, we are." He says, "You gets twenty a day. Is that all
right?" I looked at my partner, he looks at me, we don't know what
is going on. My experience with the policy was very limited. He
says, "Don't worry, everything is okay. Division is taking care of the
bureau, we take care of the men who were here before you, we take
care of you."

Q. And speaking not about your own group but about your
knowledge of the division plainclothesmen who have the primary
responsibility in the area, what percentage of the plainclothesmen
assigned to the division, to the Sixth Division at that time, do you
feel participated in the pad?

A. Everyone, to my knowledge.

Q. Everyone?

A. Everyone.

I first met Waverly Logan, formerly Badge Number 1931, and Horace Lord, Badge Number 4292, in a hearing room on the second floor of police headquarters, 240 Centre Street, shortly before ten o'clock in the morning of Thursday, February 18, 1971, as Deputy Commissioner Louis L. Stutman prepared to open a session of the departmental trial of former Patrolman Logan, who was charged with taking a bribe of $100 from a known Harlem narcotics dealer.

This was months before Logan was to appear before the Knapp Commission and tell what he said he knew about police corruption in the city of New York, and his trial evoked very little interest in the big city. A radio station microphone holder was there, but he really didn't know what was going on (and maybe nobody really did, or, for that matter, does yet). *The New York Times*'s Dave Burnham was there, the man who'd started the snowball back in 1970, but he wasn't very excited about this rather clear-cut case of the department cleansing itself of a bad apple, and as a matter of fact he was out of the room—gone to pick up a press release from the Knapp Commission, which was then just getting started—when Horace Lord took the stand in Logan's defense. From time to time a guy from the *Daily News* would drift in and out, and a *New York Post* type came and went.

The windows overlooking Centre Street were closed tightly, although the boilers seemed to be working overtime, because Commissioner Stutman likes his hearing room warm, and everybody was sweating beneath the gaze of the eyes of the photographs of all the former (and the present) police commissioners around the wall of the ancient room. Waverly Logan helped himself to a paper cup of water from the old-fashioned bottled-water cooler, which of course had no ice, waiting for his departmental trial.

The story of Waverly Logan is odd in that it ties up a number of fascinating elements concerning public corruption of the New York City Police Department and the internal corruption that has tended, over the years, to make it a tightly welded organization that tells its secrets to no one.

At the very heart of the Waverly Logan case is Harlem, that black hotbed of vice and crime, the latter almost invariably springing from the former and from the extreme poverty in which most of the citizens exist there. Gambling and the narcotics traffic are widespread, far more than prostitution (which seems to be mainly a pastime of white men), and generating more money (and therefore being more attractive to policemen) than either liquor or the fifth vice, pornography (which for some reason does not seem to be very big in ghetto areas, perhaps because of the obscene caricature of normalcy many blacks are forced to accept as a way of life through poverty, ignorance and oppression).

Estimates of the annual turnover in the numbers racket alone in Harlem range from a conservative $250 million to $1.5 billion, with the narcotics trade rivaling it in the race to produce illicit revenue. Both elements are directly tied to organized crime.

And both, oddly enough, contribute to what might be called the GHP—the Gross Harlem Product—that total of goods and services which, in the terms of Federal Reserve Board reporting, serves as an indicator of a community's or a nation's fiscal well-being. To my knowledge, no one has had the balls to do a study on the *positive* aspects of organized crime, but it seems like a safe bet (if betting were legal) that much of Harlem is supported not by welfare and jobs alone, but by the churning of money garnered illegally by thousands of numbers runners and pimps. It does, despite the rakeoff by organized crime, return to the community hundreds of thousands of dollars annually. Of the typical dollar bet on "policy"—that daily numbers drawing (sometimes drawn, sometimes based on the last three digits of the total daily "handle" at a local race track, depending on the house rules)—33 cents goes to the banker, who will arrange with God and the Mafia how it is to be split up; 25 cents goes to the runner, the man who takes bets from the citizens and delivers the winnings later; a nickel goes to the controller of the house; 34 cents goes for payoffs and expenses (only 5 to 10 percent of the total is returned to the bettors, not even in the same ballpark as parimutuel betting) and 3 cents goes to the cops. And even the cops return some of it to the Harlem economy through the purchase of goods and services.

Late in November, 1971, an eight-page bill was drawn up by a team of constitutional lawyers for the Harlem Council for Economic Development, which claims membership of more than 1,000 black and Puerto Rican businessmen, including an estimated 200 hundred numbers bankers, for presentation to the New York State legislature. Using the enabling legislation for the New York State Lottery and New York City's Off-Track Betting Corporation as precedent, the bill would legalize the numbers, and would require that 10 percent off the top be returned to the community as seed money for economic development programs. The proposed law was to be introduced in the next session of the legislature by Assemblyman George W. Miller, a New York Democrat, but was by no means supported only by businessmen. Legalization of numbers has been a policy plank (if you'll pardon the expression) for the Harlem chapter of the Congress of Racial Equality, which has charged that off-track betting was a graybelly scheme to milk even more dollars from the ghetto without returning anything; and by Howard (Howie the Horse) Samuels himself, the man who made his millions in the sandwich bag business and later became head of New York's OTB corporation. Samuels has estimated that it will take three years to legalize the numbers, although, knowing New York, there will be considerable pressure on the legislature from organized-crime lobbyists to continue the racket the way it is: tax-free and unregulated (except by the vice cops).

Money from the numbers goes to finance the importing and distribution of narcotics, of course, the two having come to be virtually inseparable. Any number of sociologists will attempt to tell you why minority-group members use drugs, but the fact remains that the incidence of drug addiction is much higher in ghetto areas—the dope is there. And police benefit from it.

Once upon a time, narcotics graft was thought to be "dirty," and it still is when you move into the suburbs and find outraged police officers reflecting the outrage of well-heeled, white, middle-class families when a swarthy pusher is discovered in their midst. Mike Hammer machine-gunned dabblers in smack with the same enthusiasm as when he was blowing holes in Communists, and in those early 1950s both classes of the enemy were seen strictly in terms of black and white.

But the pushers in Mickey Spillane's fantasies were those who spilled over into *his* city, and he seldom let his hero wander into Harlem, where dope had flourished for years, because, after all, *they are only niggers*. And this is precisely the same attitude that prevails in the plain-clothes units, black as well as white, throughout New York City. (Their attitudes are reinforced by the media, however, who consistently do not report crimes—even heinous crimes—involving victims and criminals from the black community.

New York City has for many years been divided into boroughs, divisions and precincts for the purpose of police protection, or regulation, as it turns out. Until recently each of the precincts had its own squads of plainclothes detectives, assigned to such squads as burglary, auto theft, homicide and vice. The morals squad reported directly to the chief inspector, and a separate narcotics squad functioned under the aegis of a joint federal-city program (and still does). The plainclothesmen have since been moved to the division level.

There never was a vice squad, per se, in New York City. The public morals division might be in a loose way described as one whose duties were to keep the public clean. The plainclothesmen had the handle on nearly every illegal activity that did not involve crimes against persons and/or property: dope, booze, gambling, liquor, pornography. Because of the "sensitive" nature of such investigations, the patrol division's men were seldom allowed to make arrests in cases involving vice without checking with the plainclothes detachment. This led to a centralization of control, with a minimal payoff—if the patrol units, the uniformed men, could not make arrests without permission, the bag got smaller, and less visible.

Enter the PEP squad and Waverly Logan.

The Preventive Enforcement Patrol Squad, as it is formally known, was formed in 1969 with the aim of cutting down street crime in Harlem. The idea was to use native ghetto kids, those who knew the ins and outs of the streets and the street people, so that they would bring neither a naive, Queens-cop approach nor the hardened attitudes of the force that had already been stationed in Harlem—since 1844. And it was to be a more effective force in that part of Manhattan North (which is what the cops call the division that oversees Harlem) than any that had existed previously.

Effective, it was. Soon the guys in the PEP squad, as they had begun to call themselves, were making "quality" arrests. "What they were doing, though," said lawyer Harold Foner, looking out through those dark glasses he affects, "was cutting into the regular bag, don't you see that, don't you?" He seemed to be irritable, because at this time, early in 1971, the Knapp Commission had not yet found out what was going on in Harlem, and had not told *The New York Times* or its readers; but Foner knew, and he was trying to get it across. Later, in my interview with Hugo Masini, assistant to First Deputy Commissioner Smith, Masini was to say that they had had some trouble with the PEP squad making "scores" of its own, and that PEP wasn't nearly as clean as its admirers would have it, but it is probable that Foner had put his finger on one of the troubles—the Harlem gambling and narcotics figures already had a well-established system of paying off cops, and the arrival of the PEP squad simply meant that many more mouths to feed, like an extra half-dozen relatives showing up unannounced for Sunday dinner. The other big trouble, of course, was race—the PEP squad was all black, and that led to part of Waverly Logan's problems.

At any rate, Waverly Logan was up on departmental charges. He is a tall, skinny black man, or, rather, chocolate brown, a man who, except for his height, might pass unnoticed in a crowd in, say, Albee Square in Brooklyn. He dresses well, and at the time I met him he was driving a taxicab for a living, because he was still in that special hell reserved for

New York City civil servants who have not yet been fired but who have been suspended pending a hearing.

Logan's story begins on April 22, 1970, not a full year after he had joined the PEP squad, when he busted a known narcotics and gambling figure named Joseph Spooner outside the Golden Glass Bar and Grill in Harlem. Logan and another officer were in plainclothes, and another half-dozen uniformed men were on hand to help make the collar. Spooner had a load of drugs on him, and said a few words to Logan about $600 being in it if he got off, but it was no go. Spooner's case was put through the tedious processes of the New York City Supreme Court, and came up for trial on September 3, 1970, five months later, at which time Waverly Logan appeared at court to present his testimony. Although Logan was there, the assistant district attorney in charge of the case elected to dismiss the charges against Spooner (you'll remember, a prime method of corrupt cops to get clients off the hook is simply not to show up in court; in this case, the assistant district attorney later was to recall that all records in the matter were destroyed sometime after September 23, 1970, so that he could not recall exactly why the case had been dismissed).

After the noncase, Logan dawdled in the building, and went into the men's room to relieve himself. He found Spooner there, and found Spooner trying to hand him, Logan, a roll of bills. Flustered, Logan knocked them to the floor, not knowing that the entire episode was being watched by another officer, Terence McSwiggin, who was in the building that day for another court appearance. In rapid succession:

Logan and Spooner left the building .

Over on the corner with the saloon where the vice cops hang out, Spooner handed Logan an aluminum cigar cylinder supposedly containing a cigar but in reality containing $100 in bills.

McSwiggin notified the internal affairs division that he had witnessed, in the men's room, the possible bribing of an officer.

A few minutes later , the IAD men, arriving as if Mayor Lindsay himself was about to be kidnaped, found Logan *back* in the Supreme Court building, and when he saw them he tossed the cylinder and its contents out a window in the stairwell, underwent a few hours of interrogation in the IAD central offices and was brought up on departmental charges of taking a bribe. (Spooner, to my knowledge, has never been charged with bribing a public official, and well he might not have been, since Logan never faced criminal charges of taking a bribe, that little departmental maneuver to be revealed presently.)

The first witness on that cold morning of February 18, 1971, in the superheated hearing room, was a man who identified himself, under questioning, as Terence McSwiggin, Shield Number 26326, a member of the tactical patrol force, that body of highly disciplined, dedicated officers functioning as a sort of commando unit in New York.

McSwiggin is a stocky man nobody could mistake for anything but the Scotch-Irish descendant he is; and he told his story that morning, as he had to IAD interrogators previously, in clear phrases, saying "yes sir" and "no sir" to defense counsel Foner, Commissioner Stutman and Sergeant Morton Perry, the cop-lawyer who served as prosecutor (and who is assigned full time to handling cases of this sort). Perry is a genial man, the way prosecutors always are who have to go into court with material gathered by others, like Hamilton Burger on the old *Perry Mason* show, doing the best with what they've got, only Morton Perry usually has got enough to make it stick—regardless of the criminal court rules of evidence.

"What do you think the other guys on the force are going to think about this?" I asked McSwiggin, after his testimony, in the hall.

"I don't think they know it," he said. "I don't think they know it." It is a long, honorable tradition that one cop does not rat on another, no matter how rotten he is, and there is no way many of the 31,000 cops in New York would not have learned of one officer's testifying against another downtown.

In the beginning, Patrolman McSwiggin testified, he arrived in the Criminal Court Building at 100 Centre Street, just down the street from police headquarters, at about 11:30 A.M., where he had a case. He felt nature's call, and, shortly before noon, entered the men's room on the second floor. Behind him, two men entered, then two more. One of the first two was Waverly Logan—as Harold Foner objected to this form of identification (since McSwiggin had no reason to know Logan's name, then or now), the testimony was changed to "a policeman I had seen in court before"—and then Logan was pointed out in the hearing room as the policeman. McSwiggin said he saw Logan talking to another man (later identified from photographs as Spooner) and that Logan had his left hand under Spooner's jacket, as if searching him.

"As I approached, the officer saw me, looked nervous, and he withdrew his hand," McSwiggin testified. Whereupon the money fell to the floor. The officer then looked at McSwiggin again, then bent down, blocked the money from the TAC officer's view, picked it up, and gave it back to the man, who put it in his pocket. McSwiggin said he followed the two out of the men's room. They walked together, he said, down through the lobby, and proceeded south, at which time McSwiggin lost sight of them. He then called the incident in to his precinct, and "somebody from IAD responded."

That somebody was Captain Joseph DeMartino, with Sergeant Randall Perkins and Lieutenant Frank Alioto, who at lunch the day of the hearing was careful to tell me that his name is spelled the same way as the mayor of San Francisco.

McSwiggin testified that Captain DeMartino came out, checked the first, second and fifth floors of the Criminal Court Building, with the two other officers; and then he said he waited forty-five minutes after being questioned by the IAD men before identifying photographs of the suspect (Logan) while in a car outside the building. He said he had never worked with Logan and had never even spoken to him.

Cross-examination by Foner revealed that McSwiggin had joined the force on March 1, 1967, and that his first assignment had been in the 46th Precinct. He then worked in the 23rd Precinct for three months, before being transferred to the TPF. He said he had never worked for the IAD. He said he had never seen Logan in uniform, and that the first time he had seen Logan was within the previous year, and that he had no knowledge of what Logan did in the police department, although he had an idea that maybe he had been in the narcotics field in Manhattan.

"Have you ever been in court when one of his [Logan's] cases have been called?" Foner asked.

"Once," McSwiggin said.

"What was the disposition of that case?" Foner asked.

"I don't know. I paid no attention to it," McSwiggin said.

"But you paid enough attention to know that it was called [to court]," Foner said. He then asked if McSwiggin had talked to members of the IAD before today, the trial day. McSwiggin said no, not since September 3, 1970, the day of the Spooner trial and alleged payoff.

McSwiggin testified that the case he was in court for that day was called at about 11 A.M. and that he was out about ten minutes later, because the defendant pleaded guilty. He then was told by the judge to report to a Miss Diaz in the probation office, which kept him until about 11:40, at which time he stopped off by the men's room and witnessed the Logan-Spooner incident.

McSwiggin testified that he urinated and combed his hair, and then saw Waverly Logan with his hand under Spooner's jacket, and that he saw fifteen or twenty bills fall to the floor. After the two men left, McSwiggin said he followed them until they left the building, and then telephoned the internal affairs division and said, "I believe I just saw an officer on the take."

From the time of the telephone call it took about twenty minutes for

Captain DeMartino of the IAD to get to the courthouse. In a deposition made later the same day for the IAD, McSwiggin chronicled the events of the next few minutes this way:

I informed him [DeMartino] of what had happened, described the officer to him, he took me and advised me to walk throughout the building floor by floor to see if I could see the officer. [McSwiggin had seen Logan leave the building, but apprently Logan had not yet signed out.] I went through the first floor, the second floor with no results. I went up to the fifth floor with no results, back down to the fourth floor. Checked all the court rooms with no results. I walked into the Complaint Room at which time I did observe the officer. I turned around, proceeded out of the room and was walking south down the hallway when I looked over my shoulder and I saw the officer coming down the hallway behind me. I saw Captain DeMartino and two of his officers in the hallway engaged in conversation. As I walked past them I advised them that the officer in question was coming down the hall behind me. I didn't bother to turn around, I kept on walking. When I got three quarters of the way down the hall I did turn around and I saw Captain DeMartino going into the staircase of the other end of the hallway. I waited there for approximately forty-five minutes and I called [in] again at which time they advised me to proceed to 137 Centre Street, eighth floor, which I did. I saw Captain DeMartino and he told me to wait there to sign a statement, to make a statement to him and that's it.

From noon until around 11 P.M., Waverly Logan was in continuous custody of the internal affairs division, being interrogated, transported from place to place, threatened and cajoled, with the experts in the business using the "good guy-bad guy" technique on him through the day and night. His testimony during a later session of his departmental trial, on March 2, 1971, tells a generally accurate story of what happened.

Foner, in questioning, leads Logan into telling about what happened after he left the Criminal Court Building:

Why did you go looking for [Horace] Lord [Logan's partner in the PEP squad]?
Lord had the car [Logan said]. And I had to testify for him in another case on the thirteenth floor.
What time was that?
It was approximately 12:40 when I went looking for him.
What occurred then?

I went up the street looking for Lord. I found the car [in the parking lot], and saw Spooner coming out of a bar [a hangout for cops].

(This was after the incident in the men's room. Logan, in his testimony, explained that situation by saying that Spooner had pulled his handkerchief from his pocket, and that in so doing a roll of bills fell to the floor. He said he stopped to help the man retrieve them, not seeing any denominations, shoved a handful into Spooner's pocket and mumbled something to the effect that Spooner was getting too old to go around pushing dope.)

What was said?

I asked him, "Have you seen my partner," and he said no. I asked him was he playing games with me, he said no. We talked about the bar, and I told him he was getting old and should stop selling narcotics. I told him he was through. We chatted about Harlem, and I felt him out and determined he wasn't being arrogant. He offered me a drink, I said I didn't drink. "Well," he said, "have a cigar," and he handed me the container. He said he was going home, that his car was in the parking lot. I told him that if he sees Lord to tell him I'm looking for him.

On the street?

Yes. Lots of people around.

When you talked to Spooner a lot of people were around?

Yes.

What did you do with the cigar container?

I decided to open it. I looked in it and there was money in it. Spooner wasn't out of sight yet.

What did you do?

I panicked. I went directly inside and upstairs. I went to the fourth floor to call Sergeant Jenkins [the administrative officer of the PEP squad] to tell him what had transpired.

Did you get through to him?

I saw [Patrolman] Alvarez [a member of PEP], and asked him for a dime to call. He told me how to call on Centrex. I went to the Complaint Room to call. I talked to a patrolman, he said Jenkins was out to lunch and would be back at 1. I said it was very important, to report that I'd called. Then I saw Patrolman [Richard] Ford [also a member of the PEP Squad]. The conversation with Alvarez was in court.

Tell us about that conversation.

I told him I thought somebody in the Narcotics Squad was trying to set me up. I showed him the cigar container, and said, "Ain't this a bitch," and he laughed. Coming out I ran into Ford. He also said he thought he was being set up, too, because he'd been offered money, and I told him he ought to get used to this in Harlem, it's an everyday thing, every arrest you make somebody offers you money.

Where was the container?

Always in my hand until I saw Sergeant [Randall] Perkins [member of the IAD].

Did you pass it to anyone?

I let Alvarez see into it. I told him to look here.

What happened after you left Ford?

I went down on the elevator, but never got off, came back up to the Complaint Room. To make a phone call. But somebody was on the phone, so I saw Barbara, the girl who draws complaints, and I borrowed a dime from her. I went down the staircase a couple of landings, and I stopped. I heard the door [the fire door] opening, looked up and saw Sergeant Perkins. "Are you an officer?" "Yeah," I said. He said in a friendly manner that he wanted to ask me some questions, and I said, yeah, I want to talk to you, too. He showed me his badge. Now Alioto [Lieutenant Frank Alioto, also of the IAD] comes up on the other side of me. I had the cylinder in my hand. Alioto grabbed for it, and I threw it out the window.

Why?

I panicked. But Alioto didn't look like a cop, and Perkins hadn't identified himself as IAD. Alioto pushed me against the wall and took my gun. Perkins goes down to get the cylinder. [Alioto was careful to keep his eye on the cylinder, from the window, until Perkins picked it up, thus protecting the chain of evidence for future use.] DeMartino was there. He identified himself as a captain with IAD. Before he got there Alioto said sit down and stay quiet, but DeMartino says let him talk. He then said they were gonna put me in jail. I said why you want to flake me like this, I'm a police officer, too, got a wife and family. Flake—that means put me away with false evidence. I helped Perkins locate the cylinder. All he knew was it was a flashy object. They took me down the stairs, across the street into another office. . . .

What time did you first see Perkins?

Just after 1.

Why didn't you go to the lieutenant in the sign-in room?

Our whole squad had had previous trouble with him. . . . I don't know his name. It's something like Dillinger, Dillon or something. He didn't like me, we didn't get along. I felt I couldn't go to him.

Okay. You left 100 Centre Street for where?

Directly across the street.

What happened?

They took me to the top floor. Set me down in a chair, with a tape recorder. Present are Alioto, DeMartino and others, about six people. They threatened to lock me up, mostly DeMartino. He said if I have nothing to hide and come clean he'll take care of it, but if I say nothing he'll go straight to the D.A.

Did he advise you of your rights?

He said if I called for a lawyer he'd lock me up.

(At this point the record becomes interestingly fuzzy. While Logan testified that his access to legal counsel had been denied, he said privately, earlier in the year, that the IAD men were careful to administer the so-called Miranda decision warning to him during preliminary stages of the interrogation. That decision, by the United States Supreme Court in the case of *Miranda* v. *Arizona*, set aside convictions where the accused had not been advised of his rights to remain silent and to have the advice of a lawyer. Why Logan chose to testify to the contrary perhaps will never be known, but earlier he said that he had been "Miranda'ed" while the tape recorder was running, and that in a few seconds the tape was restarted, erasing the Miranda advisement. Thus the Miranda does not appear on official police department transcripts of the recorded interrogation sessions held that day. His earlier statement was confirmed, too, independently, by Lieutenant Alioto at lunch in the headquarters lounge at noon, on February 18, 1971, when Alioto told me that Logan had, indeed, been given the Miranda warning and that he, Alioto, had administered it himself. In testimony on February 18, 1971, Deputy Inspector William Bonacum, then commander of the IAD, was asked by lawyer Foner if he had visited with Assistant District Attorney Milton Glass on the possibility of bringing criminal charges against Logan. There would be no criminal prosecution, it turned out, because Bonacum admitted to Glass that Logan *had not* been given the Miranda warning. Why the IAD was satisfied to rig Logan's case so that it would remain a department affair and not get into the spotlight of open court proceedings remains the subject of conjecture.)

Logan continued that he was questioned twice, once with the tape off and once when it was running. Transcripts of those tapes show three different Waverly Logans: the first confused, suffering, agitated, fearful; the second somewhat calmer; the third totally disciplined.

What did they ask you [Foner continued in the March 3, 1971, session]?

One question after another, all trying to ask questions at the same time. I tried to tell it straight away.

Did you deny that you received the container?

No. I told them I got it from Spooner.

Did you tell them why you threw it away?

Yes. I said I thought Perkins was from the Narcotics Squad, the same unit I been having trouble with all along.

What do you mean?

The Sheffey Complaint. I was a witness.

The Sheffey Complaint. It sounds like a movie title, and it probably could be. Little known in New York outside police circles, the matter involved one Sergeant Howard Sheffey, then president of the Guardians Association, an organization within the police department that tries to be for black cops what the PBA is for white cops (or for all cops, as PBA officials would have you believe).

Sheffey had been a cop for fifteen years, and if in full-dress uniform would have enough medals to make him the envy of a visiting South American junta leader. On August 21, 1970, around eight or eight-thirty in the evening, Sergeant Sheffey, with Patrolman Logan, was outside the 28th Precinct station house, when they heard comments from civilian bystanders about what might or might not be going on inside. Now the 28th Precinct is deep in Harlem, and when the two black police officers went into the building—specifically to the detective bureau—they found two white plainclothesmen beating on a black suspect. Sheffey then made department history—he took the incident to the hated Civilian Complaint Review Board, unthinkable for a policeman to do. Logan was a witness in that case. Later, during his questioning in Logan's departmental trial, McSwiggin—the chief prosecution witness in the Logan case—was asked if he knew either of the plainclothesmen, since all three of the white men had worked in tactical patrol. McSwiggin said no, and the matter became so important during the proceedings that Commissioner Stutman, the trial judge, ordered a confrontation between the three men, which was held Friday, February 26, 1971, at 72 Poplar Street. The results of the confrontation were that McSwiggin denied knowing the two other officers, and both of them said they had no recollection of ever knowing Officer McSwiggin.

Continuing the direct examination of Logan on March 3, 1971, lawyer Foner asked, "How long did the interrogation take?"

There were two tapes. One at 137 Centre Street, and one at Poplar Street [Logan said].

[Commissioner Stutman then asked:] Did he [Alioto] tell you you had the right to counsel?

No. He started to, then tailed off into threats and promises, with the tapes off.

What time did all this happen [Foner asked]?

I have no recollection of time.

What time did you eat that day?

I didn't eat that day.

Who took you to the D.A.?

Alioto. I asked him what was going to happen, and he said he didn't know. They brought Ford in, and separated us. Also Lord was brought in. I didn't have a chance to talk to him.

Did anybody talk to you? Did you see Bonacum in the D.A.'s office?

Yes. Alioto was with me like a guard. I asked if I'm under arrest, and he said he didn't know.

[Commissioner Stutman then interjected:] I will accept that the respondent was not under arrest, but not free to go [whatever that means.]

At about this point, the lid began to close on Logan's casket. Bonacum started talking about the car, and about the dope that was falling out of the upholstery, the glove compartment and everywhere else you could look. It was a laugh then, to everybody except Bonacum and Logan, and it is a laugh now to everybody but Logan. (And to Eddie Egan, the supercop upon whose career the book and movie *The French Connection* was based. I met Egan outside Commissioner Stutman's hearing room early in 1971, while Logan was being tried; and Egan was big and marcelled and grinning and self-confident; and the commissioner himself had called him in for an interview; and at the time Egan didn't know that they were going to get him the same way they got Waverly Logan—only this time out of simple, insane jealousy; and by December 1, 1971, seven *hours* before he would have been eligible to retire from the force, he would be dismissed for failing to voucher narcotics with the property clerk.)

There is no cop in America who deals regularly with narcotics enforcement who is not guilty, at one time or another, of possessing unvouchered dope, even if it is only during the time it takes for the officer to get back to headquarters to turn the stuff in. In Harlem, dope is the currency used by cops to pay informers, who they know are users and pushers, on the time-honored theory that you let the little fish keep swimming, in hopes they'll attract the really big ones. Catching the big ones, of course, has alternative rewards—cracking a really big ring means gaining departmental honors, publicity, community acclaim and maybe a movie contract, the way Eddie Egan did it; or maybe setting yourself up for some really big, long-term, nontaxable ice.

(It should be mentioned that trouble never seems to come in small doses, especially for Commissioner Pat Murphy, who, shortly before Christmas, 1972, girded himself and called a press conference to announce that most, if not all, of the eighty to one hundred pounds of heroin seized in the original *"French Connection"* case had been removed from the property clerk's office and replaced with a simple, harmless white powder. Murphy's face was grayer than usual that week, when he had to admit that a police officer, using a fictitious badge number, had taken the dope on a voucher, ostensibly for use by an assistant district attorney in a court case. The name that appeared on the police receipt for most of the missing heroin was that of Detective Joseph Nunziata, who had been found dead in an unmarked police car on March 27, 1972. His death had been ruled a suicide.)

During Logan's interrogation by Inspector Bonacum, around 4 P.M., September 3, 1970, the day of Logan's nonarrest, a big deal was made out of this. The taped part of the interview went like this:

> Patrolman Logan, I'm Deputy Inspector Bonacum. Also present is Lieutenant Alioto, Internal Affairs Division. When the officers from the Internal Affairs Division approached you today, what did you do with the cigar container that had the money in it?
>
> I, ah, threw it out of the window, for the reason that I that, that, I was scared, I was scared all day, that's why I called my supervisor. I was gonna throw ... I didn't know what to do with it.

Much of the next part of the interrogation was concerned with whether Logan had contraband narcotics in his car, although the method of questioning was roundabout, and even got involved with ten sets of dice the IAD had found in the Volkswagen, dice Logan claimed he'd taken out of a street game a night or two earlier.

> Do you have narcotics in your car [Bonacum finally got around to asking]?

I might have some [Logan said]. I'm not sure because I usually use my car to transport prisoners, and, ah, when I use my car to transport prisoners a lot of times they stuff things in the seat and I usually get it together, throw it out or voucher or *whatever* [italics added]. I have [inaudible] vouchered narcotics before.

Do you have unvouchered narcotics in your car now?

I, I, if I [do] it's in the bag. I might have some in the car in the bag.

Do you have unvouchered narcotics in your bag now?

[On the tape appear the sounds of an attache case being opened and closed.]

I don't have no unvouchered [inaudible]. Could have dice in the car.

All right, well listen, just say you could have. Would you permit the lieutenant to look through your bag?

[Now appear the sounds of papers rustling.]

All right. Do you smoke marijuana yourself [Bonacum asked]?

No sir.

Do you use hashish?

No sir.

Do you use any form of narcotics?

No sir, but I find a lot of old stuff pertaining to narcotics, it could, this could be narcotics by transport. Using my car for work, you know, transporting prisoners.

All right. Do you have any marijuana in your car now?

I might. I don't know. I might have some. I might have some. I might have some, that is the truth, have some.

There was, indeed, dope in the car, including marijuana, which Logan said he'd taken from a street dude.

This packet of bamboo paper [Bonacum said].

It was in, it was in [Logan stammered].

That the lieutenant handed me from your attaché case, this is the type of paper commonly used to roll marijuana cigarettes, isn't it?

It is, sir.

Well, why do you have that in your attaché case?

Usually when I take things off of people, I have dice in here and I have bamboo paper, I have quite a, sometimes I have unvouchered narcotics that I do get to voucher if I don't [inaudible].

How long do you hold these narcotics before you voucher them?

Um, maybe, um, a week or something like that.

Well, how long have you held this marijuana?

This, I might have, this, this particular bag, I might, I don't think I had it there last night. If it wasn't last night it was, the middle of last week. Cause a lot of times, I'm going to tell you, I'm going to tell you the truth, it could have been last week. I, ah, I, ah, I found it, guys when I mark a . . . guys stuff it in the seat.

Don't you search prisoners before you put them in your car [asked Lieutenant Harold Hess, his first contribution to the session]?

When you get them, you handcuff them together and you don't quite search them, you ain't got time to search them, you don't have time to search.

Suppose he had a gun in his pocket?

I mean you go over them, but you don't really search them. But I don't take, I don't take no narcotics.

All right [Bonacum said]. I have another envelope here that was recovered from the left hand map pocket of your car. This envelope contains a silver foil and glassine envelopes, there are ten silver foil and four glassine envelopes. Do you recognize these envelopes?

This I do recognize. [Five months later, at Logan's departmental trial, the defense would stipulate, without objections, that the envelopes indeed contained "junk."]

All right. What is this?

This is, ah, this pertains, I think it is narcotics.

Well, what kind of narcotics is it [Bonacum asked]?

I think, I think it's either cocaine or heroin. [From the description of the packaging, it was probably both.]

Logan said some of the dope had been left in his car by prisoners being transported, and that he had confiscated the rest of it in street raids. The interrogators went to great lengths to get Logan to tell them where he had picked up a pot pipe also found in the car, and asked him who had been with him during the time the drugs were taken.

How many men were in the team [Bonacum asked]? Sergeant Sheffey, yourself and how many others?

Just Sergeant Sheffey and myself.

You found this and you did not report it to the superior on hand? You did not report it to Sergeant Sheffey?

No sir. This I did not refer to the superior officer. I was, I had been warned about keeping unvouchered narcotics around, by the lieutenant because, he says *some outside command might grab us* [italics added], he said we should voucher, which, in all intentionally, I was going to do. I was.

What case does this marijuana pertain to [Alioto asked]?

[Logan's response was inaudible.]

It's an unmarked envelope, how do you keep track of the case [Alioto continued]?

The case.

Yeah.

I found . . .

What arrest was it in connection with? Right?

Sir, I make narcotic, I hit dice games every day, I make dice games arrests every day, and when I make the dice game arrest, I, you know, everybody throws it off them.

Well, how do you keep track of how you obtained this property? Do you make notes someplace? How do you keep an accounting of it?

I just . . . put it all together. I put it all together.

You put all the property together?

Put all the property together and voucher it.

And you voucher it?

Yeah, and then I voucher it.

And how many times have you vouchered found narcotics [Bonacum asked]?

Once before.

What quantity was that?

Ah, it was nineteen glassine envelopes.

And who was with you when you found the nineteen glassine envelopes?

It was, ah, this during the period of off duty.

On no occasion in the past while you were on duty have you vouchered recovered, found narcotics, is that correct?

Only once, the occasion I told you about.

That was when you were off duty. Now I said on duty.

[Logan's reply was recorded, in the interrogation transcript, as inaudible, but Bonacum continued:] How have you been disposing of found narcotics?

You know how it is . . .

Just tell me the truth. Don't, don't try . . .

I don't, I don't know what to say, well, like all the other ...
police officers do the same.

How do they do it?

[Again Logan's reply is reported as inaudible. It might be
assumed that at this point he asked that the tape recorder be turned
off, because Bonacum responded:] No, you have to keep it on the
record.

You have to keep it on the record [Logan asked, obviously
stalling for time to think of something that would satisfy the record
and keep him out of court]?

Yeah [Bonacum said].

Throw it down the sink [Logan said]. You know you throw it
away. You usually throw it away, everybody else, usually you know
... or something like that, you know you throw it away, you found
works and all that stuff, you know, in Harlem you come across ...

Who was the lieutenant, that warned you not to keep?

Lieutenant [inaudible] warned all of us not to, try not to, he
didn't want not to keep, he said toss your cars, when you get out of
them before you go home because it would be embarrassing for an
outside command, you get picked up like you, ah, picked me up,
you, ah, had narcotics in your car. So he told me to, he said always
toss your car. . . . So I tossed my car and I keep this in the side thing,
to put it, to put narcotics in.

Well, what did he tell you to do with the narcotics when you
found it?

He just, he mentioned toss the car.

In other words, he didn't give you any instructions how to dis-
pose of it?

Well, I guess, I guess ... I imagine, he meant ... toss the car. He
said toss the car, because it could be embarrassing if an outside
command find unvouchered narcotics in your presence. But sir, I do
not take narcotics, do not take narcotics.

What comes out of all these questions and answers is that everybody in the room, a deputy inspector, a captain, two lieutenants and
Patrolman Logan, essentially knew the answers to the questions before
they were asked. If all the "found" or "dropped" narcotics taken by
policemen in Harlem in a year were turned in, properly marked as evidence (vouchered), the police department would have to build an annex
to hold it, and it would have to be fireproof because if it ever burned
down half the island of Manhattan would be on a trip. Honest men may
rise to high rank in the police department, and do, but they do not make

it without a fairly deep knowledge of the corrupt activities of those not so honest. It has been pointed out that a corrupt policeman is by the very nature of his activities a proselytizer, needing to render all other policemen partners in his grafting, or, if not partners, silent acquiescers. Those who do not become partners either look the other way, in which case they are treated with distrust and are not allowed into the close fraternity of other cops, therefore marching their way toward retirement as lonely outsiders, or they leave the force and take jobs elsewhere. A few decide to talk to outsiders, but these are so rare as to be psychological freaks, in which case they are by definition generally not to be trusted.

What can be learned from Waverly Logan's interrogation is that police commanders have almost unlimited power over the destinies of their subordinates. It is a common police ploy to charge a civilian suspect with far more crimes than he could conceivably have committed (this is called "throwing the book" at someone), with the object that the suspect might be tempted to plead guilty to one of the lesser charges, thus getting him off the street and at the very least into the hands of a probation officer, not to mention the credit for conviction on the cop's record. The unvouchered contraband device, which the cops used to get Eddie Egan and Waverly Logan, is a heavy hammer that hangs over the head of almost every New York cop, and the smart ones know it. Logan's Lieutenant Inaudible told him, you'll recall, to be sure to "toss your car" before going home for fear that an "outside command" might discover the stuff. It wasn't a case where the lieutenant warned Logan that he should immediately voucher the junk because it is a departmental regulation; the implication is that as long as nobody but members of the PEP squad knew you had it, you were all right, but don't let an *outside command* find out, even though chances are that that same outside command is tossing its own cars before going home at night so they couldn't be busted by the PEP squad. And, incidentally, you may be sure that Lieutenant Inaudible, whoever he is, has a notation in his dossier now that he has been informing his men on this point.

(In Logan's formal departmental trial, Inspector Bonacum was asked by lawyer Foner about the elements of Logan's interrogation, and if Logan had been questioned about narcotics.

("Yes," Bonacum said.

("What did he say?" Foner asked.

("He said that he'd been warned by his superiors to turn in narcotics picked up in gambling games, but didn't," Bonacum said. He did not mention the "outside command" modifier.)

So the police department had an airtight case against Logan—they had him on the original specified charges, that he had taken ten ten-dollar bills from a known criminal (even though it was never shown that Logan had done anything to earn it; Spooner's case was dismissed, but it was an assistant district attorney who dismissed it, without conferring with Logan); and if that weren't enough they had his car chock full of narcotics, all illegally possessed by him, admittedly. He was going to be dismissed from the force—and there was nothing he could do about it.

He was guilty, of course, but what he was guilty of was infringing on the rights of corrupt cops already milking Harlem for whatever they could, and for doing it behind the backs of the men who had spent years devising a payoff system that was lucrative, essentially foolproof and even provided severance pay. This is not to accuse the officers of the internal affairs division, or of the tactical patrol force—it is quite possible for clever men to set up a situation where a victim is set up for other, entirely honest men to finish him off, believing all the while that they are doing their duty.

On June 2, 1971, Deputy Commissioner Stutman found Logan guilty of having been offered $100 by a male not to arrest him; and Logan pleaded guilty to failure to deliver narcotics evidence to the property clerk upon the completion of court hearings (that was the charge; as you know, the narcotics involved were never connected with any court hearings). On the second charge, for which Eddie Egan was fired from the force, Logan was penalized by being ordered to forfeit five days' pay. For the first, he was dismissed.

On October 26, 1971, Waverly Logan appeared before the Knapp Commission in New York City and said that he had been grafting as much as $2,000 a month in Harlem, while a member of the PEP squad. It wasn't the kind of organized take Harlem had been used to, though.

When the PEP squad was organized back in 1969, Logan told the Knapp people, he and his twenty minority-group partners felt good about it. "The men felt that they was in a new police department all by itself, that it was gonna be a good squad, have good bosses, that no holds was barred, that if they've seen a violation of the law, they was gonna make an arrest." He said that attitude lasted just as long as it took for the squad to bust the wrong numbers bank, which drew the wrath of a high police official, who threw out the arrest. The squad, somewhat disillusioned, began the kind of lone-wolf, one-shot grafting that so infuriated those who had a district organized. The PEP squad, Logan said, would look for "scores," toss whatever operation it happened to be for whatever they could get—he said he got as much as $2,000 for not going through with an arrest of a narcotics dealer—and then cut out of that precinct and into another to cover their tracks from other policemen who had been getting regular payoffs for protection from the same operators all along.

Word of these extracurricular illegal activities did get around; I was sitting in the fireplaced anteroom of Deputy Commissioner Smith one afternoon, months before Logan talked to the Knapp Commission, and asked Smith's assistant, Inspector Masini, if he had heard of the Logan case and if he agreed that Logan had been framed. "I don't know," he said. "But we've been hearing some troubling things about what the PEP squad has been doing up there in Harlem."

Logan, speaking in October, 1971, before the Knapp panel, said, "I pretty much believed that after seeing the department wasn't on the level, it seemed like everybody was taking money, everybody had contracts around, everybody I talked to was doing their thing. So after the first dollar there it seemed like it was the natural thing to do."

Harold Foner, Logan's attorney of record during all of this, says Logan is a lying sonofabitch and that the only money Logan ever got in Harlem was stuffed into his pockets the way Spooner shoved the cigar cylinder at him. Foner was in almost constant contact with Logan from the time he was suspended in September, 1970, until after his dismissal in June, 1971, during which period Logan drove a cab for a living.

"He didn't have a pot to piss in," Foner said. "I used to have him drive me around, on business, and I'd toss him fifteen or twenty dollars, and that's all he'd have to his name. When he was on the force he never smoked or drank and didn't run around, he lived with his wife and baby in Queens, so where the hell is all the money he made in Harlem?" Foner insists that Logan was talked into weaving a big story for the Knapp Commission by some "rad-lib chick down in the Village," who, romantically attracted to Logan, thought he could come out clean if he made the television screen. But while Foner insists that Logan was just stupid, he maintains, and has enough inside information to maintain with authority, that the PEP squad was as bad as the rumors that had trickled up to Deputy Commissioner Smith's office had them to be.

Shortly after Logan testified before the Knapp Commission he left the city, probably for California. Foner says Logan has reason to believe that one of the sergeants in Harlem had "a contract" out on him.

(Even in Waverly Logan's absence, Foner, as attorney of record, was appealing on his behalf in two areas. One is called an Article 78: a petition to the Supreme Court in the city of New York asking that the court overthrow Logan's dismissal on the grounds that Logan was not dismissed for discipline or punishment and that he had been deprived of his rights under Police Department General Orders 15, commonly called the policemen's Bill of Rights. The other action was a complaint filed July 7, 1971, with the United States Attorney for the Eastern District of New York under the Federal Civil Rights Law against Inspector William Bonacum and Captain Joseph DeMartino. The complaint alleges that Logan was deprived of his civil rights in the entire matter, and one section states flatly that "Patrolman [Horace] Lord was shot to death after testifying on my [Logan's] behalf and while my departmental trial was being held.")

On February 23, 1971, Mayor Lindsay, Commissioner Murphy and 3,000 men and women of the police department crowded inside and swarmed about the outside of the Walter B. Cooke Funeral Home in Brooklyn. The officers wore white gloves, and when the flag-draped coffin was carried out they snapped to attention as a bugler played taps. They had come to give a hero's funeral to Patrolman Horace Lord, one of more than 100 police officers to be killed in the line of duty in the United States in 1971; and as the casket passed by there were tears in the eyes of Londel Davis, Lord's partner, who had only been riding with him for a few months. Lord's previous partner was a man named Waverly Logan.

Lord had been with Logan that day of April 22, 1970, when Logan arrested Joe Spooner at the Golden Glass Bar and Grill—the day Spooner offered Logan $600 now and $600 later if he would either not go through with the arrest or else fix it so the case would be dismissed— preferably by not showing up in court. Logan was to say that he turned the pusher down, and Logan's supervisor, Sergeant Charles Gilliam, was to corroborate his story, and Lord knew about the offer, although it is not clear whether he was present when it was made. And he was in the courthouse on September 3, 1970, when Logan got stuck with the cigar case full of ten-dollar bills.

During Logan's interrogation that day it seemed to be important whether he had shown the cylinder to his partner.

During one session, Inspector Bonacum asked Logan:

Who did you tell that Spooner gave you money? Anybody?

Who did I tell he gave me money? Yes, I think I told, ah, Patrolman Lord, I think what he did, I told Lord and I think I showed the money to another patrolman in my unit [Logan said].

Who was that?

I showed it to, ah, Patrolman Alvarez, but I didn't tell him what it was. I said look at this, so I handed him the cigar case and he looked in it.

What did he say?

He said, oh, I don't remember what he said. Says, oh, it's an expensive cigar. I said, ah, I said, ah, something like that I know, I say I see it.

[Later, Bonacum asked:] Is your partner going to stay with the car?

I don't know [Logan said].

Who is your partner?

Patrolman Lord.

L-o-r-d? [Bonacum spelled out]?

Right.

Is he from PEP Squad too?

Yes, PEP Squad.

All right, L-o-r-d, or L-o-y-d?

Lord or Loyd [Alioto asked]?

It's L-o-r-d [Logan said].

L-o-r-d [Alioto said, finally getting it straight].

Patrolman Lord showed the money to Patrolman Alvarez [Inspector Bonacum said].

Alvarez. Also of your unit [Alioto asked]?

Yes [said Logan]. I didn't tell him what pertaining to it. But I did show him the cigar case with the money contained in it. And when I showed it to him, there was another patrolman there, Patrolman [Thomas] Rentas, but I didn't . . .

Where is he from [Bonacum asked]?

PEP Squad, but I did not show him where. I did not show him.

Ah, so now, Alvarez, Lord and Rentas . . . [Bonacum began].

[Logan cut him off:] I don't [know] if Lord, I mean, I, I didn't, I didn't, I didn't tell Lord about it. Lord was on the scene [at the Golden Glass in April]. He knew. I told him about the defendant offering me the six hundred dollars.

Yeah [Bonacum said].

He knew about this [Logan said].

Yeah [Bonacum said].

I told him about the defendant offering the six hundred dollars. He knew about this. I told him about the defendant offering me the six hundred dollars prior and when I came down to court cause he had it on him that day. He said take the six hundred dollars that day.

In another session, the same day, Sergeant Perkins resumed questioning, picking up the chain of events leading to Logan's and Lord's arrival in court. Logan had picked up Lord at his home in Brooklyn (Logan was living in Queens), and dropped him off at the courthouse so Lord could go by the property clerk's office while Logan parked the Volkswagen. He entered the building then, "signed in" and then met Lord on the third floor, after checking in at each of the three courtrooms where he had cases that day. At this point Lord asked Logan for the car keys and the parking lot stub.

Did you have a conversation [Perkins asked]?

We had, we had slight conversation.

What did you talk about?

We talked about, um, we talked about—I guess we talked a little bit about the case [in which they were to testify together, later]. Slightly mentioned the case.

Did you talk about this humidor?

No, I hadn't rec—I hadn't seen that before, I never seen that, I hadn't seen it.

You didn't have this at that time?

No.

Did you see Patrolman Lord at another time, during this appearance in court [that day]?

Other than when I told you he got the car keys from me?

That's the one we're talking about, right? I'm saying, did you see him at another time?

Another time after that?

Right.

No.

Now you did not show this humidor?

Patrolman ... Alvarez.

You showed it to Patrolman Alvarez? Not Patrolman Lord?

Patrolman Alvarez [Logan repeated].

Patrolman Alvarez [Perkins said].

[After a few more questions, during which Logan exhibited signs of being sleepy, Perkins again said:] You showed it to who? Alvarez?

Right.

Now [Perkins said], let me close the windows.

No, I ain't going to do that, I ain't going to do that. I'm scared to death. [Then on the tape is the sound of a window closing, and general laughter.]

(The IAD's interest in the cylinder and who saw it, and Logan's panic upon receiving it and his failure to return it to Spooner on the spot are mysterious, unless you are willing to accept Harold Foner's opinion that Logan was really puzzled by receiving the cylinder—but only because he thought it might have been a deal made by somebody else, who had neglected to tell Logan that he was to be the bagman. Who that somebody else might be remains a mystery.)

On Thursday, February 18, 1971, at Logan's departmental trial, Horace Lord was called to testify in Logan's behalf. It was one of the rare instances in that trial where other witnesses were sent from the room.

Under Foner's questioning, Lord said that he had been on the force since June 6, 1968, and that he had been with the PEP squad since October, 1969, and that his primary duties were to enforce street violations, including robbery, gambling, prostitution and narcotics, and that he had been selected for the job primarily because of his ghetto background.

Do you recall the day of September 3, 1970 [Foner asked]?
[Lord said he did.]
What time did you meet him [Logan]?
About 8:30 a.m.

Lord said Logan had picked him up in the Volkswagen that day, the same car often used to transport prisoners.

Where were you going [Foner continued]?
To court [Lord answered].
How many times have you and Logan been to court on Centre Street together?
Ten or eleven times. Our court days are usually the same. There are special court days for the PEP squad.
What was your first stop that day?
At the Property Clerk's office.

It developed that the case Logan and Lord were to testify in was scheduled for later in the day, and Lord was discussing the case with the assistant district attorney who was to prosecute it when the meeting with Logan occurred. Lord said he took the car, and returned at around 1 P.M., leaving the left door unlocked, then going back to the courthouse, and that he was interviewed by internal affairs later. By the time he got back, of course, Logan was already in custody.

I was in the courtroom when a messenger came up [Lord testified]. Lieutenant Gilliam had been ordered to keep me there until somebody came to get me. They did, around 3 P.M. We then went to 155 Leonard Street, and waited there, and then they took me to 137 Centre Street.

What happened there [Foner asked]?

Captain DeMartino, Lieutenant Alioto and Sergeant Perkins questioned me. There was no stenographer present. They checked my memo book, and asked me if I saw Logan today. Then the inspector came in and told me I should say I saw money, but I wasn't showed any money or no cigar container. Inspector Bonacum came in and showed me papers that Patrolman Logan had signed saying he has showed me the money and if I signed a statement like it he wouldn't have to do the same thing to me.

(Logan testified that he had not signed a statement, and that he had not been shown a transcript of his interrogations.)

Foner then established that there was a rather poor relationship between the PEP squad members and the lieutenant in the sign-in room, who was white, and then asked:

How long were you at 137 Centre Street?

A couple of hours [Lord said.]

Did you ever see Logan there?

Yes. We were taken there together.

How was he?

Very scared. He was smoking, and he doesn't smoke.

Were you threatened?

He [the inspector] said if I didn't tell the truth about Logan showing me the money they'd get me.

That night, in the headquarters lounge, where Logan was drinking, but not smoking, he shook his head and said Lord hadn't told all he knew, and that he was very disappointed in his partner. (What was he supposed to tell? Lawyer Foner tells me that Lord was to have testified that Logan was just a dope, used by everybody in and out of the PEP squad, which, quite possibly, would have uncovered a whole new nest of snakes during that routine departmental trial.) The following evening, Friday, Lord told his boss, Lieutenant Hamilton Robinson, that he planned to return to a subsequent session of the trial and testify further for Logan. (I single out Lieutenant Robinson here because, while it became general knowledge that Lord planned to return to the witness stand, Foner established Lord's intentions, later, by putting Robinson on the stand and asking him if Lord had made the statement to him.) That night Lord, Lieutenant Robinson, Lord's new partner and another officer went in plainclothes on a narcotics stakeout in a Harlem tenement building. On Saturday morning at eight o'clock my telephone rang and it was Harold Foner.

"Horace Lord is dead," he said. The staked-out cops had waited for a couple of pushers to come down in an elevator. When the elevator door opened the suspects started shooting, and when it was over Horace Lord and one of the suspects lay dead.

But at least they gave him a hero's funeral.

5

Mardi Gras
Every Friday

In my search for finite cases of police corruption—well documented and with a beginning, a middle and an end, the city of New Orleans presented itself as a near-classic case. While the investigation of the police department there in the early 1950s never really got off the ground, enough sworn testimony was taken so that a broad picture could be drawn of what was really going on in the precinct houses and squad cars. But, once again, the past overtook the present, and before I could write *finis* to that early story of grafting cops, two modern-day vice cops—plus the notorious district attorney of Orleans Parish, Jim Garrison—were indicted and accused of the same sort of crimes policemen had been guilty of a generation earlier. It would have been easy to ignore the 1971 developments, but there were so many similarities in the government's case against the defendants and the allegations of two decades earlier that the updating had to be made. The similarities, indeed, are almost eerie.

In New Orleans you only have to dig about three feet to find water, and in the old days, before the above-the-ground grave became universal there, burials were conducted by boring holes in the bottom of the coffin, after which three or four blacks would stand on top of the box until it filled and finally settled into the muck and could be covered over.

Police corruption in Greater New Orleans has always been just about the same relative distance beneath the surface, and just as difficult to keep buried, in case anybody ever tried, which has been seldom in the 250-year history of the white occupation of southern Louisiana.

It is difficult to approach the problem of crooked cops in the Crescent City with a straight face because over the years the people of New Orleans and its surrounding parishes (counties) turned out at the polls to prevent any misunderstanding about what kind of a city they wanted (even though as late as 1946 the vice squad turned out every whore in the French Quarter, handed them the name of a candidate and a list of five or six polling places where they could vote five or six times with no questions asked)—they wanted night life and fun and action, both for personal pleasure and financial reward (sailors and conventioneers seldom drop big bundles in antique bookstores); and, because there is a good, strong Christian heritage in the Queen City of the South, they wanted it to be illegal, because it was immoral.

The regulation of all this shady fun—booze, women, gambling and pornography—fell, naturally, upon the shoulders of the New Orleans Police Department and, elsewhere in the area, those of the Jefferson Parish and St. Bernard Parish sheriffs. And quite naturally, with all of this winking and blinking and backslapping going on at City Hall and as far away as the state capital at Baton Rouge, it took the cops no time at all to figure out a way to make their delicate situation pay off quite handsomely. The extent of corruption surfaced once, in 1953, enough to get a broad look at it, and then it sank beneath the surface again; and when I said it is hard to approach the subject with a straight face it is because of the pitiful figures the cops showed themselves to be during that period, serving a community only to the extent that it wanted to be served, and no more. (As recently as 1971, while the police department was considered relatively "clean" by experts, uniformed New Orleans cops could be seen slouching on street corners with their hands in their pockets, lolling in radio cars in no-parking zones, shouting obscenities at motorists, and exhibiting other unprofessional bits of behavior.)

The face sobers a bit, though, when you realize that during those years of innocent grafting, culminating in a few months' public hearings in 1953, producing sometimes humorous, sometimes horrifying allegations, the powers of darkness were closing in on the city, through the gambling interests of one Carlos Marcello, long-time associate of Meyer Lansky and Frank Costello and a full-fledged member of what you might want to call the Cosa Nostra (although presently I think it is the policy of the New Orleans newspapers to refer to Mr. Marcello as a "real estate investor"). And when the Senate Select Subcommittee on Labor Racketeering came to look into that situation in New Orleans in 1959, they were told that there was very little labor racketeering going on in the Crescent City because organized crime had gotten control of so many industries that they had been able to keep labor from effectively organizing at all, and so all they really had was *management* racketeering, which doesn't count.

Before I tell you the stories of Doris Gellman, a prostitute; Audrey C., a fifteen-year-old girl who was forced into the brothels; Annie Mae Taylor, who says the captains always go first in gang rapes inside the police station in the French Quarter; and the Gold Dust Twins, bagmen in the 5th Precinct, I ought to review, briefly, what it is that makes New Orleans what it is.

By 1712, five years before the Mississippi Company obtained control of the French province of Louisiana, the total population of the territory was less than 300, including 28 women who, virtually without exception, had been deported from brothels and prisons in Paris, so that at the risk of offending modern-day residents, it might be said that the very pollen of the flower of womanhood in Louisiana was tainted from the start.

Yet, unlike other colonies in the Americas, the crowd sent to Louisiana were not told that they would have to work very hard, and indeed they did not work at all, preferring to spend their time drinking, gambling, fighting and stealing; and by 1763, according to Herbert Asbury in his 1936 book *The French Quarter*:

> The thieves, vagabonds and prostitutes who had been sent to the New World by the Mississippi Company and the French government still formed, if not a majority, at least a large and disturbing minority of Louisiana's inhabitants. Under the lax rule of the Marquis de Vaudreuil they flocked into New Orleans from all parts of the province, and the capital city became more than ever the resort of the vicious

and criminal elements of the population who devoted themselves to stealing, brawling and drinking in the many pot houses, taverns and gambling dens which had made their appearance along the river front and the edges of the swamps. The area in which these dives were situated was the first recognized criminal district in New Orleans, and it was destined to spread during the next century until approximately one third of the old city was entirely given over to vice and other forms of crime.

By 1803, the year Louisiana officially became part of the United States, New Orleans boasted 4,000 houses, 5,000 white citizens, 2,000 free Negroes and 3,000 slaves. Rampart Street was just that—a line of fortifications—and Canal Street was a water-filled moat. The city had inherited a small police force from the French, but with increasing river traffic and an influx of tough rivermen, the gendarmes spent most of their time recovering from beatings. In 1806 they were replaced by the *garde de ville*, five officers and twenty-eight men who served not only as protectors of the city but as victims of the ruffians, who took away the policemen's pikes and sabers and beat them with them. Two years later the city organized a "night watch," that precursor of modern police departments that had existed in New York, London and other cities.

The invasion of the river men [Asbury wrote] probably stimulated the growth of the New Orleans underworld to a greater degree than any other economic reason or population movement in its history. During the first twenty years of the American occupation, the number of inhabitants in New Orleans more than quadrupled, and it has been estimated that from one third to one fourth of the increase was composed of thieves, ruffians, vagabonds and prostitutes who, with the removal of all restrictions upon immigration, had flocked into the city from the four corners of the earth. For a period of some thirty years or more some of the lowest and most vicious elements of New Orleans' population specialized in catering to the vices and appetites of the Kaintocks; after three or four months on the river, the flatboat crews came ashore demanding women and liquor, and the underworld saw to it that there was always an ample supply of both commodities.

The gambling dives in an area known as the Swamp—where for twenty years no policeman had stepped—offered crooked faro and roulette games, and for the first fifty years New Orleans was under the American flag the area above Canal Street was even worse.

Not only did the flatboat men enjoy gambling, but it was a passion among the Creoles, and when the riverboat gamblers of the nineteenth century stepped ashore New Orleans was one big casino, even before the legislature, in 1832, legalized gambling (for an annual license fee of $7,500 per operator), and even after another legislature, in 1835, repealed legalized gambling and put a fine of $5,000 to $10,000 or one to five years in prison on violators.

By 1849, there were an estimated 500 gambling houses in the city, hiring 4,000 dealers and stickmen. Keno, an early version of Bingo, became the most popular of all games among the lower and middle class.

During the Civil War, when the city was being run by Union General Benjamin F. Butler, gambling was restored, in a not unusual manner (and one worthy of many modern police departments): General Butler simply issued a military order shutting down every gambling operation in the city. Then, the next day, he issued a private notice that permitted any gambler to reopen if he would pay a license fee to the provost marshal and accept the general's brother as a full but silent partner.

By 1864 the gamblers had removed such an enormous amount of money from soldiers and paymasters that the commander of the Department of the Gulf ordered the joints closed under strict military observation.

But armies and wars come and go, and gamblers sit and shuffle their decks, and in 1869 a new legislature legalized gambling and taxed each house $5,000 a year. This is the same legislature that set up the Louisiana State Lottery, which was to run for the next thirty-nine years, corrupting politicians and instilling a love for the lottery in the people of the state (a love that endures today, in God knows how many illegal lottery companies operating in Greater New Orleans), until 1907, when it was put out of business by the federal government under an 1895 law prohibiting the interstate transportation of lottery tickets.

The carpetbag legislature's legalization of gambling soon led to an overabundance of gambling houses, many of them dishonest, and it wasn't long before the city's "respectable" gamblers were back lobbying for a change. "They were successful," Asbury wrote, "and at the next session of the legislature the license system was abolished and gambling in New Orleans was once more against the law. The larger houses were closed for a few weeks while the police, with whom satisfactory arrangements had been made, were ridding the city of the undesirables; then they reopened." The ice money to the cops was often more than the 1869 law had had the gamblers paying in taxes.

The final scheme to find some way of controlling gambling and

rationalizing the odd counterpoint of gambling and antigambling attitudes was inaugurated in 1881 by Mayor Joseph Shakespeare. The
mayor wanted to license some of the eighty-three major gambling joints
in the city, but it was pointed out to him that an amendment to the state
constitution had made gambling illegal everywhere in the state and that
you can't license somebody to commit a crime. For a while the mayor
tried suppressing the gamblers, and finally called them in and told them
that if they would pay him a certain amount every month he would keep
the police from bothering them or demanding protection money. Sort of
police protection protection. The gamblers agreed, and in return promised to run honest games. The ice money was to go to municipal good
works, and did, until other politicians and city officials started getting
their hands on the money and licensing new gamblers—some crooked—
to come in and thereby fatten the kitty. In 1888 the Shakespeare plan
was scuttled, and the city returned to the hit-and-miss system of tolera-
tion-raid-prosecution-toleration cycles, where it sits today.

Prostitution laws were as subject to change through the years as
those concerning gambling, of course inevitably winding up in strict illegality, but with an interesting interlude much akin to the Shakespeare
plan for controlling gambling.

This was called Storyville, and it came to pass simply because prostitution had, by the late nineteenth century, overflowed the bounds of all
propriety. Ministers were speaking out from the pulpit, and the police
department, in 1891, wanted at least compulsory medical examination of
all the inhabitants of the brothels, which had grown elegant, expensive
and numerous over the years. (Half a century later the cops corrupted
the entire city health department, as we shall see. This was their first
gambit.) On January 26, 1897, the city council adopted an ordinance
introduced by Alderman Sidney Story, setting aside an area in the Vieux
Carré where prostitution would be permitted, but not legalized.

This area took in the Vieux Carré plus a part of the "American" section south of Canal Street, an area of the city that for the next fifty years
would abound with brothels—or at least call girls, when things were
tight.

Parts of the ordinance creating Storyville, named after the alderman, provided fines of from $5 to $25 and jail terms of up to thirty days,
and authorized—but did not require—the mayor to close any house
becoming "dangerous to the public morals." Storyville, in final form,
amounted to thirty-eight blocks in the old city occupied only by bordellos, saloons and cabarets, and lasted until the beginning of World War I;
and it is very likely that the police department, whose rank and file and

commanders were political appointees up until the 1940s, utilized the twenty-five-year span (some of which would have touched three generations of police) to systematize the collection process, and refine the methods of extracting graft from clients who could be shut down at the whim of a detective, since the regulating was delegated by the mayor to the police department.

Storyville did not die because New Orleans wanted it dead—it was no reform movement. The federal government stopped it, beginning in August, 1917, when Secretary of War Newton D. Baker issued an order forbidding open prostitution within five miles of a military base. Mayor Martin Behrman was informed that Storyville must be shut down, and he went to Washington to lodge a formal protest, and he twice had to be notified that unless he closed Storyville it would be closed by the military establishment. All things considered—including the size of the military payroll in New Orleans—the mayor, still under protest, got an ordinance through the common council to the effect that it would be illegal to operate any brothel or house of assignation within the city of New Orleans after November 12, 1917.

(The cyclic nature of military morality is illustrated in South Vietnam, where, in January, 1972, the United States Army decided to allow whores from Qui Nhon, who formerly had hustled the downtown saloon district, to entertain their G.I. customers right in the privacy of their own barracks. The army said the move was made "in the interests of keeping the peace within an increasingly disgruntled and demoralized Army.")

The population of New Orleans in 1910, at the height of Storyville's success, was 339,075. There were 175 whorehouses, all in Storyville, and about 800 prostitutes, possibly 10 percent of them part-timers. When they were put out of work, the Louisiana Federation of Women's Clubs named a committee to help the prostitutes get back on their feet, as it were, but got not a single application for aid. It was reliably reported at the time that by 1918 all 800—and more—had been assimilated into the general population and were doing better than ever.

Prostitution is still illegal in New Orleans, of course. And it is still lucrative for everybody concerned.

Aaron Kohn today is managing director of the Crime Commission of Greater New Orleans, an agency financed (woefully) by public contributions and whose consequently small staff is almost wholly occupied with input, having neither the time nor wherewithal to utilize the kind of data-processing equipment that is needed to bring his bulging filing cabinets into the sort of order, for retrieval, that would make them priceless

to law-enforcement officers not only in New Orleans but wherever organized crime touches base. As it is, Internal Revenue Service agents and
FBI men sit at the long library table in Kohn's office and pore through
the files for days at a time, and this is where some of the 1971 federal
bribery case against District Attorney Jim Garrison was put together by
members of a federal task force.

Kohn came to New Orleans in 1953 from Chicago, where he had
won wide notice for his work with the Chicago Crime Commission, and
since then his has been the loudest voice in southern Louisiana in the
dialogue on crime and corruption. In the spring of 1971, several weeks
after the final debris had been cleaned up from one of the city's least successful Mardi Gras, Aaron Kohn and I sat down to dinner in a German
restaurant above Canal Street, ate sauerbraten, and talked about New
Orleans and policemen; and before I talk specifically about what the
New Orleans Police Department was like in the early 1950s, Aaron
Kohn should tell you some of the things he has found there:

> I came here from Chicago [he said, long before we ordered],
> which had evolved the reputation of being the ultimate in organized
> crime and the ultimate protection of organized crime. In Chicago,
> my job was on behalf of the Big 9 Committee of the Chicago City
> Council ... which came into being by pressure, and in particular
> resulted from the murder of a ward boss up there.
>
> The First Ward [I asked]?
>
> No [he laughed]. It should have been.
>
> Anyway, there was a clearly defined segment of the community
> that was your ally in the fight, always: the press, the churches and
> various civic groups. There was a discernible fence in Chicago,
> people were on one side, even though you had the gray in between,
> but there were clearly discernible segments on your side in fighting
> organized crime and corruption. And there was a fairly discernible
> segment on the other side, that you were fighting. But by God it's
> been seventeen years and I still haven't been able to determine
> where the fence is here.
>
> Now, this is very significant. In New Orleans, this condition has
> existed for so long that corruption, organized crime, is not an enemy,
> but [instead] there've been intermarriages, social relationships,
> acceptability in business. Down here also you find not only the
> behind-the-scenes *influence* of organized crime on government, but
> you find organized crime *in* government. It's so acceptable you can
> actually put them into public office and keep them in public
> office....

I've always pondered the ancient systems here in New Orleans, the charm that gives it such warmth; and no matter how bad it is, it's a very attractive kind of a community. It isn't because of the things that are corrupt and entertaining—for example, the strip joints on Bourbon Street, which have been a part of the corrupting influence on the community, are no different from strips in Chicago, Baltimore or anyplace that tolerates them, Philadelphia. The people here are not offended by corruption—on the contrary, they're somewhat entertained and titillated by it. As long as it is entertaining corruption. [Former Governor] Jimmy Davis. Earl Long and his unpredictable flamboyance. Chep [the late Mayor deLesseps] Morrison. . . . The only time I've seen them reject . . . I've seen them reject *honest* public officials who do not have entertainment value —and they reject *corrupt* officials who are offensive.

Who commit repugnant crimes [I asked]?

Who are *offensive*. Now, for example, there's been a corrupt district attorney in Jefferson Parish for as long as I've been here, seventeen years. And he keeps getting reelected, an old man, he's never hurt anybody, he . . . well, for example, to give you an idea, he attended a speech that I made, as a guest of one of the participants, in the biggest Baptist Church here, there were hundreds of people there. And with him present I spoke about his corruption and the overall corruption in the New Orleans metropolitan area. After the speech was over, he walked up to the podium, stuck out his hand and said, "Thank you for the plug, Mr. Kohn." I had been talking about his alliances with the Marcellos, the impossibility of getting [charges brought through his office involving] crime—murder, rape, robbery—committed by members of organized crime, members of the Marcello organization. Horrible crimes.

Are they crimes against outcasts [I asked, recalling Bugsy Siegel's boast that "we only kill each other"]?

No, hell no! Rape against young girls, aggravated rape, rape of a feeble-minded sixteen-year-old girl, and then putting her into a house of prostitution, and I mean a girl out of a nice, middle class family, but feeble-minded, retarded. Burglaries of supermarkets.

It seems as if the community would draw the line there [I said].

No. He just favors the people, doesn't offend anybody, never does nasty things. . . . Now, William Coci succeeded . . . Jefferson Parish Sheriff [Frank] "King" Clancy. Sheriff King Clancy had been sheriff for twenty-seven years and amassed a fortune through graft, widespread gambling casinos *et al.* during his time. After our

crime commission came into being and we started identifying publicly some of the things that were being hid from the average
person, he lost, and he lost to a young lawyer with no past record in
politics at all, Bill Coci, who then came into office under a new form
of government in 1956, and then proceeded, in a very flamboyant
way, to try to acquire as much wealth in four years as King Clancy
had done in twenty-seven years.

Between the first and second primary—and he [Coci] was running on a reform ticket—he moved his headquarters into free
accommodations in a motel on Airline Highway owned by James
Caballa, an affiliate of Carlos Marcello, and meetings with Marcello
took place there. He got into office and in no time at all his chief
criminal deputy, who was his brother, Red Coci, and his two civil
deputies ... were calling on all of the bars and clubs in Jefferson
Parish with a payoff list telling them how much it was going to cost
them to operate card games, or dice tables, and telling them that
they were going to have to take—if they were not using them—the
machines of the Jefferson Music Company and the new coin-operated distributor owned by the same people who owned Jefferson
Music Company, the Marcellos ... that they were going to have to
take their machines or they couldn't run at all.

Now Coci started getting drunk all the time, appearing drunk
in public, would show up, as he did one time when I was on a panel
in Jefferson Parish, and I'd asked that he be invited because I was
going to talk about him, and he came in drunk and stood up in the
middle of the audience with a drunken denunciation of me; and to
be denounced is all right, but a drunken denunciation, this is offensive ...

How long ago was this [I asked]?

This was between 1956 and 1960. After I testified before the
McClellan Committee. Senator McClellan sent him an invitation by
telegram, since I had testified about his activities [in 1959], to
come appear before the committee. He sent a telegram which he
released to the press denouncing Senator McClellan and refusing to
go. Now, these things were not in the acceptable pattern. There was
even a recall movement started against him. Now, there were all
sorts of intimidations against those who were attempting to recall,
but they were able to get fairly close to the required percentage of
the number of registered voters before they abandoned it. They
needed something like fifteen thousand [signatures], they got something like eleven or twelve thousand. Keep in mind that this was in

an atmosphere of terror, and they didn't have that many people who'd put their name on the dotted line, so it was quite an achievement. Well, anyhow, he only lasted four years. Then an all-American boy was picked, schoolteacher, nice, clean-cut guy, he was put up for sheriff in 1960, and it took no time at all before they had him corrupted with whiskey and women. [He] was a mild, inoffensive guy, even at times when he was publicly under attack by the crime commission, and me, I'd find myself sitting at head tables at events with him, and he was always very polite. But he got more and more involved with the whores that were provided for him by the mob, and he didn't even run the office, pretty soon two people, his top command officials, who had been in there for a long time ... were both reporting to Carlos Marcello.

And in those next four years Carlos Marcello *was* the sheriff. Because the two command officials reported to the Cosa Nostra boss, not to their own boss because he was too busy with women and whiskey. Actually, one of the old-time whorehouse madams around here [who] had been forced to move out of New Orleans and was then in operation in Jefferson Parish, and with whom I had indirect communications, as she put it, [said] he was the cheapest sheriff we ever had to corrupt around here, all it took was whiskey and tail. "Tail" wasn't actually her expression. . . .

And then he was booted out in 1964, and that's when Sheriff Al Kronovich came in. He's straight.

· · · · ·

Our last chief of police here in New Orleans [Kohn continued, as we ordered brandy] was Joseph Gruson, who built a tremendous public relations image for himself. Considering the political balance of the community, and that has to include the attitudes of the general public which build relative stability into the standards of the public officials. The public officials can, for a short while, vary from the public effort, but never very long. The smart politicians eventually find the acceptable minimums and maximums of public tolerance, and function within them. Bingo, even though it's illegal, but no gambling casinos. That's what's going on right now in New Orleans. That's what Kronovich did over in Jefferson Parish. Bingo's not legal here, but it's operating. Because of the same little old sweet ladies who today are putting on pressure, where, in New York State? Demanding their right to Bingo.

This is why I advocate the removal of every step in the criminal justice system from political appointment, or from competitive election. I'm thoroughly convinced that the police officers and the police chief, the prosecutor and his staff, the courts and their staff, the correctional system, must be taken out of the line of pressures that emanate from the public demand for special privilege, highly accentuated in the case of organized crime, that make themselves now felt in the criminal justice process.

.   .   .   .   .

Wouldn't a cop just like to be—a cop [I asked]?

Oh yeah. I see this all the time. Look, you take when Francis Gravenberg came in as police superintendent and took over the state police organization, which had never had the freedom to enforce the law. And suddenly he says, "There's only one thing is our standard, and that's the law. And don't you pay attention to anything else. As long as you enforce the law I'm with you. If you don't, out you go." You started to suggest that when a man takes over a police department he takes over a bunch of bad apples, he's got a helluva problem with those bad apples staying bad. But I saw a bunch of those bad apples turn good, they were just waiting for an opportunity to be a good officer. And they loved him for it. Guys who would loaf on the job, fart around, try to stay out of trouble— when you work in a political atmosphere where some people are protected, you're never sure which ones are and which ones are not. All you can do is really stay away from them all. . . . If he can accept that [nonenforcement], he can accept a lot of other things, something happens to his character, he can make all kinds of private side deals. . . .

I started to tell you that for a long time I was puzzled by the community's charm, which reflects certain values on the part of the people, in contrast to a very low code of ethics. And not until during a period of workshops I worked on and coordinated on youth problems in the area, back in 1966, one of the panelists I invited was a sociologist from Loyola University, and from his comments suddenly emerged the answer to my puzzle:

"You'll never understand New Orleans if you try to measure it in terms of other American cities. New Orleans only becomes understandable when you think of it as a Mediterranean city."

By God, he was right. If you tried to compare the political atmosphere of this city with that of Italy, Greece, the Arabic countries, their acceptance of corruption, their acceptance of the idea that people with power have the right to use it in any way they want to, then you understand southern Louisiana—and New Orleans.

Aaron Kohn came to New Orleans in 1953, when the city found itself in trouble, policewise. Mayor Morrison, a popular figure who was getting ready to serve out his two terms as mayor (Kohn says he was so popular he could have been mayor for life except that two terms were the legal limit) and was getting ready to run for governor, had lost, in 1949, probably the only honest police administrator in the state up to that time, Colonel Adair Watters. Morrison replaced Watters with Joseph Scheuering, under whose guidance over the next five years the morale of the New Orleans Police Department would be almost totally shattered.

Morrison could have soared into the governor's mansion if two things had not occurred. The first was the brutal murder of a tourist in the French Quarter, which prompted an outcry from even the "Mediterranean" population of New Orleans so that Morrison was forced to set up the Citizens' Commission for the Vieux Carre, one of those committees which in the long run is supposed to make sure it doesn't happen again, like the commissions that investigate nursing-home fires.

The second was our old friend from Utica, the American Social Hygiene Association, which had found prostitution policed and venereal disease controlled in a "satisfactory" manner during Watters' tenure between 1946 and 1949, but which in 1952, found conditions "blatant," concluding that somebody had to be getting paid off or it couldn't be going on the way it was.

Several private organizations in New Orleans, including the Association of Former FBI Agents, began talking with Aaron Kohn in Chicago. Kohn, also a former FBI man, agreed to come down on one condition— that the body he was to head be protected from political influence by a buffer citizens' group set up to field intrusions, take the heat and generally see that the commission did not wind up with two or three vice cops "on loan" from the police department as investigators.

On April 24, 1953, the New Orleans Commission Council, which is what they call the city council, created what came to be known as the Special Citizens' Investigating Commission, appropriated $76,000 for its work and invested it "with authority, power and duty to investigate the police department of the City of New Orleans, to make reports and recommendations, and in the discharge of these duties the committee was authorized and directed to investigate and inquire into the affairs of the police department, investigate the functions, transactions and administration and management of the department to the extent that it may be necessary or desirable."

The enabling ordinance appointed three commissioners: Dudley C. Foley, Jr., who had been nominated by the ex-FBI agents' group; George C. Stohlman, executive general agent for one of the large railroads, nominated by the crime commission; and Leon D. Hubert, Jr., professor of criminal law at Tulane University, who had been nominated by the Bureau of Governmental Research, of which he was a member. Hubert's name does not appear on the final report, however, as the result of a strange political arabesque I'll mention later. He was replaced, halfway through the investigation, by Philip Gensler.

The Special Citizens' Investigating Commission didn't last very long. While it lasted it did some intensive, solid work that eventually resulted in the incarceration of—Aaron Kohn? But that's getting ahead of the story.

The reasons cited for the creation of the commission were sixfold:

1. Lack of community confidence in the integrity and efficiency of the police department.

2. Generally observed violations of the law, accompanied by an apparent lack of enforcement by the police department.

3. Frustration of the grand jury, law-enforcement officials and the Mayor's Special Citizens' Commission for the Vieux Carré in their attempt to obtain the facts with the cooperation of the police department.

4. Charges of rape, theft, bribery and safe burglary allegedly committed by police officers.

5. Statements that the police department is underpaid and undermanned.

6. The need for a nonpolitical, unbiased and thorough investigation of the police department, with results thereof to be made available for appropriate action by the commission council, the grand jury and the community as a whole.

Kohn's investigators hit the streets, both in overt operations and as undercover men and women hanging around bars, gambling joints and, in some cases, brothels. Telephone lines were manned around the clock so that citizens, either identifying themselves or anonymously, could call in tips to be checked out further, and while some of the statements in the multivolume final report read more like gossip and scuttlebutt than serious charges, the SCIC went to great lengths to secure independent corroboration of every statement therein, discarding allegations which could not be proved to the satisfaction of the commission. From the start, the cops bugged the commission telephones, and it is ironic that one of the officers assigned to monitoring the phones on one shift became one of Kohn's most important sources of information. The cop got into the habit of calling (while off duty) to raise hell with Kohn and accuse him of undermining police department morale, and it wasn't long before Kohn recognized that he was talking to a cop; and it wasn't much longer, from the things to which the cop referred, that Kohn realized that the man had been monitoring commission calls. Kohn worked with him, talking with him the way you talk to a potential suicide, insisting that it would be a wonderful thing if the honest cops on the force were allowed to clean their own house or at least have a part in the sweeping process, and finally convinced him that the commission's and the cops' goals were identical. From that moment on the officer was a double agent, and his identity, to this day, has not been revealed. Kohn says he will never tell.

The commission broke down its investigation into categories, including prostitution, gambling, bribery and bars and clubs, and further broke it down by applying each category to each of the city's six police districts, formerly precincts. During the six-month life span of the investigation, great headway was made only in activities of the First District, which includes the French Quarter, where an ordinary citizen literally could trip over sin and corruption during a casual daylight stroll, and in the Fifth District, which included the sprawling areas east of the heart of the city and which abuts St. Bernard Parish, one of the three counties, with Orleans and Jefferson, making up Greater New Orleans.

The investigation of the Fifth District approached the ideal in extent and intensity, and reflected what might have been accomplished if the commission had been allowed to proceed with its task. From hundreds of tips and hundreds of man-days of personal surveillance and observation, corporate records and legal work, the commission was able to put witnesses on the stand, under oath, and question them about activities the commission already knew to be extant, paving the way for perjury indictments or outright confessions—which, in one case, actually happened, only far too late to do any good. The only real shakeup in the police department occurred there in the Fifth District, which was not even considered among the top three districts in terms of graft by the men on the force. But it was while the Fifth District testimony was being taken that several high-ranking police officers and a group of citizens got together in a series of late-night meetings to find somebody who would be willing to sign a petition seeking an injunction against the hearings, and they finally came up with Alois Hirt, father of the famous trumpet player and a former policeman who, according to information that had already come to the commission, had served as a bagman while a member of the force. Hirt's petition was successful in getting the hearings stopped. Mayor Morrison promised Aaron Kohn that he would see to it that the commission was given the green light again "after the elections," but of course no such thing ever came to pass.

During the investigation, the commission found some rather interesting phenomena, not the least of which was that the entire trouble with the New Orleans Police Department stemmed from the enforcement or nonenforcement of laws pertaining to bars and clubs, prostitution, gambling, all the vices. In a summary, the commission reported:

> The police also share in at least one of the apparent objectives, the monetary profits of vice and crime. Statistically, our investigators uncovered information or evidence available to the police department and the mayor [concerning] approximately three hundred sixty bars and clubs. It is pertinent to observe that public records reflect that federal gambling stamps have been issued for seventy-eight of these establishments. In some of the latter, investigators actually observed gambling, sometimes actually in the presence of passive or participating police.

At this time in history, enter "Q documents," known officially as Q-1, Q-2, Q-3 and Q-4, which got the Gold Dust Twins indicted and which, indirectly, sent Aaron Kohn to jail.

The bag in the Fifth District was traveling a long and circuitous route, finally winding up in little brown envelopes, one for each policeman in the district, with the pickup of the money from gambling joints and bars being made generally on Friday, then counted and sorted during the afternoon and evening, to be passed out in envelopes similar to those in which the cops got their regular paychecks. They called it "the Big Payroll," and it was made up in the captain's office in the Fifth District station house. (The other districts had their own payrolls, the First, Second and Sixth considered by the cops to be the fattest.)

By this time the honest cops—and some not so honest—were beginning to come forward, just a little, having some confidence—just a little —in Kohn's committee. A group of twelve present and former members of the department got together around a tape recorder and, among other interesting facts, named the bagmen in each of the six districts.

One private session (after public hearings had been enjoined) with a detective who had been a member of the police force for fifteen years, went like this:

Q. Was there ever a period in the fifteen years you were on the force where something had been done, some changes been made? I refer specifically to the time when Adair Watters was superintendent of police.

A. All I know is when Adair Watters was superintendent of police he got no foolishness from the rank and file of the police department. They wouldn't dare tell you a word about anything. I know that during that time, from my own knowledge, several of the men had to go the way I had been going all along: making loans, robbing Peter to pay Paul, loans, going into debt. They went into debt at the time Colonel Watters come into office.

Q. Under Watters there seemed to be a drop in income for a lot of the officers?

A. That is right. Quite a few of them went into debt.

Q. Men who seemed . . .

A. Men who always seemed to have income.

Q. Do you recall if after Superintendent Watters went out of office these men started to clear up their debts pretty fast?

A. I would go so far as to say that when Watters left as superintendent of police it looked like these same people started getting back on their feet.

Q. Can you mention any specific people who have that pattern?

A. One of them was Albert W., I happened to be around. He was Lieutenant W. I know he was pretty well fixed. He was in the hole and he comes right back, buying a new car and has no more debts. You notice these things, you can't help but notice them.

[Another officer, who had been on the force since 1947, the second year of the Watters interregnum, had been a member of the headquarters vice squad. He was asked if he thought illegal money being distributed in an organized manner in the police department was a fiction.]

A. No, I don't believe it was a fiction.

Q. Do you think it is happening?

A. I guess it has happened, yes.

Q. Do you think it is happening right now?

A. I don't know, I don't think it is happening right now.

. . . . .

Q. Have you ever been informed by other men with whom you have worked about the distribution of graft money in the districts?

A. Well, the closest they ever came to alluding to that was—as I say—we made the raids in the Fifth, and some of the men expressed delight. "That's good—maybe these people will deal straight with us."

· · · · ·

Q. Weren't the handbooks operating so openly that all you had to do was drive by and hear the loudspeakers on the street?

A. In this instance, St. Bernard and Tonti, I saw that from the street.

Q. Do you remember the name of the bookie operating there?

A. I put one guy in jail. I think they said he ran the place or something. He wanted to talk to me, you know?

Q. Yes?

A. Yes. I said, "Talking, like if we will make out?" I think he was trying to discuss it with me. He told me—he asked me, "Could we speak in private?" and I asked him were these his friends and he said yes, and I said, "Well, this is my partner, and we don't have any secrets, so if you don't have any secrets from your partners we can talk whatever you want right here." And he said, "I just want you to understand that I take care of the beat man." I said, "They are pretty big. They can take care of themselves." He became very tolerant with me, I guess he thought I was stupid. "You don't understand," he said. "I pay off." And I said, "Well, you should pay off, if you owe anybody any money you should pay them." So he got kind of perturbed. "I am trying to explain to you that I'm paying for protection." He was disgusted, then. He said, "Where are you from?" [I said:] "From New Orleans." "Well, where is Captain DeLatte at?" "I don't give a damn," I said. He said, "This man is a policeman's brother." I said, "Good, then you won't have any trouble getting out of jail."

· · · · ·

[During the taping session with the dozen cops and former cops, the extent of the traveling bag was examined:]

Q. In the districts, there was a pool set up from the captain down?

A. Yes.

Q. That pool consisted of money collected from the handbooks and lotteries?

A. Everything that happened to be in that district. Handbooks, lottery, card games.

Q. Prostitution?

A. Prostitution. Everything in the world that was illegal was all put into the pool.

Q. Who collected the money in these districts, the man called the pickup man?

A. He collected the bulk of it, and the other men picked it up.

Q. Who would assist those men? Who would arrange it?

A. That would be the bagmen.

Q. Do you think a man would have a job of seeing every place that was contacted every week?

A. Yes.

Q. He would be assigned to make the pickups?

A. John Grosche used a different system. Johnny Grosche used to rent a room at the Jung Hotel.

Q. When he was chief of detectives?

A. Yes sir, and they would bring it up to him.

Q. Do you remember what the room number was?

A. No.

Q. Would he himself come there and get it or would he have somebody else do it for him?

A. I understand he was there. He and Lieutenant S. Then he had strongarm men. Then he had Lieutenant R. and Lieutenant M., those were his ass kissers.

Q. Who were the hammer men in town? The ones who could try to sneak without paying off?

A. When do you mean, now?

Q. Well, if you know of any now.

A. There's not many who would do that. Chickenshits would do it, but not the guys well known in the gambling circles. They will not cheat. They will always try to pay somebody.

Q. Well, let's say, for example, a lottery company was paying off for twenty stations [sales outlets] in a district and some more stations opened up. Who would have to make sure that the money was being collected for those stations?

A. The only thing I can tell you is what I heard about it, and that is . . . the beat man, as he was going on his beat.

Q. Who would he report to?

A. Report to the bagman.

Q. There's a new lottery shop that opens up, he reports to the bagman?

A. That is right.

Q. Never to the captain?

A. No.

Q. Always to the bagman?

A. That is right.

Q. Does that mean every man would have to know who the bagman was?

A. Sure.

Q. Everybody working in the district would know who the bagman was?

A. Sure. Everytime a man wanted to open up he would go to the beat man and say, "I want to open up," and he would say, "I will send somebody over." In those days, you had two men detailed in plainclothes.

Q. They were the bagmen?

A. They were usually the bagmen.

Q. Who cut out that racket, Watters?

A. Yes. Morrison did. Morrison and Watters.

Q. It was known to everybody that plainclothesmen were the bagmen?

A. Yeah, sure. Now every man in every precinct knows who the bagman is.

Q. Why would he have to know?

A. It's common talk. When you come in on the first day you want to know "who's got the money." You find out who is holding the money for that particular watch. Let's say the preceding watch picked up the money. When they go off watch everybody wouldn't be there. When they go off they turn the money over to him and say, "That's for your platoon."

Q. Suppose you had to go off in a squad car?

A. He would give it to anybody who comes in.

Q. Would they give it to the desk sergeant usually, since he was there?

A. No. It's a funny thing, but no, they never did.

Q. They never did?

A. Not when I was in the Third District. That's the only district I spent any time in. In the Seventh Precinct, I never got any envelopes in those days.

Q. You never got any?

A. No indeed. They were scared to death of us.

Q. Why were they scared to death of you?

A. Because we were young men.

Q. They didn't know whether they could trust you?

A. That's right. There was a lot of talk about our being close to Watters. There was an old sergeant who used to plead and beg with us not to hurt him, but he didn't know what he was talking about.

Q. Is he still there?

A. No, he's up at Tulane University now, as a guard ... He would get drunk, believe me, he would be sobbing with tears in his eyes.

The collectors in the Fifth District were Lieutenant Louis G. Hill and Sergeant Clifford Reuther. Hill had been on the police force since 1929 and had been a lieutenant since 1942, and was promoted to captain the week Superintendent Scheuering took over from Watters, only to be demoted again three days later because, while his street and political friends were powerful, times had changed, and he simply had not passed the civil service examination for captain. By the time Hill got around to appearing before the citizens' committee he had been twenty-three years on the force—and had spent all twenty-three years right there in the Fifth District, except that he had been transferred to the Third in May, 1952, as the heat came on. He and Reuther rode together in the same car as partners, a virtually unheard-of practice for a lieutenant and a sergeant, and at one point, in a public interrogation, Aaron Kohn asked Hill why the two men were in plainclothes.

"During those days," Hill said, "we didn't have a detective force that they have today and the complaints came in from the station and wherever they had need for plainclothesmen, we were given that work the same as the detectives of today."

Kohn had his own version: "As a matter of fact, lieutenant, the reason that you and Sergeant Reuther were working together and in plainclothes was because it was less embarrassing to the police department at that time to be able to make the collections from various gamblers and slot machine operators, isn't that true?"

Hill denied this, of course, as he denied all allegations at that hearing, but as a matter of fact his personal income while he was collecting for the Fifth and serving as half of a two-man vice squad was something around $500 a month, with proportionately lower amounts going to almost every other cop in the district, and this was at a time when a lieutenant's salary was running under $500 a month. Hill had outlasted a dozen captains, most of whom also got their shares from him, and ran the district with something less than an iron hand. A handbook, complete with blaring loudspeakers calling the races, ran at full capacity directly across the street from the station house. The Cadillac Bar, not a hundred yards away from the precinct house, featured B-girls and a hot-seat poker game where the suckers would be fleeced and tossed into the street, and had assigned to it a uniformed policeman from the Fifth District who got $10 extra a night to make sure nobody busted up the place. At one point there were 150 federal gambling stamps outstanding in the Fifth District alone, but the only real gambling arrests ever made in the district were flying excursions out of headquarters, by the vice squad (even then made through motives of spite or revenge, rather than law enforcement); and more than thirty major lottery companies with 500 or more stations made their home base right there in the Fifth District. One notorious saloon, the Silver Star, where they didn't have television but customers could watch the fights every night anyway, was paying $20 a week for protection in 1950, a figure that was cut in half the following year as it became increasingly obvious that the New Orleans Police Department wouldn't be able to protect it much longer, and it was finally raided and shut down by the Louisiana State Police in 1951. At one point, during May, 1949, shortly after his three-day tour as a captain, Hill was the part owner of a handbook at Spain and Roman streets. Another joint where a handbook was running, Jack's Stroll Inn at 1001 Elysian Fields, was paying $20 a week and getting its money's worth using a technique really refined in old Chicago. If a raid was scheduled on Jack's Stroll Inn, the operators would get a telephone warning and move the entire operation across the street to 1012 Elysian Fields, and never miss a race.

The walls really started crumbling on Hill and Reuther on August 31, 1953, during the SCIC investigation, when a policeman, in a midnight rendezvous with Aaron Kohn, turned over four documents which had been taken from the desk of Captain Edward F. Hermann, commander of the Fifth District, in the summer of 1951. The documents were lists of lotteries, handbooks and bars and the amounts they were paying to the police, with telephone numbers to call in the event a raid was planned or discovered in the planning stages at headquarters. Handwritten annotations were fairly well established as having been made by the Gold Dust Twins (Hill and Reuther), and one handwritten set of calculations placed the total bag to be divided among the officers and men of the district each week at $1,745. These documents were used as the basis for intensive investigation of the Fifth District, and formed the nucleus of the case against Hill and Reuther after they were indicted in 1954.

They also led to the dismissal of charges against the Gold Dust Twins, and to the imprisonment of Aaron Kohn.

Now, at the beginning of the investigation, Kohn had come to an agreement with the three-man committee, including its chairman, Leon Hubert, that whenever the committee could get information of value by granting immunity from prosecution, that immunity would be granted, and in writing. And during the negotiations with the officer who turned over the Q documents (so called because of their designation as evidence) he not only received immunity, but Kohn agreed to the single condition imposed by the cop: that his identity not be revealed until such time as the police department's ruling triumvirate—Superintendent Scheuering; Joseph DePaoli, the director of traffic, and assistant superintendent Milton Durel—were no longer in positions of power in the department. (DePaoli was supposed to be supervising traffic, Kohn was to say in 1971, "but nobody was supervising traffic—he was supervising handbook graft collecting.")

In October, 1953, two months after the documents were received, Hubert told Kohn and his two committee co-members that he was resigning to run for district attorney on Mayor Morrison's ticket, hoping to use that office as a stepping-stone to what he really wanted, ultimate election as criminal court judge.

Mayor Morrison was the dominant political power, meaning that if you were going to run the district attorney's office you were going to run it the way Mayor Morrison wanted it run; but at any rate, Morrison was reelected mayor and Hubert was elected district attorney, taking office in May—just a week after the SCIC had completed its report on its six-month investigation. (That report, incidentally, was furnished to every city official when it was released in April, 1954. Today only one copy exists, and that one is in the offices of the New Orleans Crime Commission.)

It fell to Hubert to follow through with the results of the investigation, and one of his first acts after taking office was to appoint Malcolm V. O'Hara, a former law student of his, as an assistant. About that appointment, Kohn was to say, in 1971:

> Now that appointment of O'Hara is in complete conflict with the findings of our report. In that report is extensive detail about the operation of the Mills [family] of the gambling syndicate, dominated the gambling at that time, with direct evidence of corruption. Malcolm V. O'Hara is a very close friend of the Mills. His brother is married to the daughter of one of them. His father, William O'Hara, was a criminal district court judge. The O'Haras and the Millses are a part of the same political structure, also supporters of Chep Morrison.

He [Hubert] then assigned Malcolm O'Hara as the advisor to the grand jury, and nothing happened, no witnesses were called. So then I go to see Malcolm O'Hara in the D.A.'s office, and I said "Malcolm, how could you possibly give guidance to the grand jury? Aren't you very close to the Millses?"—and I'm talking about the principals now, Frank Mills, Henry Mills, Arthur Mills—and he said, "Sure, I'm with them a couple of times a week, we're best friends, I like them." So I asked him to recuse himself, and he said no. So then I go to Leon Hubert, said I don't know whether you know it or not, about this relationship, and he said Malcolm had told him all about that. He said he had total faith in Malcolm's integrity.

(A decade later, the eight criminal court judges of Orleans Parish hauled District Attorney Jim Garrison into court for saying that racketeers and vice figures had "influenced" the judges. One of the judges, Malcolm V. O'Hara, took the stand and denied that he had ever been influenced by racketeers or anyone else to quit approving expenditures for Garrison's raiding in the French Quarter, which is how the whole flap started. O'Hara and the seven other judges convicted Garrison and fined him $1,000 or four months in jail, and it took the United States Supreme Court to knock that one down.)

Kohn finally asked permission to go before the grand jury himself, and was allowed to do so, and he told the jury that Hubert and O'Hara had in their possession a report that could provide the basis for calling as many as 2,000 witnesses, including every member of the New Orleans Police Department, and when Kohn was finished with his rather vehement explication it was Hubert who said that he was sorry, but no witnesses of any sort could be called until Kohn revealed to the grand jury the name of the officer who had turned over the Q documents.

The jury demanded that I produce the name of this police officer, [said] that I lied to them, that they can't do anything, there's nobody else they can call, until they first have that witness. I'd bring in boxes of documents showing them how you don't need this man, here's all this other information, these are the places where the pickups are being made, call in the employees of these places, call in the cops assigned to these squad cars which were instructed to pick up. And incidentally, I had developed some cops who were willing to come in and testify that they were instructed to go out and pick up graft. They wouldn't call them.

What they did was indict Kohn for contempt, a charge thrown out by a judge in a different court. But the next grand jury, a few months later, cited him again for the same thing, and this time he did three days behind bars.

In the meantime, the Gold Dust Twins were moving toward some sort of reckoning. Indicted by a previous grand jury, which used the SCIC's fairly extensive report on the Fifth District plus the Q documents, and which had showed signs of trying to run away from the district attorney, Lieutenant Hill and Sergeant Reuther were tried in criminal court in 1955 on charges of conspiracy to commit bribery.

Before a five-man jury and Judge Neils F. Hertz, fourteen persons testified that handbook operations were indeed conducted at places listed on one of the documents, two handwriting experts identified the handwriting on the Q documents as being that of one or the other of the two men; the defense charged that the state's case rested on circumstantial evidence and demanded that the mystery witness who gave Kohn the documents come forward and face the two defendants, and Judge Hertz agreed and told Aaron Kohn to produce the witness. Kohn stood firm, and on Friday, August 5, 1955, Judge Hertz sentenced Kohn to ten days in the pokey plus a $100 fine for contempt of court.

The next day, while Kohn was swabbing out his cell in Parish Prison, the jury deliberated an hour and forty-five minutes and returned a verdict of not guilty for Reuther and Hill.

In a prepared statement to the jury, District Attorney Hubert said:

No society can rise above the level of its own law enforcement agency. If there is corruption in public office the laws mean nothing. A public official who is a grafter no longer serves the public. His masters are those who pay him. Once he is corrupted he can no longer do his duty to the public, because those who have paid him have a strangle hold on his will. Thus the public pays millions of dollars of tax money for the services of a good police force and is outbid by the handbook and lottery operators. If the police fail, then all else fails, for how can the district attorney, the grand jury, the court do their duty? Honest and incorruptible police are therefore the keystone of all law enforcement. What you gentlemen do from this moment until you return with your verdict will set the standard of police conduct in this city from this day on.

By God, he might have been right.

Leon Hubert never did get his judgeship, but was later to become one of the regional counsel who worked on the Warren Commission report. Malcolm O'Hara, of course, became a criminal district court judge, and was still one in 1971. Lieutenant Hill retired from the police department on August 12, 1955, five days after his acquittal, and twenty-six years and five months after he joined the force, and several years before his death. Sergeant Reuther, a few months after his acquittal, appeared before the police bureau of investigations, an internal organization which by then had gotten control of the probe and was keeping it all in the family, and spilled his guts, testifying that he was indeed responsible for the collection of graft in the Fifth District, naming several captains who had been part of the Big Payroll. It is worthy to note that nothing he said after his acquittal could be used against him, and on November 5, 1957, an old perjury charge against him was dropped by District Attorney Hubert because of Reuther's cooperation before the police board. Earlier that year, he made a small headline in the *Times-Picayune* after an incident in St. Bernard Parish. In part, the story read this way:

> Reuther said a St. Bernard deputy held him while another man slugged him. Reuther has told of graft activities in the Fifth District, which adjoins St. Bernard Parish. It is said a number of gamblers from whom Reuther has been quoted to have collected graft in connection with bookmakers and lottery operations are working out of St. Bernard Parish. Reuther's testimony before the city Civil Service Commission of collecting graft from various gamblers in the Fifth District touched off the recent shakeup in the top echelon in the police department. Reuther, now an insurance agent, said today's attack occurred without warning. He said he went into Buster's Bar in Arabi, and was having a drink when the owner of the place "came over and grabbed me by the shoulder." Then they beat him up.

The shakeup referred to involved a couple dozen captains, sergeants and lieutenants, some of whom were indicted for public bribery or malfeasance, some of whom were dismissed. Because the statute of limitations was rapidly expiring, no one ever came to trial, and many of those who were fired were reinstated long enough to get their retirement papers in, and that was that, except that the Internal Revenue Service, which got one of the copies of the Kohn report, managed to make a case against one or two captains on income-tax evasion.

And except for Sergeant Robert Brown, the name of the officer the judges and district attorney had been so anxious to hear—the one who supplied the Q documents to Kohn. The way that turned out, Kohn was able, ultimately, to force out the three top men in the police department, Scheuering, Durel and DePaoli (he did it through a long letter, made public, to the mayor, charging all sorts of bribery and malfeasance), and the three were allowed to resign, with glowing letters of thanks and recognition from the mayor; and once they were gone, the condition imposed by Sergeant Brown was eliminated, and Kohn revealed Brown's identity, and, of course, nobody was interested any longer, and Brown was never called by any official body for any questions.

Instead, he was fired for drinking on the job.

Drinking on the job had never much bothered the New Orleans cops before, particularly the vice cops in the French Quarter, where the police routinely mixed business and booze, business and broads, and arranged, among other divertissements, a fishing trip for visiting out-of-town lawmen complete with an entourage of girls out of Cody Morris' whorehouse.

In its summary on prostitution, the special citizens' commission pulled together a lot of what it found to be wrong with the vice squad, which then had the mandate of keeping the lid on activities in the Vieux Carré. A portion of that 1954 report reads like this:

> We found evidence of a well organized system within the New Orleans Police Department for the extortion of money and other things of value to protect and give profitable continuity to commercial gambling. It has become equally apparent that organized prostitution, though curtailed by effective police work between 1946 and 1949, has been permitted to return. . . .
>
> Among other contributions of [the 1950 Citizens' Committee for the Vieux Carré] was a new ordinance to express municipal laws against prostitution. This law was enacted in 1950 . . . but [is] not being enforced. One of the major contributions of the new ordinance was provision for mandatory jail sentences for repeated offenders. The records on prostitution for a seven-month period in 1953, analyzed by the committee staff, showed that in most instances police were charging offenders with obsolete ordinances which did not provide for such punishment. . . .
>
> We conclude that the New Orleans police not only do not enforce laws against prostitution, but they apparently violate them. The statutes of Louisiana define pandering in one of its forms as "receiving or accepting by a male, as support or maintenance, anything of value which is known to be from the earnings of any female engaged in prostitution." From evidence and allegations it appears that some New Orleans police share in the earnings of commercial-

ized prostitution. Sworn testimony reveals that in more than one instance certain police have made arrangements for prostitutes to be employed in bawdy houses, and fraternized in the brothels. . . . It has also been found that some police officers were recipients of extremely expensive gifts.

There is a substantial amount of evidence to indicate that the process of enforcing the laws against prostitution has [involved] a number of public officials and employees who, to protect the law violator while creating the illusion of police activity, for the record and for the press, engaged in the preparation of false police reports, and committed one or more of the following crimes: perjury, pandering, bribery, extortion, malfeasance. Testimony in the private hearings and statements by present and former New Orleans policemen, as well as other allegations, establish the existence of token or routine raids and arrests by police department personnel, involving especially the Vice Squad, now known as the Special Headquarters and Narcotics Squad. . . .

· · · · ·

The committee's investigation has provided evidence that there is collusion between prostitution and the police, and in order to provide statistics of police activity, and to pacify the public they conduct token raids, varying in number with the pulse of the community attitude. Representatives of the prostitution establishment are arrested and released and permitted to return to work, and frequently they are fined, and back to work they go. A minor inconvenience and a minor interruption written off as a normal operation complication.

The kind of climate this propagated in New Orleans is illustrated in a list of irregularities the committee cited under a chapter on police organization, adding that "far too many of the New Orleans police personnel are guilty of one or more." The list is revealing—there is nothing on it that would really upset an Archie Bunker, if he stopped to think about it. It includes:

● Theft of money and other things of value from prisoners.

● Cruel treatment imposed upon prisoners, especially Negroes.

● Rolling of drunks.

● Acceptance of money and other things of value from persons against whom they are sworn to enforce the law.

● Observing violations of the law and failing to take action against them or report them.

- Participation in violations of the gambling laws.
- Lounging in or visiting houses of ill repute.
- Sharing in the proceeds of prostitution.
- Consorting with and concealing knowledge of the illicit activities of persons continuously engaged in violations of the law.
- Open and friendly association between police supervisory officials and known law violators, to the detriment of the morale of officers of lower rank.
- Frequenting of establishments where there is gambling and drinking and/or solicitation for prostitution.
- Drinking of alcoholic beverages while on duty.
- Public intoxication.
- Public bribery and extortion.
- Intimidation of persons who attempt to exercise rights to criticize police or their employees.
- False testimony and perjury.
- Illegal seach and procedure without warrants.
- Abuse of authority.
- Token or routine raids.
- Failure to observe rules of the department.
- Sexual relations with female prisoners.

The vice squad during this time was being alternately commanded by Captain Frank Italiano, Major William McNamara and Captain Joseph Guillot, with each of the officers having his own bagman, generally his chauffeur. Caller after caller told the citizens' committee about activities of the three men, and much came out in open testimony, although none of the three was ever convicted, even though all three, along with fifteen other high-ranking cops, were dismissed from the force (and, later, reinstated, allowed to resign and collect retirement).

Besides the bars and brothels, the vice squad had another little deal going. In its final report in 1954, the citizens' committee reported on it this way:

> Several present and former members of the New Orleans Police Department told of rackets engaged in by members of the [Vice] Squad and other special details assigned to the Fairgrounds Race Track during the racing season, ostensibly for the purpose of controlling unlawful activities . . . especially in connection with the 1951 and 1952 racing seasons, when the six to eight members of the Squad worked alternate days, being paid at the rate of ten dollars per man by the track authorities. However, it was alleged that with the money collected by the Squad from bookies both inside and out-

side of the race track, the actual income of the men would vary from fifty to ninety dollars per week per man. . . .

It was alleged that the special detail was alternately under the control of Major William McNamara and Captain Frank Italiano, although Major McNamara appeared to be preferred by the track authorities. . . .

Sergeant Peter Gervais was in charge of the men from the [Vice] Squad. It was said that five or six of the major bookies were frequenters of the Fairgrounds Race Track during the season and were tolerated by police officers in exchange for a payoff of fifteen dollars per race, or one hundred dollars per day from each. It was further alleged that this total of six hundred to seven hundred twenty dollars a day was divided among the men in charge, either Major McNamara or Captain Italiano . . . and . . . others. In addition, handbooks operating in bars near the race track were said to be making payments to the special detail squad to buy them off their duty of closing up such bookies. It was said in effect that police assigned to the detail were collecting money from the track authorities to repress such operations and were at the same time collecting money from the handbook operators to permit them to operate. . . .

There is no better way to get a picture of the New Orleans, particularly the French Quarter, of the late 1940s and early 1950s, than through the eyes of one who lived there. Why Doris Gellman chose to present herself to testify before the citizens' committee in 1953 is a mystery, except that maybe she was sick and tired of the whole thing. Committee staffers sorted and sifted through everything she told them, and used only that part of her exposé that could be corroborated independently.

Miss Gellman appeared twice as a witness during public hearings conducted by the citizens' committee before the commission council, on December 30, 1953, and January 5, 1954, acknowledging that she had been a prostitute and had worked for a brothel operator named Cody Morris at 809-11 Baronne Street, the Somerset Hotel and other locations. The Baronne Street operation had been called to the attention of the superintendent of police several times since 1949, and the records show that the place was hit by the cops five times between January 1 and December 1, 1950.

In reproducing parts of Miss Gellman's testimony I am eliminating much that is repetitive or serves only to establish times and dates for the record. What emerges, I think, is the true, shabby flavor of the French Quarter.

Q. You say you have been to several other places for Cody Morris?

A. To the Waltham Hotel on Canal Street. I worked out there on call.

Q. You say that was for Cody Morris?

A. Yes. In fact, all the houses use the Waltham Hotel.

Q. What years did you work for Cody Morris, do you recall?

A. Yes, I believe it was 1945 and 1946. I worked for Cody Morris off and on. When the money wasn't good at Cody's I would go over to Walter's [Walter Noto]. If the money wasn't good at Walter's I would go over to Norma's [Norma Wallace], or either go to Bertha Anderson's. I would go wherever they had the most money.

(The Norma Wallace mentioned was a notorious madam, who became good friends with Aaron Kohn during the investigation. Afterward, when she moved out of the city and left the brothel business, she opened a restaurant up the river and sent a message to Kohn: "If I'd known how much simpler it is to sell meat rather than lease it I would have changed businesses a long time ago.")

Q. How many girls, incidentally, were working on call?

A. We always carried between nine, ten, eleven. We never carried under nine girls. We always had the demand. We had the greater amount of the cab trade. We had plenty of cab business and we had to take plenty of business or the cab drivers would go to other houses, and the operators didn't like that.

Q. We will go back to the cab operators.

A. The reason I say the cab operation [is] because Cody, Walter and Norma Wallace, that is all cab houses.

Q. With Cody, for example, he maintained a set of books?

A. Right.

Q. In which he kept a record of every date?

A. Right.

Q. So every single date that a girl has there is a record maintained showing how much the girl got?

A. Right, if it was a cab date, put yellow in his number, or if they knew him by name, like Big Nose Joe Nola, that is the driver, they would put Big Nose Nola, and we would know who it was. In other words, if it was his date, if he brought the date to the house you would mark in the books, or Miss Ione [Cody Morris' wife] would mark him down, or either Betty Ott.

Q. This is in Cody Morris' house?

A. Yes. Or either if Henry Krause was up there. He used to run a bar across the street and used to come up, Henry or Jelley Del Rio, Robert.

Q. Did you say Jelley Del Rio?

A. Yes. Robert Del Rio. They called him Jelley Del Rio.

Q. Who is he?

A. He used to be a show boy. Put on French Parisienne shows with girls.

Q. You say he put on French Parisienne shows?

A. Yes. You see, Cody had the only mirrored showroom in this city.

Q. What is a French Parisienne show?

A. Do you want me to tell you, really?

Q. Well, I think for the record it would be established as a practice, but I would suggest if possible that you describe it in understandable terms with a certain amount of care.

A. Yes sir. Well, there is two girls or either three girls, whatever a man paid for, to put on a French Parisienne show, completely in the nude, with a man. See, for a French Parisienne show, you explain it to him, tell him he was going to see a French Parisienne show with two girls and first of all the girls show him all the normal positions for normal sexual intercourse and then all the different French between men and women, the daisy chain, charm circle, and the sixty-nine.

MR. CURTIS [Henry Curtis, then city attorney]: That is very indecent. I don't see any reason for it at all, Mr. Kohn.

KOHN: May I say that these are practices going on in the community in violation of the law?

MAYOR MORRISON: Couldn't it be described in a general way as an indecent act instead of ...

CURTIS: I think that it is very improper and I advise the Commission Council that it is a very improper way of bringing out the evidence. You can bring out anything that is improper, but to put into the record indecent testimony is simply shocking and improper. I recommend to the mayor and to the members of the Commission Council that that line of testimony be stopped.

KOHN: Well, may I also say that I would agree that we should try to get in as ...

CURTIS: I see no reason at all that it should be described at all.

MORRISON: May I say that certainly the witness can testify to an immoral act without having to describe what the woman does and what the man does. I don't think that has any part here.

MISS GELLMAN: They weren't really doing it, sir. They were just putting on a show.

MORRISON: Just say an act committed in violation of the law. To say how it was committed is just a little on the shocking side, and I don't think it assists us in any way.

Q. Would you try to be a little more general, please.

A. Yes sir. It was a sex show.

Miss Gellman also testified that the charge for such a show ran from $50 to $150, and that the shows were quite popular with movie stars, celebrities, police organizations—and that once a French show was organized for the warden of Angola Prison and several of his friends.

Q. And under what name were you charged at the time?

A. Doris Gellman. It is all down on the police records, I guess. I have been in jail several times, it ought to be down there. I have been to jail many times from the houses on routine raids. They fingerprinted us and mugged us, and I guess they have the names.

Q. What do you mean by routine raids?

A. Well, see, a routine raid is like when the house is open, running wide open. If one of the girls has a beef with a guy, the guy calls the police that the girl didn't treat him right or he thinks he got gypped on the money, so he goes and calls the cops. Usually we are tipped off in advance. Somebody calls up and lets us know. So . . . the police come and raid the place, but when it's a routine raid they take two girls or three girls and, see, we go to jail in turns, all the girls go to jail in turns.

．　．　．　．　．

A. We were always charged with loitering or that type when we got arrested from Cody's. One time Harry Daniels [chief of detectives] got mad and slapped that "hold for FBI" on us and kept us seventy-two hours and then left us go.

Q. Why did Harry Daniels get mad at you?

A. I think on account he walked into the room and caught one of the girls and one of the men in a kind of an indecent act. Just what it was I couldn't say. It wasn't prostitution, but it was abnormal. It kind of made him hot under the collar. He don't go in for that.

．　．　．　．　．

Q. And when you got to court, you got the hundred dollars back?

A. Usually we were found not guilty. Even if the officers did catch us in an act of prostitution, they said we was out in the hall playing cards or something, you know, the ones that we knew. . . . We wouldn't be charged, unless the girls gave the officer some kind of reason, you know, to really press it against her. She got smart with the cop. The police don't like that, they make it rough. They can either make it rough or easy on you. Naturally, we'd be real nice to them.

Q. Was it usually true that when these raids or arrests were made that even though a police officer would find an act of prostitution going on, he would not make that charge?

A. That is right.

Q. What charge would he bring?

A. Just say we were loitering in an immoral house of prostitution.

Q. Loitering?

A. Or living in the house, take for instance that time at the Somerset Hotel.

Q. Now, just a minute, please hold on. The lady has to make the record as we go along. You said you'd been charged with loitering in this house, or charged with playing cards.

A. Right.

Q. You don't mean that was the official charge on the books.

A. Yes, that's right. That is what we told Judge Garafalo, and that is what the officer told Judge Garafalo on the stand. So I guess it was the official charge.

Q. That would be the testimony?

A. And they would give us the hundred dollars back.

. . . . .

Q. Had Sergeant Yancovitch [a vice squad member] participated in what you call routine arrests before?

A. Several times. Whenever a routine raid was made, Yancovitch would come and say, "Well, which of you is going to jail tonight?" We'd all laugh, and he'd say, "Well, whoever's turn it is get dressed in your street clothes and come on down." Then he'd take us by the door and tell us, "All right, I'll rough you up a little bit. I'm gonna rough you up a little when I take you out." And he'd give us a push. You know, whenever anybody sees a police car drive up in front of a sporting house, there's always a bunch of eyes that come in.

A. I said that one day while we were up there at 809 Barrone Street, Major McNamara had come upstairs into the parlor and Italiano and a couple of other officers, [Eddie] Schoenberger, one of the detectives on the force, came and sat in the parlor, Christine Roberts, Little Christine, Gagliano and a whole bunch of us present, including Betty Huff . . . and Cody Morris was sitting there and we were all served drinks, real whiskey for a change. And they was bragging about the TV set Bebe Anselmo was supposed to give him.

Q. Give who?

A. Gave to Major McNamara at that time. . . . That was around 1949. That's the reason I remember, because that's the time before I went to work for Anselmo.

· · · · ·

Q. Have you worked on very many occasions, in connection with that kind of work, turned over money to [Detective] Frank Marullo?

A. No, he never asked me for any. He got his from the houses, and he didn't need none from me. He used to pick up a lot of money. I think Italiano and that bunch was always together.

Q. You say he [Marullo] used to pick up money from the different houses?

A. Like when he used to come to Cody's and sit upstairs with us all and drink. See the parlors coming in, full of company, put them in parlors while they were waiting. He knew that the girls were turning dates up there.

Q. You mean he would see men coming into the house?

A. Of course.

Q. You mean he would see men going into the rooms with girls while he was sitting there?

A. Have drinks with us, sit down and talk, and sometimes he would take me to bed and Cody would pay me for it.

Q. In other words, Frank Marullo would have a date with you, and Cody Morris, the owner, would pay you?

A. Yes. He'd always pay. "Don't ask the police for money. If you want to have a date, go ahead, and I'll pay you."

· · · · ·

A. All the houses got their cut, like forty-twenty.

Q. I'm speaking from the standpoint of your share. Would you divide it with anyone outside the house?

A. No. All they'd take was two dollars a night from each one [each one's share]. It's called "towel money." But it wasn't for no towel money.

Q. What was the money for?

A. For police protection.

Q. I don't want to seem naive, but as a matter of record, what do you mean by police protection?

A. They take two dollars from each girl. Only one place they took three dollars, and that was Mabel Clinton's place. They took three dollars, but the rest of the places they took two dollars. They would call it towel money but it was police protection. We used to kid about it.

. . . . .

Q. Did you see the men to whom the money was given?

A. No sir. All I seen was those squad cars down there.

Q. You'd be on the second floor looking down?

A. The only time—one time I saw any money was one time when Duke Rutledge was there—Duke Rutledge [a policeman] and Frank Rivard [a city hall official], upstairs in Cody's, sitting down in the Number Two parlor. And I was up there just shooting the bull with them and talking with them, with Cody Morris and a couple of the girls. All the girls didn't want to come in the parlor. Some of them had old men, and their old men didn't want them to associate with the police. Jay Pierson's old man was sent up on a dope charge, so she was free and I was free, we went to bed with them upstairs, and I saw Cody Morris hand Frank Rivard a wad. I saw Frank put it in his pocket. Cody reached over, and put it in Frank's pocket, he put his hand in his pocket to shove it down or something. It was money. You couldn't help but see it was money. I was sitting right on his lap.

Q. On whose lap?

A. Frank Rivard's lap.

Q. How many times, for example, did you see Frank Rivard at Cody Morris'?

A. Well, he came over several times, he came on that fishing trip.

Q. On how many different occasions did you see Duke Rutledge there at Cody Morris'?

A. Well, he used to come over there to date Jay Pierson, a lot, although he was my date on the fishing trip.

Q. Was any money passed to Duke Rutledge?

A. I never did see any money passed to him.

Q. Did you ever see any other money passed to any other person by Cody Morris, or Miss Ione Morris?

A. Just O'Rourke.

Q. Is he the one who's called Junior O'Rourke?

A. I don't know. He used to wear a bright yellow shirt collecting money. In some kind of a beat-up looking car. Cody used to throw the money down.

Q. I'd like to show you a number of photographs of police officers—and ask if you can identify any of them as the man you've been referring to—without turning over to the back of them.

A. That's him, right here.

Q. On the back of this photograph there is the identification made by the police department itself with J. W. O'Rourke, Number 424. You say that is the man you refer to? As O'Rourke?

A. That's the one who used to come with Captain Guillot over to Frank Brown's. Used to pick up money in match boxes, and drink with us over at Cody's.

Q. When you would see this squad car and see Officer O'Rourke was there any other officer with Patrolman O'Rourke?

A. No. He used to come all by himself.

Q. In the car all by himself?

A. Yes sir, he came by himself. I know when I saw him he was by himself. When he came when I wasn't there, I don't know. But I saw him in that bright colored shirt. He still had that shirt the day when he brought us down to Judge Garafalo's court. I remember because he'd caught one of the girls inside one of the rooms having a date with one of the guys, and he said he caught us outside playing cards. Him and Captain Guillot, I know I handed him the money. I was in the room with a prick and I went to the door and I hollered for the maid, "Here, come get this." It was two tens. I can't ever forget it. I put the money right in Captain Guillot's hand. He gave the money back to the sailor and said, "Get out and don't let me catch you in one of these places again." And O'Rourke went down to court with us, and by the time it came up to trial he testified that it was all in the hall playing cards. The judge dismissed the case and gave us our hundred dollars back. That was over at Frank Brown's.

Q. How many times did you see him at Frank Brown's place?

A. O'Rourke, two or three times. I'd say two times. I want to be accurate.

Q. Alone each time?

A. Once he was with Captain Guillot. The time of the raid. Once he came up with Schoenberger.

Q. Detective Eddie Schoenberger?

A. Detective, that's right. He used to follow me around, too. He asked Cody one time to let me go on a date with three men from out of town—police officials from someplace. I don't exactly know where. Cody paid me ten dollars apiece for each one of the men, to take them over to the hotel right next to the Bamboo Lounge on St. Charles Street. It's a little hotel.

. . . . .

Q. Did you ever see Captain Guillot on any occasion at any of the houses excepting that one time you mentioned involving the raid?

A. I've seen him drive up outside the house run by Frank Brown. For awhile Brown went on his own. Tried to run the Somerset Hotel. Cody didn't like the idea of having that competition right close by and put a little heat on.

Q. How could Cody put the heat on?

A. I meant to send over whoever was on the Vice Squad at that time. Must have had something to do with that. That was the time Captain Guillot and O'Rourke came.

Q. [How did you know] that Cody Morris was putting the heat on?

A. I see what you mean, now. That was the reason why the police kept passing by there, because Cody was putting the pressure on him. Frank Brown said that Cody didn't want nobody to work but he was going to work. He was still going to make his own money.

Q. Did you from that, from any other things you have learned or observed, have the impression that Cody Morris had the ability to direct the police department to take action against a competitor?

A. As far as taking action, I don't know, but I know Cody has got pretty good pull. As you can see for yourself, he's never been arrested, just one time as a house operator, and I think that was pretty recently.

. . . . .

Q. You mentioned Cody Morris on a number of occasions in speaking about a fishing party. You said something earlier today about Frank Rivard having been there and talked about a fishing party. Were you referring to Cody Morris' place?

A. I was referring to the fishing party that Cody Morris sent me on. You see, I was working for Cody. Just come out of the hospital—I'd been sick for awhile, and Cody come down to my house and said, "Doris, they've got a fishing trip going on and I can't get nobody 'cause all the girls have old men."

Q. Would you explain that? When you say all the girls had old men?

A. Pimps. Old men.

Q. Why couldn't he send them?

A. Their old men didn't want them to go. So he asked me to go and I said I didn't have any objection . . . being that I went with these other officers.

Q. What other officers?

A. Well, there was Eddie Schoenberger, Frank Rivard, Duke Rutledge, Frank Marullo that I once had intercourse with.

Q. Cody Morris asked you to go?

A. Yes sir. He asked me to go.

· · · · ·

Q. Who are these girls? Who is Tiny?

A. Tiny's a little girl who works for Marie Bernard. I don't know her first name. That was Harry Daniels' date.

Q. Which Daniels is that?

A. Chief of detectives. It was his fishing party, see?

Q. It was his fishing party?

A. His party. Cody told us it was his party.

Q. Cody Morris told you it was his party?

A. That's right. Marie Bernard and all the houses gave him whiskey and stuff. We had cases of beer and all out there. We had a good time as far as that part. Bill Erickson was with us. Mayor Morrison's secretary. Duke Rutledge, Frank Rivard, Bill Erickson, Harry Daniels, Theophile Landry. Bill Erickson had just come from addressing some kind of a big speech or something that night. He still had his fancy suit on. We went to Forays' and had a few drinks. Went on the Airline Highway and Tiny and Harry got in his car and we stopped over by 1019½ Gravier. I waited downstairs with Dominick Battaglia's old lady.

Q. Do you know Captain Italiano?

Doris testified that she knew Captain Italiano quite well, and that he would come around for drinks at Cody's whorehouse while business was going on as usual. It was also Italiano who supervised the cleanliness and health of the prostitutes in the French Quarter.

A. See, Captain Italiano used to come around, see, we had to go around and get our blood test and smear, we had to have our paper in. He would give us a little slip with his name at the top if our blood test was negative . . . and we would have to have those into the houses by Friday. If we didn't have it by Friday, we couldn't work over the weekend. Dr. Gomila can tell you that.

Q. Every week?

A. Yes. Dr. Frank Gomila here in the Maison Blanche Building, we had to turn our little slip in, that was in all the houses, you can ask all the house operators, they will tell you.

Q. Did that happen all the places you worked?

A. You had to have this to prove you didn't have venereal disease.

Q. And to whom would you give the paper?

A. To either Miss Ione, which was at Cody's, or either give it to Betty Ott, she was handling the books up there—or else give it to Cody Himself.

Q. Was it always . . .

A. On Friday they would pass around and pick the slips up. I know.

Q. Who would pick the slips up?

A. Frank Marullo.

Q. Did Frank Marullo pick up in all the houses?

A. He picked up at Cody's. I've seen him there picking up the slips.

Q. Now did that turning in of the slip showing the doctor's examination have anything to do with . . .

A. It had on it, "This is to certify—just like I am the one— that's free from gonorrhea," and Dr. Gomila had signed it at the bottom. They'd charge you three dollars for a smear and five dollars for a blood test. The smear was once a week and the blood test was once every three months.

Q. Would anyone tell you which doctor to go to?

A. We had to go to Dr. Gomila from Cody's, but from Norma Wallace's we had to go to another doctor, but I done forgot his name. The only two doctors we went to, Dr. Gomila and I don't know who the other doctor was . . .

Q. I mean, where you under instructions to go to some specific doctor, or could you go to any doctor?

A. No. You had to go to a Board of Health doctor. That doctor was Dr. Gomila. We had to go to his office—just like that time I wanted to lose weight—he writes out prescriptions for barbiturates, benzedrine, or dexedrine—a lot of girls use them at night to stay awake—and he would write out prescriptions for it and we would get it filled. If we didn't get it that way then we'd get it from Willie's or the Circle Drugstore, or Wirth's.

If Audrey C. is alive today she is around thirty-five, and has been down twenty miles of bad road, but she was only fifteen when she was pumped into the conduit of prostitution in New Orleans. Her case, one of the rare instances of thorough police investigation in the city at that time, was built by Captain William A. Walker, Sr., commanding officer of the juvenile division of the detective bureau, who pursued Audrey's short career down some avenues which might have been avoided by a less courageous police officer.

Audrey's fling spanned the months of October, 1951, through mid-January, 1952, but it began in July, 1951, when she was seduced by a seventeen-year-old youth named Bobby Eckert. She and Bobby ran around together some in Jefferson Parish and New Orleans, while Audrey was living at a boardinghouse where she had been placed by her mother several months before. (Get one thing straight: Nobody has said Audrey was *perfect.*) On October 28, 1951, she ran away with Bobby and a friend named Frank, and in a series of stolen cars, chases by state cops and hitchhiking escapades got as far as Eunice, Louisiana, 150 miles away, before stealing another car and heading back for New Orleans. Then she and Bobby split.

On October 31, 1951, while I was walking up St. Claude Avenue with a boy named Clyde [Audrey said in a statement to Captain Walker], a man whom I know by the name of Pete [Alexander Peter Laurent] came along in his car and asked us to get in and we did, because it was raining. Pete told Clyde that he would take me to his place. Both of them knew that I was a runaway. Clyde argued about me going with Pete, because he knew that Pete was a pimp. Finally Pete took me with him. While I was riding with Pete in his car, he told me he wanted to put me to work as a prostitute. He drove me to a tourist court. . . . He took me in Cabin Number Two at about 5 a.m. October 31, 1951, and had sexual intercourse with me and also used his mouth on my private and also had unnatural intercourse by placing his penis in my rectum. The man Pete left me in the cabin and came back about 7 p.m. with a man named Moose [Marcel Hingle] and we left the cabin and rode around in Moose's car. Pete told me that Moose was going to be my old man

and that any money I made as a prostitute was supposed to be split
three ways between us, and that one of them was going to take me
up the country to work as it would be pretty good there. Pete left us
and Moose took me to his apartment at 1421 Bourbon Street.
Moose told me that he would like to buy Pete out, meaning that he
wanted to buy Pete's interest in me and I told him that it was okay.

Moose then took her out and bought her $50 worth of new clothes,
and then, on November 3, took her to a place called Joan and Frank's,
about six miles outside of Eunice (a town of about 11,000 population),
where she worked as "Vicky" or "Ginger" until November 23, when she
decided she'd had enough of the sticks and told Moose she wanted to go
back to New Orleans. Moose, with a couple of roughneck pals, took her
back to town, beat her up and put her out to hustle on Bourbon Street.
She did, for a few days.

"On December 1, 1951," she said, "Moose sent me out to hustle on
Bourbon Street, and told me to be home before 3 A.M. on December 2. I
never did go back to him." That night, while hooking at Mac's Villa
Court in the 100 block of Chartres Street, in the French Quarter, she met
Joe Gratneyese, who made the move that sent Audrey into the big time
—he set her up as his mistress in a big roominghouse on Melpomene
Street. It took her only a couple of days to find out that the house across
the street was one of ill fame, and she asked the girls there if she could
come to work. Nan Tilton, the madam, took her on, and that filled out
Nan's stable of about nine girls.

Now Nan Tilton had been running this house for twenty years, and
had never been caught or busted in any way. It was a quiet place—the
girls turned tricks in their own rooms (Audrey always used one of the
two rear rooms upstairs), and Nan often exchanged girls with other
houses, just to liven things up a bit. There was plenty of traffic to and
from the house, but during the twenty years this never seemed to bother
either Captain William J. Dowie of the New Orleans Police Department,
who lived in the same block on Melpomene Street as Madam Tilton's
operation, or Assistant District Attorney Edward Haggerty, Jr., who lived
a couple of houses away.

One of the houses Nan exchanged girls with was Gertrude Yost's
whorehouse at 935 Esplanade Avenue, which had been in business for
thirty-seven years, and, according to Mrs. Yost (then seventy-one), had
not been busted since 1918. It even had a row of personalized douche
bags, with the regular girls' names on them (flocked, you wonder?) hanging in the bathroom. It was on such an exchange visit with Gertie that
Audrey C., on December 12, 1951, ran into one Carmello Graffagnini,

alias Jack the Squirrel, one of Moose Hingle's underworld friends, and Jack the Squirrel put her to work for himself—at Gertie's—on the spot. Of course, she continued to make calls from the Melpomene Street place. During the time Jack the Squirrel had Audrey, she said she made about $800, which she gave to him, keeping only the $82 she had on her when she was arrested on January 18, 1952, by Captain Walker, after Audrey's mother had found out—a little too late—what the child had been doing in her spare time.

Everybody in the case was charged with one thing or another, except little Audrey, who was referred to throughout the police investigation as "the victim."

Some funny things happened to the charges, too. All charges against the madams (and there were two or three in Captain Walker's reports I haven't mentioned) were dropped, because, according to Superintendent Scheuering, the ladies were all to be used as witnesses by the state against the other figures. As a matter of fact, none of them was ever called as a witness.

No charges were filed against one Anthony Marino, owner of the Hour Glass Bar, who hired Audrey to work as barmaid, B-girl and prostitute for the four days she was in the street on her own.

Joe Gratneyese got eleven months in Parish Prison for his role in exploiting Audrey's talents and youth. Moose Hingle was fined $150 and given four months in jail. Pete Laurent was found not guilty of anything, and charges were dropped against the two hoods who helped Moose beat Audrey up the night they came back from Eunice.

Bobby Eckert, then eighteen, was sentenced to eight months in Parish Prison for "carnal knowledge of an unmarried female under the age of seventeen years." New Orleans knows a villain when she sees one.

If Audrey C. was alive and living in New Orleans on Saturday, April 24, 1971, she might have read with some interest the following story, which appeared on page three of the *Times-Picayune*:

> The police Vice Squad Friday announced disruption of a prostitution ring involving at least two juvenile girls, drugs and intimidation.
>
> Police and Jefferson Parish sheriff's deputies Thursday arrested six adults and a sixteen-year-old girl in connection with the ring. Three adults were still in Parish Prison Friday. One posted bond, and two others were released on their own recognizance. The other juvenile, a fifteen-year-old girl, went to police about one month ago and complained that she was forced into prostitution.

Sergeant Robert N. Frey, commander of the Vice Squad, said that the younger girl met a man who induced her to participate in immoral activity when she was hitchhiking on St. Charles Avenue not long before she went to police. The man, identified only as a white man, had not been arrested as of Friday, but was being actively sought by Jefferson and New Orleans officers. About one month of investigation and surveillance resulted in the arrest of the older girl and four adults after officers served a search warrant at 1601 Lesseps, Apartment One.

The apartment was the home of Hays G. Dugas, forty-four, and Beverly S. Banks, thirty-two, who were arrested along with the girl, Charles S. Boze III, twenty-four, of 3425 Dauphine, and Remona C. Menendez, nineteen, 1015 North Broad. The search warrant was served about 8:30 a.m. Thursday. About 4 p.m. Jefferson Parish Vice Squadsmen cooperated in the arrest of Vincent L. Giangrosso, thirty-two, 1909 Cooper Road, Gretna, and Leroy Choina, forty-five, 539 Delmar, Gretna, in Gretna.

Dugas posted bonds totaling three thousand, two hundred fifty dollars and was released from the prison Friday. Beverly Banks was still in the prison Friday. Police booked them with soliciting for prostitutes; pandering; letting premises for prostitution, enticing minors into prostitution, contributing to the delinquency of a juvenile, and possession of morphine and numorphan, two drugs which were allegedly confiscated in their apartments along with prostitution records.

Criminal District Court Judge James L. Alcock authorized release of Giangrosso on recognizance bonds totaling two thousand five hundred dollars Friday. He also authorized a recognizance bond for release of Choina from the Central Lockup Thursday night.

Giangrosso was booked with enticing minors into prostitution, pandering, and contributing to the delinquency of a juvenile. Choina was booked only with contributing to the delinquency of a juvenile. Boze and the remaining woman were still in the prison Friday. The sixteen-year-old girl was turned over to juvenile authorities.

Police said that most of the prostitution activity took place at the Lesseps Street apartment. It was alleged that the younger girl was being forced to act as a prostitute, through threats of violence. The ring was operated on a large scale in Orleans and Jefferson Parishes, police claimed. Contacts for dates were made by means of telephone calls to the Lesseps Street address.

Sergeant Frey said that the ring also employed females over

the age of sixteen, and that it was not known how many, if any, juveniles other than the two who came to light were involved with the ring. An investigation into the number of juveniles involved, as well as all other areas of the ring's activity, was continuing.

Frey said the fifteen-year-old girl, her brother and two other teenagers were given a ride by the wanted man. He persuaded the girl to accompany him alone. Through promises of gifts of a car and an apartment, the man persuaded her to engage in immoral behavior with him, Frey charged.

"He conned her," Frey said of the man's approach.

Threats were then used to force the girl into prostitution and to use marijuana and cocaine, Frey said. When the girl was scheduled to go on one of her prostitution dates, she instead went to her boy friend and explained her situation, Frey said. The boy friend took her to police. The girl received a telephone call, but no attempt was made to harm her. Although Frey felt the Lesseps Street apartment had not been in use by the ring for long, he said officers who were watching it saw numerous men, women and girls entering and leaving.

That Lesseps Street address, incidentally, is out there near the old Fifth District, the one where the gamblers had the cops tied up for so long back in the 1940s and 1950s. I mention this because in this *Times-Picayune* story the kingpin of the new prostitution ring is alleged to be Hays G. Dugas, who, Aaron Kohn says, is a close associate of the men who operate as part of the Carlos Marcello empire over in Jefferson Parish. It makes you wonder how much the girls on Lesseps Street were paying in towel money.

On Monday, March 23, 1959, the U.S. Senate Select Committee on Improper Activities in the Labor and Management Field met in Washington, D.C., to talk about New Orleans and Jefferson Parish, and try to find out how the racketeers came to dominate the coin-operated machine business there.

The cast of characters was big league—the chairman of the committee was Senator John L. McClellan of Arkansas, and also present were Senators Frank Church and Carl T. Curtis, chief counsel Robert F. Kennedy and an investigator named Pierre Salinger. And this was the day Aaron Kohn was to testify.

In reading the testimony that follows, you can hear that famous Kennedy voice as he questions Aaron Kohn. (An interesting aside is that Kohn submitted his testimony to the committee in advance, and the chief counsel agreed to accept all of it except any mention of Mayor Morrison, who had made a deal with the Kennedys to deliver all of south Louisiana to John F. Kennedy in the 1960 presidential election in return for Kennedy's support in the race for the governorship Morrison was planning to make.)

Kohn introduced a list of names and places, for the reference of the committee. It included Sheriff Coci and his brother; a number of gambling casinos in Jefferson Parish; the names of the coin-operated machine companies controlled by members of the Marcello family; Williard F. Guillot of St. Bernard Parish, owner of the Guillot Amusement Company, and, of course, the Carlos Marcello family: Carlos and his brothers, Anthony, Joseph, Pasquale, Peter, Salvatore and Vincent.

After describing the general makeup of the Marcello operation, and assuring Senator McClellan that their operations did, indeed, reach into his home state—to Hot Springs, a popular watering spot for mobsters of all sorts—Kohn continued with a description of the origins of organized crime in New Orleans, and gave a brief life history of Carlos Marcello, the head of all organized crime in Louisiana and parts of Mississippi, and his rise to power through gambling interests in his adopted country (he was born in Tunis, in Tunisia, North Africa, and the government has been trying, unsuccessfully, to deport him for decades).

By 1952 Marcello was deeply entrenched in the machine gambling business—slot machines before that, pinballs after.

The State police organization [Kohn testified] for the first time in modern history proceeded to destroy thousands of slot machines and enforced the laws in connection with them, the number of such gambling devices in the state was substantially reduced. However, in Jefferson Parish, since Sheriff Coci had been elected to office, there have been numerous instances of slot machines coming back into use. And at least one of the companies in which Marcello was a partner has been one of the operators of these slot machines. However, the recent history of Marcello's interest in coin devices has been chiefly in relationship to jukeboxes and pinball machines. One of the companies, the Jefferson Music Company, the largest operators in Jefferson Parish, is located in Gretna. The gathering of information about this company indicates that prior to January of 1942 the company was under the name of Carlos' mother, Mrs. Louise Marcello, but that about that time, however, she sold the company to another son, Vincent Marcello, who was then a minor, who by court order was given the authority to engage in contracts. At that point the size of the company is somewhat indicated by the fact that Vincent paid seven thousand dollars and reportedly took over the entire business, which then included forty-nine slot machines and fifty music boxes, sixty-two pin games and other equipment spotted in about eighty-four locations, mostly in the Algiers section of New Orleans. Then it appears in 1944 from the record that Vincent and Carlos formed a partnership in the Jefferson Music Company, which has continued to be the key management figure.

McClellan, at one point, asked about Kohn's testimony involving the Coci deputies who were making the rounds of bars in Jefferson Parish, harassing the operators until they agreed to put in the Marcello-owned machines.

This is the case where the law enforcement officials who are supposed to enforce the laws muscle in and tell the operators or the business owners that they have to change from one machine to another or from one company to another in order to operate [McClellan asked]?

Yes sir [Kohn said]. It did happen. I might point out in passing that the same thing was done some years back in the City of New Orleans in connection with the organization of operators of pinball machines in order to force people to join an association. Law enforcement officers harassed operators, locations, until the operators joined that association of operators.

(Kohn, throughout his testimony, answered specific questions about Jefferson Parish, where the mob made its headquarters and did a certain amount of business, and he was never fully successful in getting into the city of New Orleans, where the mob did not make its headquarters but did most of its business, because, as mentioned previously, New Orleans was Mayor Morrison's town.)

The committee heard several bar owners testify about being bullied by deputies into changing their coin-ops, and when Kohn was recalled he told the story of Will Guillot of the Guillot Amusement Company, headquartered in St. Bernard Parish. Counsel Kennedy asked if there was any relationship between Guillot and the Marcellos, and Kohn replied that there was—and with the police, as well.

Will Guillot—his full name is Williard F. Guillot—and his son, Glen, run the Guillot Amusement Company [Kohn said] and operate jukeboxes, pinball machines and slot machines. The headquarters for their operation is in a bar known as the Corrine Club, in which Guillot also runs a handbook and has other forms of gambling. Over a period of years gambling has repeatedly been found by our investigators, and, incidentally, as early as January of this year, Guillot was arrested and charged with handbook gambling. About 1953 or 1952, about that time, or perhaps just before the time Francis Gravenberg, the new state police superintendent, started smashing slot machines, Guillot bought some slot machines for delivery to his place in St. Bernard Parish. . . . When these machines were delivered to Guillot, he paid part of the bill in cash, and the balance of it, believed to have been four thousand dollars, was handled by issuing a check. The check bounced and there were persistent efforts made to collect on it, which failed. Then an attorney for the vendor asked the sheriff of Jefferson Parish to issue a warrant for the arrest of Guillot in St. Bernard Parish, and they ran into a great deal of trouble getting the warrant served. Then he received a telephone call from Carlos Marcello, who said, "Stay right where you are, I am coming over." When he came over to this lawyer's office, he demanded to see the check. It was shown to him. Marcello tossed, I believe it was four thousand dollars in cash down, tore up the check, dropped it on the floor, turned around and walked out.

Kohn told a horror story about the ruthlessness of Guillot in the control of his distributorship. It began with the running out of the juke-box-pinball business of a man named Mitchell Morehead, who ran the M&M Amusement Company. After a series of unpleasant run-ins with the Guillot people—including cops who were working for him—Morehead gave it up, and only returned to the trade one time, when a friend, a Mrs. Irma Lowe, and her partner, Mrs. Ruth Sanders, who had opened a small restaurant on St. Bernard Highway, asked Morehead to sell them a jukebox on a chattel mortgage. Kohn told what happened then:

> They were told to get their jukebox from Will Guillot, which they did, but it never worked. They were having a lot of trouble with customers putting their coins in and not getting their plays back. They would have to give the money back to the customers, but they could never get the money from Guillot. About a month went by without the machine operating properly, with Guillot telling them he was too busy with his handbook during the day to do anything about repairing the machine or have it repaired. They finally got Guillot's permission to bring in another machine, and this is when the women went to Morehead in New Orleans.

A few days after Morehead's new Seeburg machine was installed, about 7 o'clock at night, the front door of their small restaurant burst open. At this time there were two women and a male customer, when through the door came Will Guillot and his son, Glen, and a man by the name of Clem Nunez, who worked as a mechanic in this coin device business.

They [the women] claimed Guillot had a gun in his hand. As he came in he started shooting at the jukebox. Clem Nunez pulled out a blackjack and for the next five hours, approximately, there was a reign of terror inside this little restaurant. When one of the women, having no phone available at the location, started to go out the door to use the phone at a fire station across the street, she was told that if she went out of the door she would go out feet first. They broke up all the stock, that is, Coca-Cola, beer, excepting for what beer they drank themselves they destroyed, broke mirrors, smashed the cigarette vending machine, and during the course of this on two separate occasions pairs of deputy sheriffs walked in. When the first pair walked in they recognized the men and they immediately turned around and walked out again. Not very much longer afterward another pair of deputies walked in and started to do the same thing, but as they reached the door on the way out one of these three men picked up a beer bottle and threw it at the back of the deputies' heads, and it shattered on the door jamb. The sheriff turned around and said, "You fellows better cut it out or you will get in trouble," and quickly walked out again. About midnight another deputy sheriff came in in civilian clothes, wearing a gun, and threw the two Guillots and Nunez out of the place. The women attempted the next day to have a complaint accepted by the district attorney's office and it was refused. They also went to the clerk of the court, who refused to accept a complaint. Finally they found one justice of the peace who was willing to accept the complaint. It was sent to the sheriff's department and the two Guillots and Nunez were then arrested and charged with disorderly conduct, threatening to do bodily harm with a pistol, and destroying private property.

The restaurant never opened again. The women tried to sue Guillot, but Will Guillot, in the presence of witnesses, said that if Mrs. Lowe started walking into any courtroom to sue him she would never reach the courtroom alive. Morehead tried to sue for damages to his jukebox, but never found a lawyer willing to take his case in St. Bernard Parish.

In the spring of 1971, I asked Aaron Kohn whatever happened to this evil old man, Will Guillot.

"Oh, he's still over there," Kohn said. "As a matter of fact he was raided last year in connection with gambling, he and his son. They have a place over near the stockyards over in St. Bernard Parish, where he runs a handbook, and a bar, a restaurant."

Two years after that hearing Kohn was to get a chance to tell his stories again, this time before the Permanent Subcommittee on Investigations, headed by Senator McClellan and with an illustrious membership: Henry M. Jackson of Washington, Sam J. Ervin, Jr., of North Carolina, Hubert H. Humphrey of Minnesota, Ernest Gruening of Alaska, Edmund S. Muskie of Maine, Karl E. Mundt of South Dakota, Carl T. Curtis of Nebraska and Jacob K. Javits of New York.

Kohn appeared, and ran through many of the same facts about Carlos Marcello and his rise to power in Louisiana, and went into detail on the town of Gretna, the parish seat of Jefferson Parish and headquarters for the mob, and after he was finished Senator Mundt made a statement—in the form of a question—that may sum up what Louisiana is about:

> The mysterious thing to me, and the thing that started to disturb me when we had Marcello with us before [Carlos Marcello had been called, and refused to answer], is that here is an illegal entity, a man so contemptuous of America that he has lived in this country more than half a century without ever becoming a citizen, a man that the federal government could deport if the federal government really wanted to deport—the Justice Department in the United States today could deport him in the next thirty days if it wanted to, if it worked on it—how an immigrant like that can delay through the courts his deportation. When our committee some time ago finally put the bee on the Justice Department, they did deport him for a fortnight or two down in Guatemala, but yet he comes back and here he is.
>
> This is an astonishing and a shocking thing and discloses once again that in America the reason criminals of this kind continue to succeed is because of an indifferent attitude on the part of the public that does not hold the feet of its law enforcement officials to the fire and say, "We are not going to continue to let you accept underground political contributions; or things of that nature." It is preposterous to have a Senate committee sitting here all this time, day after day, trying to study the problem of organized gambling, when you almost have a sign out on the place, you have an address, everybody knows where it is, 326 Huey P. Long Avenue, Gretna,

Louisiana, and yet the State of Louisiana has the power to stop it and they do not stop it. Your commission, as I understand it, is a volunteer group that has gotten together trying to put a little decency into Louisiana, is that right?

Aaron Kohn's response was simple. "Yes sir," he said. "Trying to make law-enforcement-men's aim integrity rather than collusion."

The abandoning of a community to the forces of organized crime may be the most significant result of the corruption of a police force, but is is not the most difficult to stomach. The climate of police corruption —taking a buck or two or even $75,000—always seems to include an atmosphere of good, clean fun—cops even banter with the people they are shaking down. But it seems that as police officers exercise their discretionary powers over other people, the mood of the cops becomes brutal and cynical—hateful, if you will. Those who come under their power without money to buy favors or political influence with which to barter are treated with contempt, because the currency of the times has become money and power, not justice and humanity.

The special citizens' committee in New Orleans dipped into the area of this sort of police brutality in its 1953 investigations, and came up with dozens of cases—none of which could illustrate what I'm talking about more clearly than that of Annie Mae Taylor, an admitted prostitute, who was serving a brief term in Parish Prison for simple robbery, and who gave a statement to the committee's investigator in the prison on November 18, 1953, about the things she'd seen.

She was first asked about her "knowledge and experience" with police officers in the district stations.

A. Well, the first I seen of it was in the First Precinct when it was at Tulane and Saratoga. They used to put the colored upstairs and the white downstairs. At that time the floor was made with holes in it and we could look down in the holes and see the white cells. If a white woman would come in there and she would be drunk, they would line up and take turns with her and they would come from the higher ups. First it would be the one with the white cap and then it would be the ones with the stripes on their arms and then the lower ones. Just the plain officers.

Q. By taking turns with her, do you mean having sexual intercourse?

A. Yes sir. The high-ups would go first and then they would go out and then the little plain officers would take their turns. Since I got in the First District at St. Louis and Rampart, the cells are made so you cannot see in them very good, unless a person is close to you. One night, one of the officers came around and he called us to see if we were asleep. We played off like we were asleep and Number 5 cell had a little humpbacked white lady. He went up to the door and he stayed a long time. When he left the bar, he passed Number 6 and wiped himself off with toilet paper. At that time, she called over in the cell to another white girl they called Big Mamoo and told her like this, "Do you know that so and so asked—do you know that son-of-a-bitch asked me to give him a French date?" She said, "Well, honey, did you give it to him?" She said, "Lord, no." And then the other girl said to her, "Well, he stayed back there a mighty long time." And then that's when I said he came this way wiping off himself.

Q. Do you know of other instances where officers have had sexual intercourse with prisoners?

A. Yes. Willie Mae Duet went up to take a shower and fifteen officers had intercourse with her. She came down and told me she had come sick because so many had fooled with her.

Q. And she was menstruating when she came down and she believed that was caused from having sexual intercourse with so many men?

A. Yes, sir, because there was nothing wrong with her when she was sitting up there, because we had been talking and standing by the bars and when she came out it was running all over on her feet because she didn't have on no stockings.

Q. Are there any other things that you would like to relate at this time?

Annie Mae told a story about a night she insulted a drag queen, who happened to be a favorite of the cops, and as a result one of the cops, whom she called "Mr. Clarence," followed her home when she was out with a date, watched as she entered the privy in her back yard (while her date waited outside), and then arrested her for prostitution, later reducing the charge to no visible means of support (she had had 68 cents on her when she came out of the outhouse).

"You refer to Mr. Clarence. Do you know the officer's other name?" the investigator asked.

"Clarence . . . ," she said. "He is on the Vice Squad."

Q. Do you know Lovenia Parker?

A. I knew her by sight but I didn't know that was her name . . .

Q. What happened to her? From your knowledge or hearsay.

A. All I can say, but I didn't see anything, is that she got a lot of extra undivided attention. She was really petted and well taken care of and all day long she had some officer to talk to her and they was always taking her in and out of the cell. She didn't do nothing most of the time but cry, cry, cry.

Q. What did you hear regarding the officers having sexual intercourse with her?

A. She told me everytime they come in they was asking her the same thing and this one promised to let her out and that one promised to let her out and she had told me that she went with three of them that promised to let her out and none of them hadn't let her out. She told them she wasn't going to take that story any more.

. . . . .

Q. She told you that she had had intercourse with three officers and they wouldn't let her out and she wouldn't have intercourse with any more. Is that right?

A. Yes sir.

Q. Do you know what she was charged with?

A. I believe loitering.

Q. Did she tell you that she was only fifteen years of age?

A. Yes sir.

On December 3, 1971, a whole flock of chickens came home to roost when a federal grand jury indicted ten men on a single charge of conspiring to bribe law-enforcement officials to protect illegal gambling operations. If there is any substance to the government's allegations, the case appears to be a classic example of how a vice squad was utilized as the chief tool of an illegal operation to remain in business, and how vital to organized crime the traditionally organized vice squad has come to be. An entire generation grew up between Aaron Kohn's 1953 hearings on police corruption and the time of the 1971 indictment, but some of the names span that generation, and the industry involved—gambling—dates back to the riverboat days.

The biggest name on the indictment, of course, is that of Jim Garrison, who came into office as district attorney of Orleans Parish as a "reformer" in 1962, in the wake of the police scandals of the 1950s, even though he was already famous for his nighttime cavorting in the French Quarter; and he proceeded to "crack down" on vice in the Vieux Carre, taking particular aim at strip joints and B-girls. Tall—six feet six inches —and of classic D.A. appearance, Garrison was the darling of the voting population, was elected and then reelected twice without the aid of the traditional political machine and became, in his own words, a man who could deliver or not deliver the New Orleans vote—by far the most important in statewide elections—to the man of his choice.

He received national publicity in 1967 when he contended that the John F. Kennedy assassination was the result of a conspiracy based in New Orleans, and that Clay Shaw, a highly regarded business figure in that city, was central to the conspiracy. His case fell apart, and Shaw was acquitted of all charges; and it is widely believed that the entire episode was fabricated in an attempt to jazz up a fading career, much the same way the late Senator Joseph McCarthy embraced the China Lobby and anti-Communism as a method of forestalling the obscurity toward which he seemed to be rushing at full speed. Garrison, pleading not guilty to the 1971 bribery charges (and to a companion indictment charging him with income-tax evasion during the years when he was alleged to have been taking bribes), accused the government of a "plot" against him, a way of discrediting him because of his investigation of the Kennedy assassination.

Also named in the indictment were Frederick A. Soule, Sr., a captain in the New Orleans Police Department who, from June 30, 1968, had been assigned to the investigative staff of Garrison's office, and who, from May, 1962, until his transfer to the district attorney's office, had been commander of the vice squad; and Sergeant Robert N. Frey, who, when Soule moved to Garrison's staff, replaced him as head of the vice squad.

The other seven defendants were members of the New Orleans gambling fraternity, all involved in the operation of pinball machines, which are not illegal in the state of Louisiana or the city of New Orleans as long as there is no payoff in money. These machines are of the "Bingo" variety, where the player feeds nickels into the machine in an attempt to raise odds, shift possibilities of winning, and where a single game, played by a self-styled expert, can consume $2 or $3 worth of nickels. The machine itself registers no payoff, except that "free games" are recorded on the backboard, and these free games run to 999, which means that a player who compiled the maximum number of free games would be eligible, in a tavern or restaurant where the payoff is made by the bartender or operator, to receive nearly $50. It is theoretically possible to start with a single nickel and run the machine up to 999, but the odds against that are roughly equivalent to being dealt thirteen hearts at the bridge table.

The machines, mostly manufactured by the Bally Corporation of Chicago, generally replaced the one-armed bandit type of slot machine around the nation after many states legislated the jackpot out of existence in the late 1940s and 1950s (the military, of course, which was so moral about the possibility of vice in New Orleans corrupting its personnel during World War I, retained the slots in its servicemen's clubs in Vietnam until tales of corruption in 1970 forced the Pentagon to get rid of them), and in New Orleans alone the Justice Department estimated that the "Bingo" machines were doing $15 million a year in business—all of it illegal.

It took a federal strike force a year to develop its case against the ten men, and to do it they dipped into the past and brought to the surface Pershing Gervais, a sleazy one-time New Orleans cop who admittedly had taken graft while a member of the force, and who had been chief investigator for Garrison's office since Garrison first came into office. In the preliminary presentation of its case, the government did not say what it was they had on Gervais, but it must have been plenty because they were allowed to wire him and his environs for sound; and it is Gervais' activities that form the heart of a fascinating 113-page affidavit—signed by Floyd D. Moore, chief of the intelligence division of the Internal Revenue Service, who served as head of the strike force—which accompanies the indictment. (United States Attorney Gerald J. Gallinghouse released the affidavit to the New Orleans newspapers, which immediately started printing parts of it, only to be the target of a Garrison suit seeking an injunction against publication of the document because, Garrison said, it would prevent him from being able to get a fair trial in New Orleans, although, if what Aaron Kohn says about the "Mediterranean" quality of south Louisiana is true, the document surely would lead to acquittal—and perhaps the governorship.)

According to the affidavit, Garrison, Soule and Frey were each getting up to $500 a month from the pinball-machine operators (the men who owned the machines and placed them in "locations"), with Gervais acting as the go-between, or bagman, if you will. Gervais described the payoff system for the strike force, including naming the pinball operator who, in years past, had been designated by the others to deliver the money, and he said that the relationship first began in 1961, when Garrison first ran for office, when the pinball operators gave Garrison $10,000 for his campaign. He said that when regular payoffs began in 1962, the amount was $3,600 every two months, but that over the years the payments varied, dropping as low as $2,700 bimonthly and going as high as $4,400. The high figure was the current one when Gervais told all to the feds on August 31, 1970. Gervais said that he kept anywhere from $700 to $1,400 as his share, passing the rest of it to Garrison.

The strike force told Gervais that they intended to move against the pinball machines soon, and that if they were going to make any kind of a case they would have to do it soon and do it electronically; and so on November 14, 1970, Attorney General John N. Mitchell authorized the installation of "electronic listening devices on [Gervais'] person, his telephones and in any rooms under his dominion and control," most of these rooms being on one floor or another of the Fontainebleau Motor Hotel in New Orleans, where Gervais was doing his bagwork. The monitoring, by special agents of the Internal Revenue Service, began on November 16, 1970, and just in time—on November 24 and 25, a band of FBI agents, part of the strike force, executed 1,350 search warrants throughout Louisiana and Mississippi under the Gambling Devices Act of 1962, which required registration with the Attorney General all sorts of gambling devices, including the pinballs, and seized 3,000 pinball machines, 1,000 slot machines and $150,000 in cash. This, in pinball circles in New Orleans, was an ass-buster, and the scramble began. (It should be noted that the 1962 act used by the law-enforcement agencies in 1970 indirectly resulted from the Senate hearings before which Aaron Kohn testified in 1959 and 1961.)

The affidavit says that on December 1 Captain Soule called Gervais and said that because the bottom seemed to be falling out of the industry the payoffs were likely to stop, and much of the rest of the affidavit is concerned with efforts of Soule and Gervais to hold the thing together, to keep the protection money coming in even though there wasn't much left to protect, hoping that it would all blow over on the federal level and that the legislature, scheduled to meet in May, 1971, would ignore the expected four or five bills to outlaw pinball machines of all sorts, gambling type or not. About the only machines now operating were owned by one company whose managing partner had had the foresight to actually register his machines with the government and, according to the Gervais tapes, had tried and tried to get the others to do it, but they wouldn't listen.

Sergeant Frey, then the commander of the vice squad, hadn't been involved very long before the ax fell, according to the affidavit. (Aaron Kohn, in the spring of 1971, even as Uncle Sam was sorting his evidence, vouched for the vice squad chief and told me, "Bob Frey is doing a damned good job.")

The story of Frey's alleged involvement is told in the affidavit, as follows:

> On December 3, 1970, Captain Frederick A. Soule Sr. of the New Orleans Police Department met with Pershing Gervais in

Room 376 of the Fontainebleau Motor Hotel in New Orleans. Soule said that right after Joseph Giarrusso retired as superintendent of police in New Orleans [Giarrusso retired on August 21, 1970], Boasberg [Louis Boasberg, partner in a pinball company and one of the defendants in the case] came to Captain Soule and told the latter that no one can get to Sergeant Robert Frey . . . and asked Soule to talk to Frey; that Soule then invited Sergeant Frey on a trip regarding an extradition matter (on September 2, 1970, Captain Soule and Sergeant Frey delivered a state of Louisiana's governor's warrant to the Colorado Springs, Colorado, police department and took custody of a prisoner named Paul David Pierce, who had been charged in Louisiana with possession of narcotics) at which time Soule told Frey about previous and current payoff arrangements for pinball protection and solicited Sergeant Frey's agreement to take payoffs for protection of pinballs and that that was when it started with Frey. Captain Soule and Gervais went on to discuss how Boasberg, after initiating the corruption of Sergeant Frey, then began to delay and negotiate regarding amounts of payments. . . .

The following conversation, at this point, is alleged by the government to have taken place between Gervais and Soule. The writers of the affidavit chose to excise dirty words, because, after all, this is a moral society, and so I am following their style of letting you fill in the blanks:

GERVAIS: He [Boasberg] started you and then wouldn't come up . . .

SOULE: He started—wouldn't come up because he, he told me . . .

GERVAIS: Why didn't you tell him, you ———, you the one that's . . .

SOULE: In the meantime, I speak to Callery [John Aruns Callery, another gambler-defendant, through whom the money to Soule had allegedly been paid during the years], you know, and I tell Callery, I said, uh, I said, look, uh, I got Frey and wants to go and I said uh, I said, uh, how much you think we ought to hit Louis [Boasberg] for? He said, well, look the son of a bitch owes me for the Legislature, I'd like to get something for myself. I said, I tell you what, I said, before I get you to accept anything . . . if you're going to handle it, you tack on your, your five hundred for you and ask for two thousand, so I met Louis myself when I came back, we had arranged to meet . . . I said look, we want two, it's going to cost . . .

him two thousand, we want Callery to handle it cause we been dealing with Callery, deal with Callery, he says, oh, I'll get that, that's
fine, so he went back to each one of them guys [the other pinball
operators] and wanted them each to come up with a share but they
wouldn't do it.

GERVAIS: With him.

SOULE: They wanted him [Boasberg] to go [provide the entire
payoff amount himself] this time, and he wanted them all to share
it, so he called me back and he says, Freddie, he says, uh, none of
them will go, he said. I'll go for a thousand, he said, but none of
them will go. I says, well ———, take a thousand. So I go see, so I
come back and I talk, I talk to, ah, Aruns [Callery] and the son of a
bitch . . . so he [Callery] says, well, whatever you want to do, I said,
well, I'll take that and that'll take care of me and Frey and you can
run the other business, so then I come and tell Louie, okay, we'll,
we'll take a thousand. He says, all right, the first of the month.

GERVAIS: He's a stalling ———.

SOULE: So the first of the month comes and he [Boasberg] still
don't come up, he, then I, see, we knocked a few machines off, he
wants to see me, I go see him, it's about the sixth, I said, well, you
know, you never did come up, he says, well, let's start the first of
next month. He said, I'll tell my people to quit paying off [paying
customers for free games]. But that's all I ever got, the first of the
month, he always wants to start on the first and he don't want to
catch up.

GERVAIS: No. He's a bad ——— man.

SOULE: Yes, he is.

GERVAIS: He started the thing and then he wouldn't come up.

SOULE: That's right.

GERVAIS: Let me ask you this, though, if he started it and
wouldn't come up, how did you finally get the ——— money?

SOULE: Well, all I did was tell Callery—after I met with Louis,
I tell Callery this was what went on, you know, cause Callery's been
square with me.

GERVAIS: Yeah.

SOULE: So, uh, Frey was knocking the piss when, when he
didn't come up on the first, Frey went out and knocked the piss out
of about ten of them, you see. (The Sunday, October 4, 1970, edi-
tion of the *New Orleans Times-Picayune* carries a story that on
October 3, 1970, the New Orleans Police Department Vice Squad
confiscated ten Bally in-line type gambling pinball machines from

nine establishments in New Orleans, where seventeen persons were arrested for making illegal payoffs to players of pinball machines for games won.)

GERVAIS: He did, he did, huh?

SOULE: And I told Callery, I said, we've got ten, he said, wait a minute, and that's when TAC [TAC Amusement Company, one of the pinball companies) come up with the ———— money.

GERVAIS: Oh.

SOULE: So, uh, TAC come up with it, Frey called the investigation off, so we got five hundred apiece from TAC.

GERVAIS: Uh huh...

SOULE: That went on for, for ...

GERVAIS: A couple of months.

SOULE: Two months, and then we were gonna knock them off again and so Nims [Robert Nims, another defendant, of the Lucky Coin Machine Company, Inc.] come up.

Then, according to the affidavit, Soule, having gotten the operators in line, the FBI raids having tightened up the money situation, said that Frey could expect to get something more starting around the beginning of 1971.

According to the affidavit, long conversations were held about who was going out of business, who was staying in and how they would manage to stay in business. One operator wrote all his locations and told them, officially, to stop paying off on the machines or else to pay off only in merchandise, which was legal, but he did not expect the owners to comply, his sole purpose in having sent the letters being to provide a possible defense in case he needed it as a defendant in a trial. The economic result of the FBI raid was disastrous, too, it seems. One operator said the FBI had picked up about 360 of his machines, and that it was costing him $16,000 a week in lost income. In a meeting on March 13, 1971, between Gervais and Boasberg (the operator who had written the locations asking them to stop paying out), the conversation, according to the affidavit, went like this:

GERVAIS: But the ———— letters are going to kill the business though, I mean, if you really ———— toe the line with them ———— locations, and, don't give them no help at all ... ———— I think the business would just die off.

BOASBERG: Most people would pay—if, if, if Garrison, Giarrusso and Aaron Kohn walked in together, they would pay them off. Those people are desperate for money, Pershing.

GERVAIS: They are going to pay regardless.

BOASBERG: They can't exist.

GERVAIS: No matter what you tell them.

BOASBERG: Do you, do you realize how many places have got games in the city right now that are starving to death?

If things were tough on the pinball owners, they were getting precious little sympathy from Soule, Garrison and Frey, according to the affidavit. They kept the pressure on, through Gervais, although at one point Frey was reportedly a bit scared, and, while he didn't want to give up the money, would just as soon have been out of the whole mess. Various methods were discussed of eliminating payments while the heat was on, including credit and retroactivity, sounding something like the President's Cost of Living Council trying to figure out Phase II.

SOULE: You see, the ———, we carried him for the whole month of December, he was supposed to, he said, look, he wanted to give us two apiece [Soule and Frey], two hundred apiece, so I, I told, I told Frey and Frey didn't want to fool with it, I went back and said, look, we going to carry you, don't wor— we'll take care of you but we don't want a dime, he said, I'll give you a nice Christmas present, I, I said, okay, he never came up with no f—— he never came up with nothing for me.

GERVAIS: Nothing [laughter] . . .

SOULE [laughter]: But I wasn't expecting nothing, but we didn't, didn't, didn't touch a machine in the whole month of December.

It came out that Soule's father had worked for Boasberg for many years, and still did at the times the tapes were made, and one of the reasons Soule didn't bicker over the missing December payment was that the gambler had treated his dad "real good," and, back in the early days of World War II, had sent Soule $50 a month to tide him over while he was in the army.

There was also a little falling out among the defendants about who was putting up how much money and giving it to whom. Keep in mind that before the specific time mentioned in the affidavit, Callery allegedly had handled the Soule and Frey money, giving it directly to Soule, and had allegedly delivered only the Garrison money directly to Gervais— and, incidentally, "taken care" of the legislature as well.

Garrison was even unaware at this time that either Soule or Frey was on the take, according to the affidavit, so closely had these cards been played to the chest. On March 9, 1971, Gervais went to Garrison's home, his body fully wired for sound, to deliver money and carry the operators' request that Garrison intercede on their behalf with Governor John McKeithen, whose efforts would be needed, the operators thought, if any antipinball legislation would pass in Baton Rouge.

GERVAIS: Now, Boasberg today told me that he's been told two things—A, the legislature wouldn't go into it, and B, yes, they would go into it, so he really don't know.

GARRISON: Well, I think I've helped the governor enough and gotten to know him well enough that it took this—uh, uh, one reason it took us so long to get to know each other is because we're very much alike really as far as relating, you know, I don't relate to real easy, neither does he.

GERVAIS: Uh huh.

GARRISON: But, uh, he trusts me now, where he's long since stopped trusting a lot of people around him 'cause I've never let him down.

GERVAIS: Uh huh.

GARRISON: And, uh, if it's down to the governor, I think I can stop it.

GERVAIS: Uh huh.

GARRISON: By just plain asking ...

GERVAIS: Right, 'cause he knows ...

GARRISON: I can talk ...

GERVAIS: Well, it's the thing they most afraid of.

GARRISON: I, I can talk a little trash with him.

GERVAIS: Yeah. Now, Boasberg, boy, he's a whining, grimy ———— to get money out of but, uh, uh ... I mean, he stalls and stalls, see, and I was sweating April out because I figured April the first, the leg ... he will stall us until after the Legislature meets but there's no way he could stall us until May ... so, uh, now, you see, Soule, I talked, I talked to Soule yesterday, when, when the April payment comes, after that, Soule says he wants more money ... he said, they will come with more money and the only way you get their attention like Sou——— ...

GARRISON: Where does Soule come in?

GERVAIS: Soule—gets money for him and Frey—since he's on the—Soule's always gotten money.

GARRISON: Oh, he's not with me any more?

GERVAIS: Yeah, he's in your office.

GARRISON: Oh. I see.

GERVAIS: But he's handling the thing for the Vice Squad.

GARRISON: Oh, oh [laughter] ...

GERVAIS: You know, he always did, you see ...

GARRISON: I didn't know that.

GERVAIS: Yeah, he always did.

GARRISON: You mean even Frey, who's been a pain in our ass, is, uh, all right as far as this thing, this, uh, area is concerned?

GERVAIS: Him and Soule is making the money.

GARRISON: Okay.

Much of the negotiation reported on in the tapes involves Gervais taking over as bagman for all three, with the money now, for the first time, coming openly from the other defendants.

On February 10, 1971, Callery met with Gervais at the Fontainebleau, and, according to the affidavit, Callery began a discussion of the payoffs since August, 1970, and said that he understood that Boasberg gave Captain Soule $1,000, "and if he did, that is all he has put up"; that Lawrence Lagarde of the TAC Amusement Company paid two $1,000 payments for Soule for September and October, and that the payments to Soule and Gervais since August had been made by TAC and Robert Nims, another defendant. The affidavit continues:

Callery stated that "we" gave four thousand dollars to Soule and four thousand four hundred dollars to Gervais for a total of eight thousand four hundred dollars, none of which was put up by Boasberg. Callery said that he recalls that Lawrence Lagarde put up five thousand of the eight thousand and four hundred dollars. With respect to the forthcoming reduction of the share of the payoff to be made to Jim Garrison, Callery stated that he thinks Garrison would be foolish to take it; that he has a chance to get out of the deal, forget about it and let it die. Callery stated that Boasberg put up two thousand dollars for the payoffs on August 1, 1970, but has not put up anything since. Callery stated that the payoffs to Gervais were one thousand eight hundred dollars years ago, 1962, when the original deal was made; that he added two hundred dollars a little later for Gervais, and that he subsequently added another two hundred dollars to "take care of some of the boys on the Vice Squad." Callery stated that he talked to Jim Garrison and that Garrison understood the cut in the payments; that when Callery talked to Garrison, Garrison said he had read about the FBI pinball raids in the papers and that "When the cow is dead, there's no more milk." During the conversation, Callery was told by Gervais about the latter's meeting with Louis M. Boasberg and John J. Elms Jr., and their agreement to pay one thousand dollars every two months retroactive to January 1, 1971. Callery replied that he doubted that Jim Garrison would take that reduced amount but he might. Callery stated that he believed he owed it to Jim Garrison to go and talk with him about the decrease in the payoffs since he [Callery] had made the original deal. Callery said that he told Jim Garrison that there was only one man [Boasberg] still operating; that he [Callery] was no longer involved in the payoffs because he had had a "package going," but that the "package had been dismantled."

Would Garrison or would he not take the lesser amount? The affidavit claims to know the answer (at least two payoffs to Garrison, all in marked money, are claimed by the government to have occurred):

On February 25, 1971, Pershing Gervais drove to the residence of District Attorney Jim Garrison, 4600 Owens Boulevard, New Orleans, Louisiana, for the purpose of delivering a blue envelope containing one thousand dollars in United States currency, which had been furnished to him by Special Agents of the IRS, and which had been previously substituted for the one thousand dollars delivered to Gervais by Captain Frederick Soule Sr., on February 19, 1971. [Soule, according to the affidavit, got the money from a man named Harby Marks, also a defendant and a trusted employee of Boasberg).] The currency consisted of twenty fifty-dollar bills with the following serial numbers. . . . Gervais told Jim Garrison of his meeting with Louis M. Boasberg of New Orleans Novelty Company and John Elms Jr. of TAC Amusement Company, and stated that he had received one thousand dollars for the months of January and February, 1971; that in March he will receive another one thousand for the months of March and April, 1971; and that the one thousand dollars every two months would be the new reduced payoff until after the Legislature meets, in May. When Gervais produced the envelope with the money in it, Garrison snatched it from his hand and Gervais said, "You burned my fingers! Bring the butter up! Here . . . Jesus Christ, you burned my fingers, James."

During this visit, Garrison also explained how he was going to approach the governor in the antipinball legislation matter, and I include it, because if it is true, it verifies much of what has been theorized about New Orleans:

GARRISON: . . . But I am going to tell John [Governor McKeithen], John, don't kill yourself as senator.
GERVAIS: By attacking this?

GARRISON: You might not be running in '72—you might be running several months later . . .

GERVAIS: For the Senate, for the Senate, huh?

GARRISON: Yeah . . . New Orleans, always think of New Orleans —the Irish Channel and the Ninth Ward. He will understand.

GERVAIS: Uh huh.

GARRISON: He will understand. The Irish Channel and the Ninth Ward, a guy got a bottle of beer, on a pinball machine, bang, bang, he gets another beer, bangs it—that's New Orleans.

GERVAIS: Yeah, yeah.

. . . . .

GARRISON: The Channel, baby, and the Ninth Ward, 'cause whoever I'm for, they're for.

GERVAIS: Okay.

GARRISON: In other words, I'm gonna guarantee him . . .

GERVAIS: Okay, that'll satisfy him . . .

GARRISON: Don't worry, I'm going to tell him, look . . .

GERVAIS: See, I haven't committed, I haven't, I said, listen, I don't know anything, I can't give you no answers, I have to [find] out [referring to the pinball operators] . . .

GARRISON: John, I'm going to tell you . . .

GERVAIS: I even said, listen, I might have to bring this package back to you [return the $1,000 if Garrison refused to take that small amount] . . .

GARRISON: No.

GERVAIS: [Laughter.]

GARRISON: Don't bring him a dollar.

GERVAIS: Okay.

GARRISON: Tell them this, tell them I'm gonna, I'm gonna go to John and tell you you happened to be my personal choice but if I change my mind at the last minute and name Carlos Marcello, he will be the next Senator from New Orleans.

(McKeithen did run for the Senate in 1972, as an Independent. He ran third, with 124,181 votes, behind J. Bennett Johnston, a Shreveport lawyer, who rolled up 544,100 votes. The Republican candidate even beat McKeithen, by about 90,000.)

The affidavit trails the marked money delivered to Garrison right up to the point where $1,100 of it was used by a Garrison aide to pay a bill at the Fontainebleau. The affidavit also claims to know what happened to Soule's money, too, but it goes back a number of years. In the government's affidavit, the tape transcript shows Captain Soule and Gervais chatting on March 2, 1971, in Room 752 of the Fontainebleau, discussing how Gervais had handed all of the money over to Garrison, not keeping any for himself, and this apparently prompted Soule to reminisce a bit:

SOULE: Now, when I run, when I was running the [Vice] Squad [1962–68], I used to get seven and a half a month.

GERVAIS: Seven and a half a month?

SOULE: 'Course that was only, only for me and that's what I got.

GERVAIS: Jesus Christ, that was pretty good.

SOULE: Well, that's all I got, that's why I say, you, that's what I got, I had to be tough with them, you see, he [Callery] used to tell me if TAC ain't come up, I would knock the piss out of TAC, you understand, but they all coming up and I was getting ... seven and a half a month. Plus what I was getting from you, so ... so, uh, I used to get about fifteen hundred every two months, you see.

GERVAIS: Every two months, that wasn't bad. But, listen ...

SOULE: But I, I was getting that even before I was doing business with you, that was the only thing I was out getting, you see when I ...

GERVAIS: Well, you had to get that the minute, you got, they must have got you in the Squad, huh?

SOULE: Yeah. Well, as soon as I got in there, I knew Aruns [Callery], Aruns approached me and, uh—well, first I was getting less, he was coming with just for Boasberg and this and I started rapping a few other ...

GERVAIS: [Laughter.]

SOULE: And he said, look, you want to take this down and take this and so, anyway, I had, you know, it kept going up and up.

About a month earlier, on February 11, in another meeting between the two men, according to the government affidavit, Soule told Gervais, in what is rather a poignant revelation, about his savings:

GERVAIS [laughter]: You got money in legitimate savings account?

SOULE: I got about ... fifteen hundred dollars.

GERVAIS: Fifteen hundred? You ain't going to get much on that, Freddie.

SOULE: No, well, that's all I can afford to put in there. No, I got, I got a few thousand dollars, I got ———— safe box.

GERVAIS: But you can't ———— ———— with that money.

SOULE: No.

GERVAIS: You let that money out, you'll be in real trouble.

SOULE: I got about seventy-five thousand.

GERVAIS: Do you? If you admit that, you ————, you must have a hundred fifty.

SOULE: No, no, I'm, I'm ————, I'm telling you straight. Most of it, you know ...

GERVAIS: Yeah, made with them things [pinballs].

SOULE: Most through you [laughter].

GERVAIS: Yeah.

SOULE: I, well, I, tell you the truth, I, everything I got, I got either through you or Callery.

GERVAIS: Yeah.

SOULE: Everything I got.

GERVAIS: Boasberg, huh?

SOULE: Boasberg never did give me but one time, that's all. I got everything from Callery.

At this point the federal strike document paraphrases the conversation:

Soule said that he can't do anything with that seventy-five thousand dollars except when he gets old, just before he's ready to die, he'll give it to his children and that their problem with that amount of money will be less than his would be. Soule said that if he wanted to spend that money he'd have to say he won it gambling and pay taxes on it and for that reason, "I have to live modest, I can't spend it."

Soule told Gervais the bank where he kept the money, and sure enough, according to the affidavit, the G-men went to the Irving Bank and Trust Company, 111 East Irving Boulevard, Irving, Texas, and found $75,000 in the safety deposit box rented by one Frederick A. Soule, Sr. The IRS also took a look at Soule's income-tax returns for 1965, 1966, 1967, 1968 and 1969, and found out that the only income he reported was from the city of New Orleans, uniform allowances, state of Louisiana, *Fairgrounds Race Track* and interest income.

The kind of protection all of this alleged bribery bought, of course, is nebulous. On May 3, 1971, just six months before the indictment was handed down, Harby Marks, the trusted Boasberg employee, came over to the Fontainebleau to see Pershing Gervais, this time in Room 358, and allegedly bringing an envelope containing $2,000, half of which was for delivery to Soule. During the conversation Marks said that Frey's vice squad had recently grabbed a pinball machine at the Broad Inn, 131 South Broad Street, and that Boasberg wanted to know whether it was a "routine raid" or just what the hell.

After he left, Gervais called Soule and asked him to drop by the next day. When Soule arrived, the government affidavit says, Gervais handed him an envelope containing $1,000 in marked $50 bills, watched as the investigator counted it and then put the arm on him about the vice squad arrest:

> SOULE: Broad Inn?
>
> GERVAIS: Yeah.
>
> SOULE: Who's that?
>
> GERVAIS: Boasberg, you knocked him off.
>
> SOULE: Oh, yeah, yeah, you told me.
>
> GERVAIS: 131 South Broad, Friday. He asking questions, what am I going to tell him?
>
> SOULE: Uh, you know, tell them, you could say ... I have to find out more facts about it, Frey told me to ask you something about it.
>
> GERVAIS: Fro—Freto and another guy.
>
> SOULE: What kind of case they made, did they get paid off, did they ...
>
> GERVAIS: I don't know, I don't know a thing about it, they asked me to find out about it.
>
> SOULE: Uh ...
>
> GERVAIS: Got to give them some kind of answer, 'cause they caught me cold, you know.
>
> SOULE: Yeah, I know they knocked him off Friday.
>
> . . . . .
>
> GERVAIS: What did, what did, uh, Frey say about it?
>
> SOULE: Well, he said that they accidentally knocked them off ... So he said, it's just, just something he put them out to do ...
>
> GERVAIS: Yeah. He's going to get the report on them some ———.
>
> SOULE: I'll get the reports. Yeah, I, it's probably, they witness a payoff, you know, and under those conditions difficult to control.
>
> GERVAIS: He didn't ask you when he told you they got them— you can't call him and ask him, huh?
>
> SOULE: You let, let me go see him and talk to him 'cause he's ...

GERVAIS: He afraid—to take a phone ...

SOULE: No, no, no ...

GERVAIS: Just be good if you could just ask him not ... whether, you know, what kind of case it is. I'd love to let them know.

SOULE: He wants you to let them know right away?

GERVAIS: Well, it's, he's just a little nervous, said, listen, this is a funny situation, I'd like to kind of relax them.

SOULE: Well ————, they didn't do anything ... whole two months went by—not like they ain't had it in four months.

GERVAIS: Yeah.

SOULE: Yeah, I understand your point, right.

GERVAIS: See, I would just like to be able to go right back and tell them something.

[Here, according to the affidavit, Gervais asked the hotel telephone operator for 822-3912, identified as a "straight line" to Sergeant Frey, and then Soule took the phone.]

SOULE: Yeah, Bob, how you been?

Fine, how things going?

Man, you busy this morning.

.   .   .   .   .

Okay, then, Bob, listen, I wanted another thing I wanted to ask you, remember the case you told me you made, I think it was one day last week ...

Was that ah, uh, did they get, get actual, did they witness a payoff, or ...

I see, they, they, they got the payoff itself.

Right, right.

Okay, then, Robert ...

Okay, fine, man.

Yeah.

Right, very good.

Okay, Bob, hey look, I'll see you tomorrow, I came up to see you this morning, but, uh, you weren't there ...

I wanted to see you, uh, you know, I got something important to tell you about, I wanted to see you.

Okay?

All right, see you later.

Right. [Hangs up.]

They went to the place and got paid off [for free games], just an accident, that's all, tell 'em it's just one of those things, it was an accident.

GERVAIS: Did he say it was an accident?

SOULE: They got, they gotta expect that 'cause they gonna be after 'em all the time.

GERVAIS: Yeah, well, I mean, he didn't have no drive on, or nothing?

SOULE: On, no, no drive, no. You know he just can't control these kids at all times.

But they used to, in the old days in New Orleans, didn't they?

Charisma lives in New Orleans. While still under federal indictment, Jim Garrison petitioned the United States Supreme Court to kill an injunction barring him from taking another crack at Clay Shaw on perjury charges. That was on September 20, 1972, just a month after Garrison succeeded in forcing his main opponent in the August Democratic primary for the Louisiana Supreme Court into a runoff election, despite the impeccable credentials of the other candidate, Civil District Court Judge Walter F. Marcus, Jr., and despite the bribery indictment.

In the runoff on September 30, 1972, Garrison lost by a little more than 15,000 votes among more than 192,000 cast in the four parishes that make up the Supreme Court district in which the two ran. The vote in Orleans Parish—where Garrison would run if he sought a fourth term as district attorney—was close, 60,561 to 49,808 in favor of Marcus.

The ninth ward and the Irish Channel (Wards 10, 11, 12 and 13) failed him, but not by much: out of 16,311 votes cast in the ninth ward, Garrison lost by 541; out of 22,812 in the Irish Channel, Marcus' lead was only 764 votes.

It is of some interest that no gambling legislation passed the Louisiana legislature in 1971, but in 1972, after the Garrison indictment and the departure of McKeithen as governor, a law was enacted banning the type of pinball machine with a "knockout" button underneath (the button the bartender would press to eliminate the free games after the cash payoff to the winner).

6

Victims
and Villains

During this guided tour of the darker labyrinths of man's activities, I've tried to maintain the central theme of this book: that the hypocrisy of American society, which wants to indulge itself yet keep its morality intact, at least insofar as the bulging statute books are concerned, must bear the ultimate responsibility for the corruption of police departments throughout the country. And that corruption, without exception, originates in the squads and divisions directly concerned with the enforcement of laws intended to eliminate immoral behavior—laws against gambling, against the sale and use of narcotics or other dangerous drugs, laws against prostitution and pornography and laws seeking to control and regulate the use of alcohol.

And who really cares about these laws, except for the police and the lawyers, whose ranks swell each time a new ordinance is enacted? Who really cares except the Women's Sodality (except where the enforcement of the gambling laws affects bingo)? Who really cares except local temperance groups and the Advertising Council, which pumps a great deal of tax money into Madison Avenue in the form of ads against drunken driving, junkie teen-agers and smut peddlers? All of these forces are as innocent and as well meaning as the Puritans and the Inquisitors, who, in the name of God and Morality, once decided to rid the world of heresy, by violence if necessary; and the innocents find themselves in a strange alliance with the purveyors of illicit merchandise and services in that while the former act from "conscience" and "civic well-being," the latter know that a dollar made from an illegal activity is a dollar in the bank, tax-free, with the bite taken by a protecting law-enforcement officer far less than that demanded by Uncle Sam from a legitimate corporation (if, indeed, there is such an animal in the second half of the twentieth century in America).

In Miami policemen fled or went to prison because of their alliances with gamblers and prostitutes; in Utica policemen—and prostitutes—did substantial terms in maximum-security prisons for entering into arrangements with each other. Police across the Mohawk Frontier, thanks to the alliance between the vice cops and the gamblers, have mostly remained out of jail, although their communities are infested with the leaders of organized crime. Commissioner Patrick V. Murphy in New York City is trying desperately to patch up a department shown to be so riddled by corruption in the plainclothes ranks as to be virtually beyond repair. Chicago has yet to see what the generations-long entente between the vice cops and the gangsters will bring in the way of punishment for the corrupted officers. New Orlean's police department was almost torn apart by the influence of the gamblers and the pimps.

We *are concerned* with the possibility of our police departments becoming corrupt, and for two reasons: The first is that the policeman is the sole guardian of the public safety, the man who stands, gun in hand, between a tired bookkeeper going home at the end of a long day and the mugger in the jungle through which the honest citizen must pass. He maintains the integrity of the "safe corridor" from the office to the home; and then, as the street lights come on, it is the function of the police officer, as it was, historically, of the old night watch, to see that no harm comes to those who think they have earned a good, safe night's sleep. If for any reason we believe that the policeman is not enforcing one law—a law against, say, rolling dice in an alley—then in the early hours of the

morning we are apt to awaken uneasily and wonder if that same policeman is taking a dollar or ten or a hundred to ignore the violation of
others laws, such as housebreaking. The cop is our first line of defense
against the jungle, and as we see the first small crack in that line, we
begin to suspect the strength of the entire structure.

The second reason for our concern is that the first dollar bill handed
to a cop by what the newspapers call a "vice figure" *invariably* leads to
the take-over of a community—and perhaps a nation, if we are too late
—by the forces of organized crime, call it the Mafia, the Cosa Nostra, the
mob, the syndicate or what you will. These forces are already major
political, corporate and community influences in Chicago, New York,
Miami and New Orleans, and in each case they gained their first toehold
by being allowed to function by a police department that knew, instinc-
tively, that the community wanted these certain functions—card rooms,
pinball machines, brothels, bingo nights, saloons and strip joints—to
exist.

Through the years, especially the years since Prohibition, organized
crime has gained enough power, money and influence to be able to put
its own candidates into public office—sometimes national public office
—and therefore control the actual appointment of police chiefs and
other law-enforcement executives. (It should be noted that in January,
1971, James F. Ahern, chief of the New Haven, Connecticut, police
department, resigned, warning that organized crime was threatening to
control the entire city. and charged that some city officials had failed to
support his efforts against the Mafia and his program to "reorganize"—
read reform—his force of 430 men. In resigning, Ahern, who had been
the only law-enforcement officer on President Nixon's Commission on
Campus Unrest, said two of the five voting members of the police board
of commissioners had failed to back his order declaring a notorious Mafia
hangout off limits to cops, and that the board had interfered in promotions and had opposed all his efforts to suspend or dismiss officers. In
New Haven, Ahern was quoted by the *Los Angeles Times* as saying:
"there are vast amounts of money available from gambling and other
illegal activities that could be used to try to corrupt police, the courts
and city officials." Ahern, later to write a book, *Police in Trouble*, was to
have considerable to say about the difficulties of being a cop, but little to
say specifically about the situation in the town that Yale University calls
home.)

While the matter of police corruption becomes of intense public
interest, especially in the community where it is exposed, the link
between the vice cop who does or does not make an arrest and the forces

of organized crime is seldom made, and solutions to the problem of such corruption rarely get to the heart of the problem, which is, of course, community hypocrisy. The International Association of Chiefs of Police, headquartered in Gaithersburg, Maryland, did not even acknowledge the existence of police corruption formally until recently, even though the IACP's survey teams had been brush-fighting such corruption for many years through "study" and "recommendations for reorganization" of agencies where such trouble had been known to exist. The recommendations were followed in some instances; and it is ironic that a survey report a decade ago of the Seattle Police Department, a report whose recommendations were not followed, except in a halfhearted manner, was echoed by a second IACP report after the current police scandals erupted there again. (These later suggestions were implemented, for the most part, but the department, I was told by Chief Tielsch, abandoned some of the proposals as being "inappropriate" to the situation there.)

New York's Commissioner Murphy attacked the problem (very likely on the grounds that the best defense is a strong offense) in an address to the seventy-eighth annual conference of the IACP at Anaheim, California, on September 27, 1971.

> ... the crime I wish to speak about to you today is a different sort of crime. A crime which is not loud, but quiet. Not violent, but insidious.
>
> It is the crime that strikes at the rule of law itself ... bribery. There are two sides to the crime of bribery. There are those who accept bribes and there are those who offer them and the two are equally guilty. ... From the time I first assumed the position of police commissioner, I made it quite clear that imaginative and innovative change would be the main thrust of my administration. My main objective then as now is the revitalization of the New York Police Department and the restoration of public confidence in it. The means to that end, in my estimation, is strong leadership and tighter control and discipline. ...

Murphy said that while he considered the percentage of New York cops who are corrupt to be quite small, there are so many cops in New York (31,000) that

> hence, that small number could be significant. The question of just what I mean by significant is probably going through your minds right now. And let me answer it this way. One corrupt police officer, I say, is one too many. There are, of course, those who chant, "Let's

face it, some corruption in any police department is inevitable." I refuse to join that chorus.

I say we cannot be equivocal. We cannot countenance any corruption at all. Police corruption is too grave a matter. It undermines morale. It undermines discipline. It destroys public confidence in the police. And that takes years to rebuild. . . .

Murphy then outlined the reorganization he had begun in the department, including the fact that "corrupt policemen will not be tolerated," and then went into the matter of the people who are doing the bribing—a class D felony in New York.

> Any businessman, any intelligent person would agree that no sale can be consummated without both a buyer and a seller. Police corruption is no different. It cannot exist without both the giver and the taker. Obviously, therefore, only one-half of police corruption is the police officer—the other half is the briber, the ordinary citizen, and this is the person at whom I am taking dead aim. Corrupt police officers are made, not born. They do not become corrupt by themselves. Bravo, you might say. Let's get these crooks, the gamblers, these narcotics pushers and fences who bribe policemen, and while I do not want you to believe for one minute that I have overlooked or excluded such criminals in the orders I have issued, they are not the singular object of my dissatisfaction. . . .

At this point Murphy told how tough things are going to be for the driver who tries to buy his way out of a traffic ticket—the usual first result of any exposure of police bribery—but then he gets to the real question:

> Why does police corruption continue? Because a large proportion of the public contributes to it or condones it. It could be said that police are more frequently tempted to misbehave or provided with more opportunity to succumb to temptation than members of any other profession. Why?
> Because there are too many people in this world, businessmen and private citizens alike, who want to perform activities forbidden by the law. They want to skirt the law. They want to cut corners for bigger profits. They are willing to pay police officers not to enforce the law. . . .
> The crucial point to remember is that police officers are strongly influenced by the society in which they work. I believe that

you—I believe that all of us—desire integrity in our police departments. I would like to spread the word throughout this great nation, just as there is no such thing as a slightly corrupt police officer, there is no such thing as a slightly corrupt citizen. There is no such thing as an unimportant bribe. . . .

Murphy said it, but he offered little in the way of guidance for a nation faced with the kind of immorality he described.

And I say a *nation*, and not just a world, because police corruption *seems* to be a unique American disease, particularly in the form in which we see it from day to day. It is not, of course, unique here; it is simply that this nation was begun 200 years ago with an oddball combination of guidelines: a Bill of Rights and a Constitution which, among other things, promised citizens for the first time in history such a thing as "due process of law," meaning that those in power would not be operating through sheer whim; and the Puritan Ethic, which somehow saw debtors' prison (actually not abolished here until a third of the way through the nineteenth century) as a violation of civil rights but overlooked the implications of the chastity belt (now enjoying a revival in Great Britain). In most other countries the *pure* police officer is not only not demanded, but not expected (much the way it was when I was a youngster in East St. Louis). The history of police authority in Central Europe, for instance, would show that the citizenry might have far more gratitude for being spared a pogrom than resentment over being taxed a few pennies for selling beer after hours. What Haitian would grumble about *only* paying the Tonton Macoute for being allowed to break the law? (I was strolling with a friend through the infamous Pig Alley of Juarez, Mexico, one evening in 1954, where at least seventy brothels were operating extralegally, as in old Storyville, when my companion was arrested and jailed for urinating in the gutter by a police officer who had been lounging in the doorway of a bordello, stationed there to insure a peaceful evening. But who cared? Certainly the citizens of Juarez are grateful when the police are not exercising *political* persecution, far more pervasive and sinister in all of Latin America than a mere two-buck bribe from a gambler.)

Where police *are* found to be corrupt abroad, it is usually for the same reasons as in the United States. High-ranking members of the Paris police force are even now destined for prison for their roles in the 1971-72 "French Connection," a multimillion-dollar heroin deal that also involved United States authorities. In New Delhi, it was reported in 1971 that police were paying up to $400 to secure postings in precincts where the graft was most lucrative: areas where illegal hawkers of wares and illicit liquor sellers might be shaken down. (The Hindustan *Times* reported that it was suggested that such regulatory function should be taken away from the police and handed over to the Municipal Corporation and the Central Excise Department.) Such corruption, however, would seem to be of small concern in a nation where due process is far less important than securing the next bowl of sour rice.

One of the most important cases of police corruption abroad has come to light in Great Britain, where some thirty-five officers from Scotland Yard have been suspended and are awaiting trial. It is interesting to note that these are not the uniformed cops, but members of the detective bureaus—the men charged with the enforcement of vice laws and the regulation of gambling—which is legal in England, although totally bogged down in a quagmire of technicalities and nitpicking regulations, the sort of overregulation that can lead to police corruption almost as quickly as total prohibition. The situation in Great Britain, however, is not nearly as disturbing as that in the United States—the thirty-five suspected cops are a *really* small percentage of the Yard's 21,500-man force, and perhaps one of the reasons for such a low percentage was quoted by Quinn Tamm, executive director of the International Association of Chiefs of Police at the Attorney General's Conference on Crime Reduction held in Washington on September 9, 1971: "Some years ago," Tamm said, "when Sir John Knott-Bowers, who was at that time commissioner of Scotland Yard, was in the United States, he was asked what basic differences he saw in the British system of law enforcement and that of the United States. He stated that in England the public hired the Bobby to enforce the law and then assisted him in enforcing it. In the United States, he said, the public hired the policeman to enforce the law and then dared him to enforce it."

It may be that it is time to begin reversing this situation, but few have come up with anything near a solution to a problem that almost defies description—a problem that may even be further compounded by the general malaise that has affected almost all blue-collar workers in America at mid-century, from General Motors assembly-line workers to bus drivers. (James Ahern, in his book, describes the ennui of a policeman's life in brilliant terms, and it may be that the law-enforcement profession was a victim of malaise long before it overtook the general public.)

For solutions, police experts rely heavily upon inspection and the pinpointing of responsibility to combat corruption within a department, but this breaks down in city after city as the inspectors themselves, with the captains, become tainted, as happened in New York and Chicago; and even while the inspection-responsibility syndrome is functioning properly, it is only because the *possibility* remains that policemen will become corrupt, a possibility that escalates immediately into *probability* once the department's guard is lowered, even slightly. The inspectional services division of the police department, therefore, is roughly equivalent to a first-year medical student trying to treat a sophisticated case of cancer using only those techniques he has already learned—even as we realize that the techniques of graduate physicians have not yet been able to find out what the disease is, let alone conquer it.

Some work is being done at American University in Washington, D.C., in the area of federal assistance in the inspectional area, although just how such a system might operate is vague—and unlikely, given the American myth of states' rights and its accompanying slogan, "Federal Aid Means Federal Control." However, the Justice Department's Law Enforcement Assistance Administration has for several years been channeling vast amounts of cash into local police agencies, watching dumbly as the local cops buy new uniforms, chrome-plated whistles, tear-gas grenade launchers, and, in at least one case, tanks. There is no reason why such funds should not carry limitations on their use—Ahern suggests training and education instead of gadgetry and pomp—and there is no reason why their distribution should not be tied to a federal inspectional service not unlike the General Accounting Office, Congress' watchdog agency over funds appropriated for other purposes equally susceptible (especially in the military) to boondoggles. The best estimates of the International Association of Chiefs of Police indicate about 40,000 police agencies in the United States, employing 430,000 persons, with virtually no coordination between any of them. (Even where there is some coordination, things seem to fall apart—a crime-computer system allegedly linking the District of Columbia with its Maryland and Virginia suburbs carries stolen-car reports as much as two years old, nobody ever having bothered to reprogram after the car was recovered, leading to a great deal of hassle and unpleasantness between the cops and the citizens.) As I pointed out earlier, much police corruption occurs in metropolitan areas with many smaller communities and fragmented law-enforcement agencies, and it is in such areas, I think, that LEAA coordination might help pull things together.

Such a concentration on police techniques and organization, however, ignores the national morality—the true cause of police corruption, the "part II" of the bribe, as Commissioner Murphy put it. In *Police in Trouble,* Ahern wrote:

> Clearly the entire problem of consensual crime [victimless crime] has fundamental and far-reaching implications for the police role, which encompass considerations of individual rights and liberties and the citizen's relationship to his government—all of which police must monitor in some sense. But in precisely what sense? And to what extent? Until very recent years police have been expected to lurk in train stations attempting to prevent or detect homosexual rendezvous. They have been expected to peek into windows in attempts to catch consenting adults in acts of "lascivious carriage." To good cops, such assignments are meaningless and degrading. To bad ones, they are a license to harass those whose conceptions of what is moral are different from theirs. In both cases, the effects of these assignments have been detrimental to police, and it is difficult to see how they have profited communities. It is a condition of the policeman's job to work in such gray areas. The law is constantly changing, community values are constantly changing, and even notions concerning the most fundamental of human rights and obligations are slowly changing. In the midst of the flux created by these changes, the professional policeman can function. He must function. But he cannot function if he is expected to enforce laws such as those against gambling and marijuana—unenforceable attempts to legislate individual morality.

Robert K. Woetzel, professor of international politics and law at Boston College, wrote in *Current History* in June, 1967:

> It is true that law can help to enforce moral standards, but, in a pluralistic society with different moral creeds, this would seem not to be the main criterion for legislation. According to the American Law Institute's model penal code, which has been adopted in Illinois, a crime is a real or threatened injury sustained without consent. Many of the actions upon which organized crime feeds, and which are proscribed in law thus creating a vacuum into which the underworld steps, are not crimes in that sense. They may be immoral actions from one standpoint or another—such as drinking, or extra-marital sexual activity. But they do not constitute real or threatened injuries which would qualify as crimes. Furthermore, in many cases the prohibitions involved represent impositions on members of other religious faiths. For example, Roman Catholics must

have felt severely imposed upon by Prohibition, as Jews may be offended by Sunday closing laws, or agnostics by antibirth-control legislation.

With all this, it is too easy to say that the vices—almost the sole source of serious police corruption—should be legalized, because it is not quite certain that American society in the second half of the twentieth century is ready for an environment awash with gambling casinos, street-walkers in the suburbs, dull-eyed junkies taking up curb space, X-rated movies at the neighborhood theater and ginmills running full blast twenty-four hours a day, even if it meant a totally incorruptible police department, which, of course, it would not.

An enlightened group of citizens, called the National Commission on Marijuana and Drug Abuse, on March 22, 1972, presented its findings to the White House, Congress and the various state governments. The 178-page report urged lawmakers to eliminate criminal penalties for the private use of marijuana, but at the same time to keep the drug an illegal substance. The commission said it could find no evidence that moderate use of marijuana is either harmful or unhealthy, or that it leads to the use of more dangerous drugs, or that it causes criminal or aggressive behavior. At the same time, Raymond P. Shafer, the commission chairman, noted, "We don't want the sanction and approval given to this psychotropic substance only to find later on, as we have with tobacco and alcohol, that we shouldn't have." He also said that all the scientific information on the possible dangers of long-term marijuana use has not been collected.

The commission recommended that state and federal laws retain stiff penalties for the sale or for the possession of more than an ounce of marijuana, with penalties against growing the weed and using it in public. Police would be able to confiscate small amounts of marijuana they find in public places, and this, Shafer said, would help to discourage its use. Earlier in the year, in an interim report, the commission had released partial results of its study showing that 24 million Americans over twelve, or 15 percent of the population, have used marijuana, and that almost 40 percent of people between eighteen and twenty-five say they have used the drug—which statistics mean that the "discouragement" the commission would like to see would have to affect an awful lot of people who would have to carry little scales around with them to make sure they didn't have more than an ounce.

If the commission wants a reading on how their "benign-neglect" marijuana program might work, they might ask Buzz Cook when he gets out of prison how he enjoyed the gambling "tolerance policy" in Seattle.

I have stressed changing attitudes toward narcotics use in our society because it is the "vice" that has been the most repugnant to Americans, and the one, until recently, from which even grafting cops were reluctant to profit. In Utica, you'll recall, one brothel was shut down by the vice cops simply because a known dopehead was hanging around there.

The other vices are also getting a closer examination around the country, although liquor is so enmeshed with various state and local pork-barrel legislators that it may never be free enough of regulation to eliminate the possibility of profit by liquor-control authorities, including policemen. For instance, I am sure that the cops who hang out in the saloon where I eat supper cannot have failed to notice the black men coming out of the liquor store across the street with cases of half-pints of whiskey, although it is conceivable that the officers have known of an eccentric who elected to buy his booze in half-pint bottles—by the case—with no intention of resale at double the retail price after 2 A.M.

Prostitution is another double-barreled mess. A lot of people drink, but the percentage of people who copulate reaches near totality, and a lot of them do it with people not legally entitled to participate, and a lot of them pay for the privilege, and this is when it becomes a crime—for the woman, not the man.

There has been a lot of noise about making prostitution legal, but it is not likely that such a law will pass in many states, particularly since so many state legislators, no matter what kind of a Saturday night they had, generally show up in church Sunday morning, accompanied by the wife they stepped out on just the night before. It *is* possible that some states might choose to ignore prostitution and place it in sort of a behavioral limbo, electing to utilize other laws already on the books (such as disorderly conduct, simple assault, disturbing the peace) when a couple of whores spill out onto Main Street in a fight over a john, or when a drunk is rolled by a ten-dollar Saturday-night special in a cheap hotel. Again, this would place the police in the position of determining when a crime had been committed, but it *would* take them off the pussy posse, where so many man-hours are wasted across the nation. And it would offer some protection to the well-behaved call girl, just as the same laws offer protection to the well-behaved surgeon—he can take your liver out if he wants to at the hospital, but is subject to arrest if he pulls a knife on you downtown.

Gambling is the vice closest to being legalized in all of its forms.

Several states have lotteries, and more will have them within a year, and, if things go budgetwise as poorly for the United States as a May, 1972, Brookings Institution report predicted, we may expect a national lottery before too many sessions of Congress have passed...

Many cases have been made against legalized gambling, of course, most generally based on the fact that, because it has been illegal for so long, only the gangsters know how to run the game. Howard Samuels, head of New York's Off-Track Betting Corporation, has largely disproved that argument (he made his personal fortune making plastic sandwich bags, not dealing faro), and it is possible that even a state-run casino could be operated free of mob control and even free of police graft, provided that the enabling legislation was clear and straightforward, and without the kind of loopholes that have turned the licensed-beverage industry into the mishmash it is today.

Even the numbers racket, that multibillion-dollar source of ghetto revenue, might be sanctified by state law. Ralph Salerno, a former policeman and a consultant to the Off-Track Betting Corporation, came to Washington on May 25, 1972, to tell the Washington Lawyers' Committee for Civil Rights that illegal lottery gambling cannot be stopped by police, but that a well-run legal operation not only could force organized criminals out of the business (and by inference eliminate the temptation of police graft), but plow more money back into the community—probably in the form of taxes.

These are some of the ideas and suggestions for a solution. Perhaps they are not enough.

In his book *Crime in America,* Ramsey Clark said:

In our turbulent times, when youth seriously questions the purpose, the integrity and the effectiveness of our laws, we must have the courage to face honestly and answer truthfully such difficult issues as the continued prohibition of marijuana and other mild stimulants and depressants, gambling, prostitution, abortion and sexual relations between consenting adults. Nothing is worthwhile for the individual, or for his society, unless his own actions are honest. The failure to face and answer such issues is as dishonest as the false answer. The consequence in the lives of millions is immense.

There are still many, nurtured on the Puritan Ethic, who believe drink and debauchery are so much more alluring to the multitudes than justice and rectitude that they conceive of goodness as merely self-denial. They insist that the law prohibit those who would not deny themselves. But prohibition is impossible. Forces more powerful than the fear of police are at work. If society really intends to control gambling, drugs and prostitution, it must work to educate, to humanize, and to civilize.

Laws that cannot be enforced corrupt. Partial enforcement of laws against known violators is inherently unequal except in the most sensitive and skillful hands, and usually even then. We become a government of men rather than of laws, where men choose who will be arrested and who will remain free for the same infraction. Those arrested are bitter, while those permitted to continue unlawful activity corrupt others and themselves. The watching public is cynical.

Shortly after Congressman Claude Pepper broke his "news" about the existence of police corruption in Washington, D.C., I met him for lunch at the Congressional Hotel, where there is a dining room reserved exclusively for Democrats, just to try to find out if he really knew something or was being taken for a ride by staff members who might like to parlay a juicy little televised hearing into a career success story; and when I told him, finally, that we would have corrupt police as long as we had a corrupt society and corrupt congressmen and unenforceable laws, he asked me what he could do about it; and I sat there ever so long a time with visions of Bobby Baker and Abe Fortas and Paul Powell and Adam Clayton Powell and Dita Beard running through my head, and it came to me that there was nothing he or anybody else in power in American could do about it; and I believe he thought I was crazy when I advised him to turn his committee's attention to street crime, with the idea that if we are going to be plundered from above at least we should be able to crawl home and sort our food stamps without being mugged on the way.

When the Pennsylvania Crime Commission issued its interim report early in 1972, it said:

> The disease of police corruption substantially weakens the fabric of public safety and undermines the public's respect for law, order and justice. By lessening the worth of individuals, it can, in part, act as a catalyst for police brutality. The first victims of police corruption are the urban poor. According to preliminary analysis, the areas in which they live have the highest potential for corruption. The police themselves suffer from this malady. In the words of Adam Walinsky, "And there are other victims, the police themselves. They have been the killers, above all, of their own hopes,

their own self-respect, their own dreams of pride and excellence, and a holy career in the law."

To combat this disease effectively there must be that rare thing—a coalescing of public outrage and official courage. . . .

And, in his *Current History* article in June, 1967, Robert K. Woetzel said:

What Alexis de Tocqueville stated in his *Democracy in America* over a century ago is still true today: the public may be excited over a particular issue such as an abuse of justice in a particular jail or an especially brutal slaying, but it tends to ignore the larger problems which gave rise to it. The only solution may be a *modus vivendi* which will satisfy the tastes of the public and at the same time reduce violence and other by-products of syndicate operations —at least until the people have learned that it is impossible to outlaw sin and that control of crime requires a closer look at ourselves and our national character.

INDEX